Teaching social education
and communication

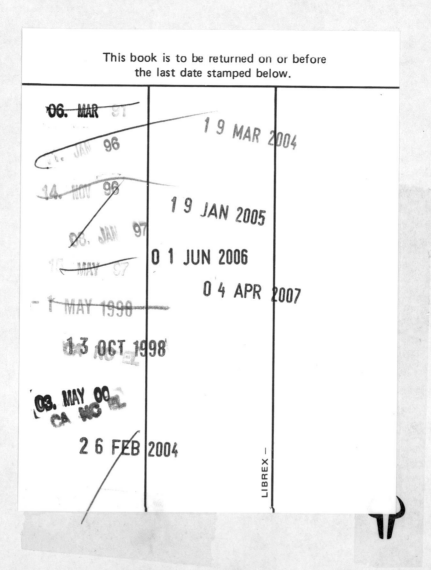

This book is to be returned on or before
the last date stamped below.

06. MAR 97

19 MAR 2004

14. JAN 96

14. NOV 96

19 JAN 2005

08. JAN 97

0 1 JUN 2006

15. MAY 97

0 4 APR 2007

1 MAY 1998

13 OCT 1998

03. MAY 00
CA NCEL

2 6 FEB 2004

LIBREX —

Teaching social education and communication

A practical handbook

Christine Butterworth and Monica Macdonald

Advisory editor: Andrew Nash

HUTCHINSON

London Melbourne Sydney Auckland Johannesburg

Hutchinson and Co. (Publishers) Ltd
An imprint of the Hutchinson Publishing Group
17–21 Conway Street, London W1P 6JD

Hutchinson Publishing Group (Australia) Pty Ltd
16–22 Church Street, Hawthorn, Melbourne,
Victoria 3122

Hutchinson Group (NZ) Ltd
32–34 View Road, PO Box 40–086, Glenfield, Auckland 10

Hutchinson Group (SA) Pty Ltd
PO Box 337, Bergvlei 2012, South Africa

First published 1985
© Christine Butterworth and Monica Macdonald 1985

Set in Times 10 on 12pt by AKM Associates (UK) Ltd
Ajmal House, Hayes Road, Southall, London

Printed and bound in England by
Anchor Brendon Ltd, Tiptree, Essex

British Library Cataloguing in Publication Data
Butterworth, Christine
   Teaching social education & communication.
   1. Social skills——Study and teaching
   I. Title   II. Macdonald, Monica
   303′.07   HM299

ISBN   0 09 161121 0

Contents

Acknowledgements

We owe a great deal to student teachers we have worked with and to the FE students they teach. We hope they will find this book useful. Acknowledgement is also due to the following for permission to reproduce materials in this book:

Joyce Anlezark, Open University; John Bazalgette, The Grubb Institute; E. Carroll, Bogle-L'Ouverture Publications Ltd; Andrew Naylor, Further Education Unit; Muriel Preshley, CET; Routledge & Kegan Paul Ltd; Pauline Willis, *The Guardian*; Mantz Yorke, Manchester Polytechnic.

Introduction to the book

Social education has been part of the school and immediate post-school curriculum for decades, accompanied by competing justifications for its inclusion and constant disagreement about its purposes.

The view that it should provide education for 'responsible citizenship' has perhaps the longest history. In schools this has resulted in social-studies teaching being communicated to the students in much the same way as the discrete subject areas were taught – pre-selected content acquired in a predominantly passive way.

Those who designed social-studies courses used the criterion of 'relevance' to select topics which they hoped would motivate students. This may have been well-intentioned, but since the relevance was defined in advance by the teachers the topics that were chosen were bloodless or trivialized versions of events in the students' real experience outside the classroom. Social studies remained a low-status subject in the school timetable and in its most limited form was accused of merely providing a second-rate kind of social training.

Even the 'new' sociology that informed social-studies teaching during the 1960s and early 1970s, whose ostensible aim was to help students expose and challenge the status quo, merely replaced one particular view of society with another. A commonly stated aim within this tradition was that students should develop a 'critical awareness' of society. This critical view originated from someone else, however – the students still did not act as their own experts, nor take their own experience as the subject matter.

There has always been agreement at a general level that social education should successfully provide a means of dealing with matters of real importance to students in their lives outside the classroom. This subject matter is by definition going to be sensitive, emotionally charged, controversial and frequently politically (with a small 'p') uncomfortable for teachers and schools. By the mid 1970s the school-based form of social education still lacked the means of dealing with such material inside the classroom. Part of the explanation for this lack of progress can be found in the innate conservatism of schools as organizations and in the absence of new influences on teaching methods.

Teachers needed methods which would help students develop an articulate, critical view of people and organizations that influence their lives. This would necessarily include teachers and schools. Schools are (on the whole) undemocratic organizations which have lacked the will to foster such radical activities. Teachers themselves lacked practical methods for achieving such aims, so were stuck in a position in which they could perceive opposition in the classroom only as a challenge to their control rather than as a legitimate critical viewpoint which they could seek to develop with students.

In the late 1970s and early 1980s other models of learning began to influence the field. Significantly, these came from outside education (from industrial and management training and from programmes developed for disadvantaged adults in prisons and hospitals). Equally significantly, they involved methods that had been used predominantly with adults, and which were therefore more suitable for older students.

Renewed debate followed the spread of these social-skills training methods into further education courses. The rapid development of something called 'social and life skills' in post-16 education was largely a consequence of the requirement that it should be a part of all government-funded courses for the young unemployed.

The introduction of 'social and life skills' in its turn generated arguments about political manipulation of the curriculum and revived the debate about the limitations of behaviourist models of learning and about the desirability of using a 'trade' model of skill practice to develop social understanding and competence. Within this model too, student autonomy seemed as far away as ever.

The spread, initially in further education and later in schools, of courses like City and Guilds 772 Communication Skills, 365 Vocational Preparation (General) and the B/TEC provision meant that, through integration and the resulting liaison between different subject specialists, communications and general-studies lecturers were drawn into life-skills and ultimately social-education teaching. The development of the Certificate of Pre-Vocational Education (CPVE) will doubtless continue this process.

The previous experiences of these English or liberal-studies lecturers led them to emphasize the development of language skills, aesthetic appreciation and creativity, political literacy and media studies. Their perspectives and priorities influenced the selection of issues and the strategies employed. Where a programme of staff development was sensitively implemented, members of teaching teams benefited from the exchange of ideas. Social education and communications emerged as even richer brews.

One of the newest developments has been the 'person-centred' approach to social education. This approach is indebted to American human relations and counselling theories and is exemplified by the 'Lifeskills' materials written by Hopson and Scally. This seeks to involve students in activities that reflect their own personal ambitions, their views about themselves and their relationships. It supplies a method for achieving the closer focus neglected by other forms of social education, but in doing so loses the wide-angle view of social institutions that content-based social-studies teaching attempts to give.

All these forms of social education are still practised. The consequent diversity of content and methods is confusing to anyone unwise enough to look for a single, constant definition of the field. The contrasting, often conflicting, views held by the proponents of these various approaches reflect their own beliefs about how individuals can and should learn, and the different social and political values underlying the picture of society which they seek to present to the student.

Viewed with a jaundiced eye, this kind of diversity can seem nothing less than a shambles. That familiar hypothetical figure, the Martian-in-the-classroom, might well conclude that anything goes as far as social education in the 1980s is concerned. In our view it is more useful to see this diversity as something that tutors can make positive use of. With the ideas in this book we hope to encourage an informed eclecticism which will allow tutors to select the kind of teaching they feel most able to do, synthesizing the best elements of the different approaches and making good their deficiencies.

We believe that the present variety of approaches and methods, combined with the best of the innovations introduced in the vocational-preparation field (induction, negotiation, counselling, profile assessment) means that tutors now have a real opportunity to devise student-led courses which can genuinely increase student autonomy, and at the same time extend their own professional competence. Such courses could also be a force for change in the institutions where they are implemented, though it is much easier to change the behaviour of individual students and teachers than to have perceptible effects on organizations. However it is certainly true that it is now possible for the tutor in this field to open up discussion with the students on how courses are run and on how the institution itself operates, in a way that is not available to teachers of other subjects. In this manner it would be possible to close the gap between the formal and the informal curriculum – indeed to make the first become the subject of the second.

The chapters that follow contain our suggestions for putting these ideas into practice. The themes we have chosen to explore are not novel or unique. A quick glance at the list of topics will confirm that our ideas about the areas with which social education should deal coincide with those of many other tutors and producers of teaching material.

This apparent agreement over common themes is worth exploring. Why do the same issues keep coming up? Our answer to this question is that these preoccupations (relationships, unemployment, finding a job, moral issues, political awareness) are inevitably produced by the situation in which young people find themselves in the 1980s. They spend longer than ever before in social institutions where older people continue to take decisions on their behalf. They find themselves effectively disenfranchised economically and politically, fenced off from important sources of experience. The extended apprenticeship may have been intended to allow more time in which to prepare for engaging in a complex and fast-changing society, but one does not learn about things by being kept out of them.

We believe that a view of young people that acknowledges that their most important problem is this lack of autonomy and their most important need the means for attaining independence should provide the background against which tutors design their courses. This overall view of the situation of young people explains our commitment to elements like induction and negotiation, in which students are involved in planning their own courses, and to guidance, counselling and profiling as ways of giving them a voice in the selection and assessment of their activities.

Autonomy cannot be achieved until the students develop skill and confidence in asserting themselves, in expressing their ideas and opinions and in negotiating with others. Communicating is a highly complex activity. Students need help in developing their ability to select the appropriate medium, register and tone. Social-education and communication teachers should work together to ensure that language skills are developed alongside social skills. Indeed, the two are inseparable.

The aim of a social-education programme should be to help students develop and articulate their beliefs and views about themselves and their society, and better to equip them to act in their own interests. No one approach from those described earlier would be sufficient to do this, though each has something distinctive to offer.

Students will gain a great deal from being helped to perceive and understand that aspects of personal relationships follow certain patterns and that with practice their competence in these areas can be increased. They also need opportunities to hear their own unique voices, a chance for creative self-expression and time for reflection. They derive a sense of responsibility and increased confidence from taking part in practical and concrete activities that have visible effects on people and organizations around them. Such opportunities need to be complemented by the chance to develop their understanding of large-scale trends, processes and political decisions which are beyond their range of immediate experience but which nevertheless produce results that affect them. Understanding and competence may result from distinct learning patterns, but they necessarily complement each other. In our view the field of social education is now sufficiently broadly based to provide you and your students with methods for dealing with the whole spectrum of social experience.

Common-core aims and objectives

In 1977 the Further Education Unit published a document called *A Basis for Choice*. This contained an appendix in which were suggested some aims and objectives that might serve as a guide in the development of vocational-preparation courses. Although the list was intended largely for discussion, it rapidly gained currency as it stood, and continues as the basis for much curriculum development.

The 'ABC' list is revised from time to time in line with current thinking; below is printed (by kind permission of the FEU) the 'Common-core checklist' as published in *Common-core teaching and learning* in January 1984.

FEU COMMON CORE CHECKLIST

An appendix to *A basis for choice* gives a series of aims and objectives which it is suggested might be the core of studies on a vocational preparation course. It was not suggested that this checklist was in any way prescriptive; indeed its dynamic nature has always been stressed, as has its responsiveness to local conditions.

There have already been suggestions that the checklist should be modified to include, for instance, computer familiarisation, and what follows is an amended version of the checklist.

The prescribed objectives are described in terms of a combination of observable performances to be expected of students and learning experiences which they should be offered. The commentary in italics following each objective is not prescriptive, but offers illustrations, examples and suggested methods.

For convenience, the objectives are grouped under the headings of the core aims. Some referencing has been used to indicate where an objective/experience is not intended to represent, necessarily, the order or organisation of the learning. Neither does the number of objectives in any group necessarily represent weighting. Some difficult time-consuming and important activities may be stated quite briefly.

- ● Part of Induction Phase
- ★ a new item

Aim 1

To bring about an informed perspective as to the role and status of a young person in an adult society and the world of work.

The students should

● 1.1 Describe a typical organisational structure of at least 2 different types of workplace or organisation, and relate this structure to their respective functions
This should include:
identification of component functions (e.g. sales, storekeeping, production, maintenance, professional services, administration, book-keeping) and who performs them (e.g. a department v one man as part of his job) distinguishing between large and small-scale organisations, and productive and service industries (e.g. garage and clothing factory).

● 1.2 Visit a place of work, relevant to their interests, and describe
  (a) the working conditions and tasks of new entrants
  (b) the range of decisions which can legitimately be made by these young workers
  (c) to whom they are responsible
  (d) with whom they have regular working relationships
  (e) training and career prospects; entry requirements

The information should, preferably, be gained by interviewing young workers, perhaps using a tape recorder or questionnaires (ref Aims 2.3 and 6.3.2).

●   1.3   Interview at least two adults workers about their entry to working life and the factors which influenced their subsequent job progress
e.g. relatives, friends or workers in jobs of interest (This may best be done in pairs if strangers are to be interviewed).

●   1.4   Make comparison of different working situations, using the information gained by themselves and others
Students might compare notes in discussion, with regard to both similar and different jobs. Note should be taken of any variations in perception or experience due to differences in the cultural background of those interviewed. There may be a need for tutors to compensate here for lack of information due to inadequate interviewing skills.

1.5   Describe the relevant trade union organisations within a particular firm or organisation, and their method of operation; identify and discuss any differences between the system observed, and the significance and functions of trade unions in general
Students should be able to use correctly such terms as: differentials, collective bargaining, closed shop, shop steward.

1.6   Describe the basic management structure within a particular firm or organisation; identify the channels of communication to and from the young workers, and the area of responsibility of their immediate supervisors
e.g. whom to see about a day off, faulty equipment, pay queries. Who has the authority to give instructions and about what?

1.7   Use the knowledge and insights gained as a basis for analysing factors influencing job choice, job satisfaction and relative rewards
e.g. (factors influencing rates of pay) skill, unionisation, social status, difficult conditions, age, qualifications e.g. (factors influencing job satisfaction) responsibility, prospects, social environment, usefulness, wage levels. A suitable method might be for students to rank a list of jobs according to a selection of factors, and then to discuss the differences between their own judgements and the actual position as reflected in wage rates, etc.

Many of these objectives may be achieved simultaneously with some of those in 9.2 (politics), 9.12 (economics), 10.4, 10.5 (technology), 2 (career choice) and 6.3 (communication skills).

Aim 2
To provide a basis from which a young person can make an informed and realistic decision with respect to his or her immediate future.

The students should

●   2.1   Participate in the construction of self-profiles, which analyse and evaluate their own characteristics, preferences and capabilities
e.g. ability to relate to colleagues or strangers, physical fitness, willingness to travel, reaction to routine, aptitude for calculation, any sensory or physical disabilities (ref. 3.1).

- 2.2 Present their self-profiles to colleagues and compare them with those of the rest of the group
  including:
  checking self-image against the perception of others; comparing the reactions of others to similar factors. This may enable the teacher to establish a group identity, and the students to gain practice at relating to others in a group (ref. 6.3.15).

- 2.3 Obtain, by a variety of means, information on the characteristics of the range of job opportunities available to them and how to gain access to these opportunities.
  e.g. (characteristics) entry qualifications, working conditions, training, prospects, job location e.g. (methods) consulting reference books, interviewing people, visiting job centres, listening to local radio, consulting careers officers (ref. 6.3.4 and 6.3.5).

- 2.4 Relate this information to their own profiles, and discuss the alternatives open to them
  Use could be made of the careers service here, and attention paid to changes in the students profiles during and since their time in school. Care may be needed to avoid sex-stereotyping.

2.5 Recognise the risk of future unemployment, understand its causes, and know the steps they can take to mitigate its effects on them personally (including knowledge of government schemes, voluntary opportunities, entitlement to benefit, the possible advantages of mobility and the possibilities of self employment)
  e.g. (causes and risks) decline of industries, and regional variations in job opportunities; technological developments (ref 10.5, 10.4)
  e.g. (schemes and opportunities) YOP and FE courses; useful unpaid work (CSV, local hospitals and community projects); social security regulations; the possibilities and difficulties of moving to another area; the possibilities of co-operatives and the knowledge and skills necessary to advertise and sell one's own labour, or to set up one's own business (ref. 9.10, 8.2).

2.6 Experience at least three different types of task, and evaluate their responses to them
  e.g. a heavy physical task (mixing concrete), manipulative task (assembly work), clerical task (filing). They should preferably come from more than one sector of employment. This job sampling may well be conducted in conjunction with the activities required under Aim 3.

Aim 3

To bring about continuing development of physical and manipulative skills in both vocational and leisure contexts, and an appreciation of those skills in others.
  Work in connection with objectives 3.1–3.4 in particular, will form part of the Induction Phase but all the objectives in this section should be worked towards throughout the year and also in the course of vocational and job specific studies.

The students should

- 3.1 Develop an awareness of their physical and manipulative abilities through experience of both vocational and leisure activities, and understand the implications of these for future job choices

This is a general objective to which much of the practical activity in the course should contribute. It should also influence the self profiles (ref. 2.1, 2.2). The leisure activities should include a choice of group and individual activities designed to satisfy a variety of student preferences (team games, gymnasium activities, dancing, pottery, etc.).

● 3.2 Experience the physical demands of some occupations, assessing (a) their reactions to physical conditions and (b) their ability to learn to cope with them

e.g. guided experience of being out of doors, standing, lifting and carrying (in the course of workshop activity, as an approach to physical education, etc.).

★ ● 3.3 Experience the manipulative demands of some occupations, assessing their reactions to these demands, and their ability to learn to cope with them

e.g. handling/constructing laboratory apparatus; making small-scale constructions, working accurately, and at speed, using a keyboard.

● 3.4 Experience the effect of working for an extended period of time between breaks, and the demands made on their concentration and physical stamina

work-place sessions as opposed to school periods.

3.5 Perform tasks to a set standard and in a given time, working co-operatively when appropriate

including the appreciation of
– the difference between the application of set standards at work, and the 'grading' of tasks by teachers in schools
– the need to 'pace' one's effort
– the need to protect the safety of colleagues.

3.6 Understanding the properties and uses of a range of materials, and practice using a variety of tools and processes appropriate to these materials

e.g. wood, paper, metal; cutting, joining, assembling, copying; appropriate safety procedures – all in the context of vocational and creative leisure activities (ref. 10.4).

3.7 Work on tasks where measuring and estimating of materials and time are required, to ensure accuracy and precision

e.g. typing, picture-framing, wallpapering.

3.8 Work on tasks where aesthetic judgements of shape and colour are required

e.g. choosing materials or designing for appearance as well as strength; painting for appearance as well as protection.

3.9 Observe a skilled practitioner at work, in an area of their choice, and appraise the judgement and skills involved

e.g. (areas) typing a letter; panel beating; connecting a tap; bathing a child; plastering; 'throwing' a pot. Social and aesthetic judgements may also be involved, as may the ability to plan (ref 8.2). The appraisal is probably best developed through group discussion.

★ 3.10 Be introduced to examples of complex equipment, in order to develop confidence in its use in the future

e.g. machine tools, electronic equipment, microcomputers.

Aim 4

To bring about an ability to develop satisfactory personal relationships with others.

The student should

4.1 Experience, directly and vicariously, a variety of personal encounters and a range of responses in them

e.g. (encounters) receiving instructions; being asked for help, receiving a complaint – in direct experience (such as those involved in 1.2 and 1.3), role-play, film or literature

e.g. (responses) aggression; sympathy, evasion.

4.2 Describe several patterns of behaviour, and analyse the interaction in terms of the roles of those involved

e.g. (patterns) use of authority or status; effect of aggression or appeasement; use of reason or emotional pressure

e.g. (roles) parent and child; supervisor and worker; student and teacher.

4.3 Identify and practice alternative responses

e.g. being aggressive, conciliatory, submissive, understanding, distant – probably in role-play – (possibilities of video).

4.4 Consider the merits of these responses in various situations, and with regard to various types of encounter

e.g. dealing with authority, the family, the peer group, individuals of the opposite sex (probably through group discussion) (ref. 5.5).

4.5 Predict the changes in role likely to occur for them in the near future

e.g. student to wage earner, child to parent.

4.6 Be aware of contemporary social conventions in various contexts likely to be met, and be able to adopt behaviour appropriate to their own goals

e.g. at work, eating out, in a library; self-presentation at interview; attitudes to those in authority; language and behaviour whilst in contact with the public (ref 5.4).

4.7 Describe some of the categories by which they classify other people, and become aware of the indicators they and others use to allocate individuals to a category

e.g. (categories) old/young; friendly/unfriendly; kind/unkind; social classes, cultural groups, sexes

e.g. (indicators) dress; accent; non-verbal behaviour.

Aim 5

To provide a basis on which the young person acquires a set of moral values applicable to issues in contemporary society.

With reference to

(a)   their present situation
(b)   a predictable future working situation
(c)   some wider current issues.

The students should

5.1   Be prepared for common moral dilemmas
e.g. individual v group loyalty, what constitutes 'stealing' at work, quality of workmanship, tax evasion, 'a fair day's work for a fair day's pay', sexual or racial discrimination.

5.2   Give reasons for certain moral 'rules' and decisions
e.g. keeping promises, returning lost property, being faithful.

5.3   Apply relevant moral terms to specific situations
e.g. integrity, corruption, cheating, fairness, in contexts such as sport, examinations, strikes, 'perks' at work.

5.4   Describe the prevailing moral code of given groups
e.g. cultures, ages, social groups, occupations (e.g: soldiers, doctors, sexes).

5.5   Formulate their own codes of behaviour in relation to certain issues and dilemmas, coping with clashes of principles
e.g. honesty versus loyalty, in relation to issues such as those described above.

5.6   Describe and analyse the moral consequences of actions
e.g. driving without insurance, the conception of a child; concealing information at interview (ref 9.1.4 also).

It is anticipated that many of these objectives (especially perhaps 5.1, 5.3 and 5.6) might be dealt with in the course of such things as practical sessions, or discussions about economic issues or work experience.

Aim 6

To bring about a level of achievement in literacy, numeracy and graphicacy appropriate to ability, and adequate to meet the basic demands of contemporary society.

6.1   **Numeracy** The student should be able to

6.1.1   Add, subtract, multiply and divide whole numbers, basic fractions and basic decimals

6.1.2   Given an awareness of their own abilities and future needs, decide when to use calculators, tables, pencil and paper or mental arithmetic, and be prepared to learn any required techniques.
What does their intended job require (a) of necessity, (b) for convenience?
What are their personal needs?

6.1.3   Interpret place value

6.1.4   Convert fractions to decimals and vice-versa

6.1.5   Use standard units of measurement, read graduated scales, and make approximate conversions between imperial and metric units
e.g. through the interpretation of plans and preparation of materials in the course of a project.

6.1.6   Read the 24-hour clock, and train/bus timetables. Make estimations of time.
e.g. planning journeys (ref. 8.2).

6.1.7   Interpret and use tables of figures
e.g. bank statement, temperature conversion, football results.

6.1.8   Make approximations and estimations, and assess the accuracy of results obtained by a calculator

6.1.9   Apply and interpret ratio and proportion
e.g. preparing mixtures, scale on maps, wage increases.

6.1.10   Calculate averages
e.g. average wage rates.

6.1.11   Calculate percentages
e.g. VAT, discounts, tax rates.

6.1.12   Make elementary algebraic substitutions
e.g. using a formula to determine one unknown.

6.1.13   Describe the properties of common shapes, and measure angles.

6.2   **Graphicacy**

6.2.1   Make calculations and estimations of perimeter, area and volume or right-angled figures, circles and cylinders
e.g. estimating quantities of materials.

6.2.2   Interpret and present graphs, charts and maps, choosing an appropriate form for their purpose
e.g. understanding of gradient of axes; pi-charts, bar-charts, etc. in the contexts of newspapers, textbooks, student projects (ref 10.1).

6.2.3   Appreciate perspective in space, photography, etc.

6.3   **Communication** The student should

6.3.1   Read and understand data in a wide variety of forms and identify the points of a given text relevant to a particular purpose
e.g. instruction manuals, notices, letters, labels (see also 6.1 and the rest of 6.2).
e.g. read a manual in order to know action to take in case of a breakdown.

6.3.2   Be able to read and understand questions and requests
e.g. questionnaires, memos, worksheets.

6.3.3   Be able to distinguish fact from opinion, identify emotive and ambiguous statements, and identify instances where expert advice is relevant to a matter of opinion

e.g. sales literature (including comparison of products); political speeches (ref. 9.1).
e.g. medical opinion on when to return to work (as opposed to an opinion on what is funny).

★ 6.3.4   Find and use information from a variety of given sources, including electronic information sources
e.g. dictionaries, catalogues, indexes, encyclopaedias, Prestel etc. (ref 9.17).

6.3.5   Listen to, and understand information and requests given orally
(ref. 3.5, 4.1).

6.3.6   Be able to communicate competently in written form; organise content, write effectively and with observation of the conventions of legibility, spelling, punctuation and grammar
e.g. formal letters and reports, informal notes and messages.

6.3.7   Explain and describe events, processes and opinions sensibly and clearly in writing
e.g. accident reports, operating instructions, arguing a case.

6.3.8   Make notes for own use
e.g. on visits, from books, during talks.

6.3.9   Be able to express tabular or graphic data in written form or vice-versa
e.g. diagrams, charts, sketch maps, statistics (ref. 6.2, 10.3).

6.3.10   Fill in forms correctly
e.g. driving licence applications, job applications, insurance claims.

6.3.11   Speak audibly and give clear verbal explanations of processes/opinions/events to a variety of audiences
e.g. friends, acquaintances, strangers, etc.

6.3.12   Make a disciplined contribution to group discussion
e.g. following some procedure; accepting and responding to others' views.

6.3.13   Use the telephone effectively

6.3.14   Experience and practice various kinds of verbal encounter, and evaluate their own strengths and weaknesses
e.g. negotiating, advising, persuading, justifying; using simulations, role-playing, mock-interviews, etc. (ref. 1.3, 4.1).

6.3.15   Experience membership of, and practice communication in, a variety of groups
e.g. formal, informal; large, small; decision making; task-centred; competitive and co-operative (ref. 9.2).

6.3.16   Experience various roles in these groups
e.g. leader, recorder, participant, chairman.

6.3.17   Experience the communication requirements of certain jobs and evaluate their reactions to them, and their ability to learn
e.g. with children, in an office; with customers; with VIPs (ref. also 2.1, 2.3).

6.3.18   Participate in planning and creating an example of a particular form of communication, matching the form to the purpose
e.g. TV (video) programme; audio tape; newspaper; exhibition.

6.3.19   Critically appraise examples in a medium of communication with which they have experience
e.g. TV, records, radio, books; identifying style, imagery, the message being transmitted, the audience for whom it is intended, influence of the technology, etc.

Aim 7

To bring about competence in a variety of study skills likely to be demanded of the young persons.

It is suggested that these study skills should be introduced as a specific group learning activity early in the induction phase, but that subsequent practice should come from following the course itself. This practice should subsequently be reinforced and evaluated on a tutorial basis.

The students should

7.1   Learn how to take notes, or use given notes for their own purposes
e.g. when preparing an essay; when hearing a talk.
Different strategies are possible.

7.2   Know how to gain access to appropriate works of reference
e.g. location of library; use of index.

7.3   Appreciate when to 'skim-read' and when to read for detail, and practise both techniques

7.4   Practise discussions and questioning
e.g. with teachers, with colleagues, with experts, co-operative learning.

7.5   Gain some appreciation of effective learning strategies and how to deploy them for their own benefit in the planning of their learning
e.g. aids to memory, such as mnemonics; simple psychology of learning, such as knowledge of learning plateaux, attention spans, and methods and effects of practice.

7.6   Experience a variety of learning situations and evaluate their reactions to them
e.g. formal talks, group talks, programmed learning, individual study with text books, using a library, role-plays and simulations; identifying which methods suit them best, for a given purpose
(These situations will normally occur naturally in the rest of the course; a separate session may be required only to evaluate them.)

Aim 8

To encourage the capacity to approach various kinds of problems methodically and effectively, and to plan and evaluate courses of action.

The students should

8.1   Examine and appraise given faults, problems or events, working individually or in a group.

e.g. faulty equipment, college over-crowding, a fall in sales, lung cancer, by

8.1.1   Thinking up alternative solutions or explanations
e.g. 'brainstorming' sessions in groups; listing alternatives without evaluation ('lateral' or 'divergent' thinking).

8.1.2   Identifying what evidence would support a statement or a guess and what would cast doubt on it
e.g. logical deduction of consequences, probable implications.

8.1.3   Considering or eliminating alternatives, in a systematic way
e.g. the need to hold some variables constant or have a 'control'; taking into account previous experience; the probability of certain causes; distinguishing between cause and correlation.

8.1.4   Generalising as appropriate from previous experiences or data
e.g. including discussion of the degree of confidence which is justified, the effects of further evidence, etc.

Special sessions in problem-tackling or scientific method may appeal to some students. Others will respond better if these objectives are dealt with in the natural course of activities and discussion occurring in the rest of the course. In the latter case, students should still be made aware of what constitutes a scientific approach, and in either case, experience should be given of problems which do not have one clear solution, as well as those which do.

8.2   Experience the process of planning an event or course of action, working individually and in groups
e.g. a journey by public transport, a visit to a factory, making an object, applying for a job, buying a vehicle, by

8.2.1   Identifying the nature of a problem, and collecting relevant information
e.g. factors involved; factual data available; sources of expert advice.

8.2.2   Working out alternative strategies and predicting their likely outcomes
as a pencil and paper exercise; as a topic for group discussion.

8.2.3   Choosing and implementing a plan, and adapting it to circumstances as appropriate

8.2.4   Evaluating the effectiveness of the plan, and identifying lessons to be learned
student performance should be judged with regard to this, rather than success or otherwise of the plan.

★   8.2.5   Develop the capacity to learn with computer assisted methods, using appropriate equipment.

Aim 9
To bring about sufficient political and economic literacy to understand the social environment and participate in it.

Section 9.1 describes a procedure by which the political dimension of issues which arise during the course can be analysed. It is not intended that these objectives

should be learned in isolation. The issues that may arise among the students, or through an account in a case-study, the press, TV, etc.

The students should

9.1   Appraise a policy dispute by

9.1.1   identifying the cause of disagreement
e.g. goals, values, methods (especially if allocating resources), results (ref. 9.11).

9.1.2   saying what further information they need, and where it can be found
(ref.6.3.4)

9.1.3   identifying where and by whom any decision will be made
e.g. in a local authority, by the housing committee; in the college, by the Academic Board.

9.1.4   indicating who is likely to be affected by various policies and in what way
identify likely supporters/opponents (ref.5.6).

9.1.5   Describing alternative ways of influencing the decision, and evaluating their relative merits
e.g. by forming pressure groups, writing letters, visiting, organising petitions, writing to newspapers; evaluating through discussion (ref.8.2.).

9.1.6   describing the issue using some basic political terms
e.g. conflict, power, consent-dissent, order-disorder, rules, compromise, consensus.

9.2   Analyse and appraise some groups to which they belong, and describe the methods by which decisions are reached in them
e.g. family, youth-club, class, student union; formal and informal groups.

9.3   Develop an awareness of the workings of formal decision-making groups by
i.e. groups which have rules of procedure

9.3.1   experiencing membership of such a group
e.g. class meetings, or in role-play simulation

9.3.2   experiencing/discussing different systems of voting
e.g. for nationwide referenda, general elections, class representative, goal of the month.

9.3.3   listing the conventional order of items on an agenda, and explaining their meaning and usage
e.g. minutes, standing items, AOB.

9.3.4   visiting and observing a public decision-making body in action
e.g. local council, college, Academic Board.

9.4   Gain a basis for evaluating national politics by being able to

9.4.1   Name the major political parties, their leaders, and describe major and/or distinctive items of policy
e.g. analysis of statements, actions, manifestos (ref.6.3.3); critical evaluation of media reports.

9.4.2   Describe in general terms, how local and central government relate, and the role of the EEC
   e.g. probably approached through case study of a given issue.

9.4.3   Indicate which Departments of Government are responsible for decisions which may affect the students personally
   e.g. fundings of the college, repair of roads, law on speed limits.

9.5   Check and explain a payslip
   e.g. deductions, tax-coding.

9.6   Balance income against expenditure and keep necessary records

9.7   Make value-for-money calculations and estimations
   When shopping; various sizes of product, special offers in shops (ref 6.1).

9.8   Plan an estimate personal budget for a typical working week in their intended jobs
   e.g. travel costs, meals, entertainment, accommodation, etc. (ref. 11.5).

9.9   Describe the function and use of a bank account, the Giro, building society, HP and credit cards
   e.g. comparative interest rates; conditions of use; etc.

It is recommended that the achievement of the following objective be promoted through the use of a simulation or business game, which enables students to discover the various factors involved from experience or as a result of their own investigation (ref.8.2). Presentation of the material in the form of a series of lectures, or a conventional text book, would not be appropriate.

9.10   Investigate how a business is run by identifying the factors involved in
   (i)   deciding what to sell
       e.g. market research, effect of competition, design of product
   (ii)   choosing location
       e.g. availability of labour, raw materials, transport, location of customers and competitors
   (iii)   borrowing money
       e.g. banks, shareholders
   (iv)   employing people
       e.g. wages, national insurance, legislation
   (v)   buying raw materials
       examples from manufacturing and service industry
   (vi)   calculating overheads
       e.g. rent, rates, advertising, office staff, maintenance, etc.
   (vii)   selling product
       e.g. functions of sales staff, customer relations, determining prices.
   (viii)   calculating profit/loss
       e.g. simple accounting
   (ix)   what happens to profit/loss
       e.g. interest payments, taxation, reinvestment, dividends.

9.11 Discuss the factors influencing the variable price of certain items, and arguments for and against state intervention
e.g. houses, fresh fruit, fuel.

9.12 Explain a selection of firms or organisations in basic economic terms
e.g. capitalist, co-operative, nationalised enterprises.

9.13 Investigate the sources of central and local government income, and where it is spent
case studies, use of reference texts, interpretation of tables and graphs.

9.14 Read some common legal documents and be able to answer simple comprehension questions on them
e.g. guarantees, HP contracts, rental agreements.

9.15 Visit a court of law, and discuss its procedures, personnel and atmosphere.

9.16 Demonstrate knowledge of their rights with respect to arrest and bail, by role-playing typical incidents and evaluating alternative courses of action
e.g. an incident involving the police (a) when the individual has broken the law and (b) when the individual is in the right
e.g. discussion of principle v expediency, rights and duties; discussion with the police representatives.

9.17 Use a simple reference text to determine their rights/duties in specific cases relating to the laws as it affects the consumer, the motorist, the employee
e.g. NCCL guide, Department of Employment publication (ref. 6.3.4).

9.18 Distinguish between criminal and civil law, know the usual order of proceedings through the courts, and compare the function of tribunals
perhaps via case studies.

9.19 Be aware of sources of legal aid and advice.

Aim 10
An appreciation of the physical and technological environments and the relationship between these and the needs of man in general, and working life in particular.

The students should

10.1 Participate in a group conducted survey of local amenities, which identifies some characteristics of the locality
e.g. surveys of leisure facilities, open or unused spaces, distribution of shops or industry.

10.2 Visit a social welfare centre as a basis for discussing personal and community responsibility for others
e.g. old folks' homes, centres for the handicapped, day centres (ref.4.1, 4.6).

10.3 Identify and assess the nature of environmental problems, through such issues as housing and transport
e.g. (a) use local photographs, sketches and taped interviews to argue for and against various forms of housing and (b) undertake a costing exercise of daily travel

*to support cases for and against private and public transport schemes (ref.8.2)
referring to the notions of continuity, change, cause, effect, etc. as appropriate
(ref.8.1.4).*

10.4   Examine at least two different industries or places of work, identifying
e.g. a production and a service industry.
  (i)   the enterprises, their use and dependence on energy
         *e.g. what fuels are used, and for what, the ecological and environmental
         implication of their use*
  (ii)   the production methods and materials which are used
         *e.g. mass production, batch production, unit production; the processes which
         are mechanised and how this compares with the recent past and predictable
         future (ref.1.3); the effect of this on changes in materials.*
  (iii) the division of labour and the nature of individual jobs
         *e.g. the effect of fully automatic, semi-automatic or manual control on the
         nature of jobs;
         the effect of the use of power, production methods and materials on working
         conditions, skills required, etc. (ref. 1.2).*

10.5   Appraise the implications of some current developments in technology
         *e.g. as observed in the above industries or as currently highlighted in the news.
         Discussions of economic, social, environmental and psychological implications (e.g.
         capital investment required, scale/location of industry, effect on employment and
         ownership, pollution, power requirements, changes in status of jobs, etc.).*

Aim 11
To bring about a development of the coping skills necessary to promote self
sufficiency in the young people.

The students should

11.1   Be able to plan and prepare adequate meals
         including budgeting, shopping and costing.

11.2   Use and maintain every-day machinery and equipment
         *e.g. fit an electric plug, use a launderette, iron a shirt. Willingness and confidence,
         and a knowledge of how to learn these things are intended, rather than
         comprehensive practice.*

11.3   Apply simple principles of health care, hygiene and physical fitness to their
every-day lives
         *knowledge of the effect of drugs (coffee, aspirin, tobacco, 'hard' drugs, etc.);
         symptoms, prevention and treatment of common ailments and diseases; access to
         facilities and activities for developing and maintaining fitness (ref.3.2).*

11.4   Practise simple first-aid techniques dealing with cuts, sprains, burns, etc.
Know when to call in expert help.

11.5   Investigate and use sources of information regarding the finding and
maintenance of accommodation
         *e.g. use of press, adverts, agencies, rental and purchase, regulations and
         procedures; do-it-yourself manuals.*

Aim 12

To bring about a flexibility of attitude and a willingness to learn, sufficient to manage future changes in technology and career.

Introduction

There may be said to be four elements necessary to produce this flexibility;
(a)   Possession of commonly used and transferable skills and capacities
(b)   Realisation of the need for flexibility
(c)   Ability to identify the underlying principles of a process or activity
(d)   Experience of and confidence in one's ability to transfer learning from one context to another.

It is hoped that many of the transferable capacities – element (a) – are already embodied in the other core objectives.

Element (b) will be encouraged by the economic and technological objectives included under Aims 9 and 10.

The need for (c) is part of the rationale behind the prescription of much experiential learning and project/case study/simulation activity in the core.

Element (d) entails the following general objectives, which will relate to much of the activity in the course as a whole, affecting the teaching approach as much as the content.

The students should

12.1   Whenever they develop a particular capacity in a given context
e.g. measuring up; estimating materials; following an instruction manual; giving instructions; fault finding.

12.1.1   Identify other contexts in which the capacity could be useful
e.g. similarity between: assembly instructions and recipes: and adjusting bikes or sewing machines.

12.1.2.   Be given practice at applying relevant aspects of previous learning to a new situation
Having identified a transferable skill, practise transferring and adapting it.

12.1.3   Identify any other activities at which they are likely to be successful, on the evidence of this learning
As a contribution to the self-profile (ref.2.2, 2.4). What do they enjoy doing? What kind of learning comes easily to them?

Courses based on ABC

Courses based on ABC common-core-curriculum aims tend to include the following elements:

- the provision of a curriculum framework as against a prescribed and possibly restrictive course
- a common core introduced through contexts selected to be relevant to specific students, courses, and local areas
- an integrated course as against separate subjects
- a negotiated curriculum based on student's expressed needs

- the development of transferable skill competency through a range of vocational and practical contexts
- an emphasis on experiential as against reception learning
- a narrowing of occupational focus and choice as students proceed through the programme
- profile assessment achieved through regular guidance and counselling
- progression to other schemes of vocational education and training and to academic courses

The table given here (Table 1.1) shows the relationship between the principal ABC aims and the structure of this book.

A BASIS FOR CHOICE: COMMON-CORE AIMS	Chapter	10 What is an adult?	11 Widening social relationships	12 On from the course	13 Unemployment	14 Getting the message across	15 Receiving the message	16 Values and choices	17 Getting involved
1 To bring about an informed perspective as to the role and status of a young person in an adult society and the world of work.		⇗	✓	✓	✓	✓	✓		✓
2 To provide a basis from which a young person can make an informed and realistic decision with respect to his or her immediate future.				⇗	✓				
3 To bring about a continuing development of physical and manipulative skills in both vocational and leisure contexts, and an application of those skills in others.		✓	✓	✓	✓				
4 To bring about an ability to develop satisfactory personal relationships with others.		✓	⇗			✓	✓	✓	
5 To provide a basis on which the young person acquires a set of moral values applicable to issues in contemporary society.		✓	✓			✓	✓	⇗	✓
6 To bring about a level of achievement in literacy, numeracy and graphicacy appropriate to ability, adequate to meet the basic demands of contemporary society.				✓	✓	⇗	✓	✓	
7 To bring about competence in a variety of skills likely to be demanded of the young persons.						✓	⇗		
8 To encourage the capacity to approach various kinds of problems methodically and effectively, and to plan and evaluate courses of action.				⇗	✓	✓		✓	✓
9 To bring about sufficient political and economic literacy to understand the social environment and participate in it.		✓			✓	✓	✓	✓	⇗
10 An appreciation of the physical and technological environments and the relationship between these and the needs of man in general, and working life in particular.				✓	✓				
11 To bring about a development of the coping skills necessary to promote self-sufficiency in the young people.				✓			✓		✓
12 To bring about a flexibility of attitude and a willingness to learn, sufficient to manage future changes in technology and career.				⇗	✓		✓	✓	✓

⇗ Indicates a KEY aim

✓ Indicates a subsidiary aim

Table 1.1 This matrix shows the links between our topic chapters and the ABC aims

PART I

Strategies

1 Introduction to Part I

As a preface to our suggestions for lesson content, we begin with an exploration of teaching and learning strategies. We believe that your students' progress will be influenced by the *way* you teach as much as by *what* you teach.

Many of the strategies cited will seem familiar, but we hope that some of the ideas will be new to you and that these may inspire a fresh way of looking at your teaching.

There are no definite statements nor rigid guidelines – just points and suggestions. Whenever it seems appropriate we have referred to relevant theory and research. If you have the time and inclination you can follow these up and study the field in more depth.

Some of the strategies require specific physical conditions – a large room, generous blocks of time, or particular resources, for example. Most can be used by any tutor with any students anywhere.

How to use
There is no particular recommended sequence for reading, no intended order of importance. In each section is a full description of the strategy concerned, followed by a quick-reference guide to this strategy – when to use it and when not, how to do it well, and how to take it further.

Although we realize that you are probably working under pressure and may wish to use this manual simply for quick reference, we do still urge you to read the full rationales for the strategies. You will find practical hints and suggestions throughout the text; in any case, we feel that the theoretical underpinning is important if you are to get the most out of the strategies.

There is also a lot of interlinking. The case-study strategy, for example, cannot be applied in isolation. Case-study work may also involve a visit, a short burst of exposition from you, and a workshop session. And it will certainly involve discussion, asking questions and some small-group teaching.

We hope that you will find *all* the strategies relevant at some stage for your particular type of vocational-preparation involvement. If you look at the ABC aims (pages 13–27) you will see that these call for a variety of teaching approaches. It is this variety of learning experience that should keep both you and your students alert and motivated to get the most out of the content of your courses.

There is one final and important point that you must bear in mind. However imaginative, worthwhile or positively challenging a strategy may appear, you should never ask your students to do anything that you are not willing to do yourself.

2　Discussion and small-group teaching

2.1　Discussion

Perhaps the first thing to establish is that when we talk about 'discussion methods' and 'small-group teaching' we are not referring to the same processes.

Discussion is an activity in which a number of participants express and weigh different viewpoints. There need not be a final, correct judgement on the subject matter. Alternatives are put forward for consideration and group members should be willing to adjust their opinions and accommodate their thinking one to another. Everyone should begin with a willingness to listen to, to evaluate and perhaps to be influenced by the views of others. And one of the more difficult tasks for you as tutor is the fostering of respect for these other opinions.

Students may not be used to learning through discussion. They may need help in accepting the changed role of their tutor; their previous experience of teaching may be of the direct transmission of knowledge achieved solely through exposition lessons. They may therefore be insecure in a large- or small-group discussion, preferring a more passive, recipient role. It is therefore important that you make clear to the students what is expected of them. However the discussion is organized, there needs to be an agreed procedure and a carefully planned framework.

Discussion has many ends. It can be used to foster the growth of interpretive skills, to teach the students to think. It can contribute to the achievement of objectives in the 'cognitive domain' (by increasing knowledge and understanding) and in the 'affective domain' (by developing awareness or modifying attitudes and values).

Discussion is not the same as either question-and-answer or formal debate. In a *question-and-answer session* you may manipulate the verbal interaction to achieve predetermined outcomes; typically you remain the focus of the group's attention. Questions are most effective if open, allowing a range of student contributions and answers, but they may tend more frequently to be closed, requiring specific responses. For a full exploration of the variety of questions in teaching, see Barnes and Todd (1977). In a *formal debate* the participants assume defined roles and take up in advance stances in relation to the subject matter and to each other. The procedure follows accepted conventions and rules. In *discussion*, by contrast, contributors may assume and shed roles at any stage: the subject matter will shift and develop naturally unless a leader focuses and controls the direction.

The tutor's role

Leading a discussion is not easy. To attend to individual contributions while maintaining an overview of the general direction, to foster respect and tolerance for all participants, and to manage the group without dominating it, require the combined skills of a choreographer, juggler and politician.

The presence of a tutor alters the social and power balances of any group. However much you may wish to be 'just another member of the group', you never can be; the aura of authority cannot be dissipated so easily. As well as being *in* authority you are seen as *an* authority, and must therefore be particularly careful not to present your values and attitudes too forcibly. You should also take great care regarding ongoing evaluation of the ideas and opinions expressed by group members. If you engage in on-the-spot criticism, students will become inhibited and very reluctant to state their views.

The discussion leader's role could involve presenting the problem and defining the task. Throughout the discussion you would prevent inappropriate digressions and at the end you would sum up. Ivan Illich (1971) argues against the need for such an 'authoritative presence' to structure the discussion.

Stenhouse (1972) stresses that a group can only function well when all the members are clear about their position *vis-à-vis* the tutor. It is therefore important that you make clear to the group your intentions in such behaviour as actively participating in the discussion, chairing neutrally, and playing devil's advocate. Sometimes the deliberate withdrawal of the tutor from a group can increase participation in discussion by freeing the more nervous students from the fear of having their contributions assessed.

Group dynamics

Some awareness of the theories of group dynamics can help. The social and personal relationships between individuals will influence the conduct and outcome of the discussion as the participants project their personalities and react to one another.

You need to be aware of possible reasons for silence or aggression. You need to be able to control your own hostility or insecurity and to deal tactfully with such feelings in others. There are many reasons why you may decide to intervene in a discussion. It might be to ensure relevance or to change the direction. There might be a need for clarification or for greater precision. It might seem the only way to encourage reasonableness and to foster respect for differing viewpoints. A quiet student might benefit from a direct address or from non-verbal encouragement to participate. A too-voluble student might need gentle persuasion to make way for others, thus ensuring a more equal balance of contributions.

Encouraging participation

There are various techniques that can help to increase participation. Individuals usually give signals when they are getting ready to contribute: you should be alert to act on eye contact, indrawn breath, shifts in seating position and the like, which may signal this readiness. While a student is speaking it is best not to maintain eye contact with him or her. If you do there is an implication that you will take up the thread once the contribution is made, and all too often an intended discussion can become a series of dialogues. It is better to glance at others in the group, in the hope that the speaker also will vary eye contact so as to address other, more responsive participants and ultimately to obtain reactions from them rather than from you. It is wise not to answer any questions that can be answered by other group members.

2.2 Small-group teaching

Many of the observations made above regarding discussion methods relate to small-group teaching also; indeed discussion is the usual purpose of such groups. There are, however, considerations of organization and management which are specific to small-group work.

A major aim of group teaching is that through interaction students accept more responsibility for their own learning and for that of their peers. Your own role will differ according to the purpose of the group. Frequently it will be that of facilitator; learning will then be student-centred rather than teacher-centred. This implies that although you will have to expend considerable time and energy in creating a suitable environment for learning to take place, the final role will be supportive rather than dominating or directly manipulative.

Setting

Thought should be given to the environment. Is the room large enough for several small groups to work without distracting each other? Can the seats be moved into circles, C-shapes or U-shapes? If there is a focal point in the seating plan – say the head of a table, or the 'centre' or edges of a horseshoe – you could alert the group to the likely outcome: that the person sitting in such a position may find himself or herself assuming leadership, as contributions will tend to be addressed towards that point.

Group composition

There has been research into the effect of group size on learning and social interaction (Gibb, 1951). It is generally accepted that small groups (groups with four, five or six members) are more effective in problem-solving tasks than are larger groups. Certainly it is more likely that quieter students will participate if the group size is kept to this level. An alternative is to sub-divide larger groups for at least part of the session.

Should the groups be self-selecting? It is probable that one of your aims is to enable all the students to contribute. In this case it would be wise to ensure the separation of the quiet students from their more extrovert peers. That way the noisier ones, because they are in separate groups, do not prevent the quieter ones from participating. Another reason for assigning students to groups is to achieve a spread of knowledge and expertise: this may be appropriate if the intended outcome is a solution to the problem or the completion of a task. The best compromise may be to vary the approach, allowing students to choose their groups when such concerns are not paramount.

Materials
Thought should also be given, well before the lesson, to the need for back-up materials and information. If the groups are to function smoothly such resources should be present in the room. Impromptu trips to the library are distracting at best and destructive at worst.

The contract phase
Students may be unsure as to their role in discussion. To help prevent anxiety you need to spend adequate time explaining the purpose of the activity. This is sometimes referred to as the 'contract phase'. If a task is set it should be set at an appropriate level so that all the students, or the groups at least, can cope with it. It should be possible to achieve a solution or outcome within the time available; and the task should motivate students by engaging their interest or arousing their curiosity.

Some groups may be formed simply to reflect on an issue, rather than to accomplish a task. The process of discussion, of considering alternatives, may well be more valuable than any end-product, such as a specific solution.

The tutor as facilitator
Once the environment has been arranged and the contract negotiated you may wish to stand clear of the activity. The decision as to whether to circulate and monitor the groups' progress or to remain on the outside is often a difficult one; it may well depend on how well integrated the group is.

In some types of group work a recorder may be nominated in each group to sum up the discussion for the class as a whole. Occasionally you may feel a need to guide the groups if they appear to be digressing or if tolerance and mutual respect are lacking. Conflict does not always interfere with learning, but at a certain level intervention may be advisable. As always, such decisions rest with you.

Related to your role as facilitator is your role as creator of climates conducive to psychological safety. The humanist psychologist Carl Rogers (1969) refers to a specific kind of facilitator. As a participant in group discussion his facilitator shares feelings and thoughts in a way that helps to develop a safe climate, which in turn reduces defensiveness and encourages freedom of expression. The facilitator's behaviour sets the mood of the group, and elicits and clarifies the purpose of any discussion; it allows the group to see the facilitator as a 'flexible resource to be utilized by the group'. Eventually, in Rogers' model, he or she becomes a participant in the group on an equal basis with the others. Earlier we said that you could *not* become 'just another member'. Once again it is up to you to decide upon your role and the degree to which you can merge with the group.

Leadership style
The effect of leadership style on the learning environment has also been investigated. The best known classification remains that of White and Lippit (1960). It was originally used to describe youth-club leaders. Relating this work to teaching, White and Lippett's 'authoritarian' system describes a learning environment that is teacher-centred with an emphasis on formality, competition and punishment. The 'democratic' system favours participation and co-operation; and the *'laissez-faire'* system stresses freedom, is student-centred, and offers little guidance.

In the original experiments the subjects worked hard in the presence of an autocratic leader but motivation and concentration ceased in his absence. Little initiative was shown in dealing with problems and there was a dependence on the leader for approval. This authoritarian social climate appeared to engender personal frustration which was sometimes expressed in aggressive behaviour. Under the *laissez-faire* leader the work was uneven, sometimes disorganized and apparently aimless. Under the democratic leader, however, the subjects worked regularly even when unsupervised. Their conversation was more related to the task in hand. It was the democratic climate that produced the greatest amount of friendly behaviour amongst the subjects and between them and the leader. The work of Morton Deutsch (1949), contrasting co-operative and competitive groups, offers similar conclusions.

It would seem therefore that group teaching is most likely to be successful if you can manage the learning environment so as to secure a psychologically safe, democratic climate in which you can function as facilitator and occasional guide. The precise way in which this might be achieved will obviously differ according to the type of group work chosen, your own personality and teaching style, and the students' learning styles.

Fostering group cohesion
Whatever the type of leader, just being in a group affects the learning of each individual. A general aim of all group teaching will be the fostering of supportive, sympathetic relationships between group members. The degree of group coherence and interaction can be a major factor in determining whether learning takes place.

You should also be alert to the social undercurrents in any group. It is important to notice if hostility is usually directed towards particular individuals or if some students' contributions appear to be over-valued by the group. While recognizing that your intervention cannot solve all the social problems of an unpopular student, tactful guidance and careful organization of groups can help such a student to make a useful contribution and thereby gain group approval. The more positive self-image that should result will obviously play a part in helping the whole group function effectively.

Some words of caution

All group teaching, and some methods in particular, has inherent dangers: tutors need to be alerted to these. It is easy to place students in threatening, even frightening situations that force them to expose aspects of their personalities, beliefs and attitudes which they may not be ready to submit to group examination. The necessary strength of character – toughness, or whatever we choose to call it – may not have been developed at that stage; group exposure can be a shattering experience. Professional counsellors and therapists are trained to deal with such situations; in general teachers are not. It pays therefore to think very carefully about what you are requiring of the students before beginning an activity. Possible outcomes should be anticipated: if the situation becomes disturbing you have to be ready to use your own social and interpersonal skills to calm the students and to allow time for gradual and gentle debriefing, to re-establish calm, 'everyday' levels and forms of interaction.

Assessment

Presuming that you have proved to be a paragon of tact, understanding, and organization, and that you have successfully created an environment conducive to co-operative learning, a final task will be to evaluate the process and outcome. This is of particular importance where the objectives require an assessment of students' contributions to discussion and their ability to co-operate with others.

There are various techniques for assessing such teaching methods and students' progress. These vary from subjective, impressionistic summaries to detailed checklists and analyses. Frequently such assessments are recorded as statements or as points on a scale on a student profile. If you would like to use a systematic analysis, the Flanders Interaction analysis may be worth considering. Both that and Bale's Interaction Process analysis are described by Donald Bligh (1971) in a collection of conference papers on group discussion. But often careful observation of students, recorded simply as individual descriptive statements, is the most useful approach. Such statements might include reference to the student's level of contributions, to his or her demonstrated ability to learn from a group pooling of knowledge and to his or her adjustment to group work, including supportiveness to others and willingness to take the lead when appropriate. Some groups that meet frequently over a long period can be taught how to take this task on for themselves. Such self-evaluation is after all a valuable part of the learning process. A sample observer's checklist is given on page 183 of *Lifeskills teaching*. An evaluation the results of which are not shared with students is, in any case, contrary to the spirit of the facilitating role.

2.3   The strategies

This section describes several different types of group organization. You may think of others and, in any case, you are encouraged to combine the alternatives in new ways to suit your particular requirements. The selection of a particular strategem, in this case a specific type of small-group teaching, will obviously depend upon your objectives. The choice will also be influenced by the varying learning styles and preferences of the students, by your own personality, teaching style skills, by the subject matter of the lesson and by the environmental factors or constraints. The following suggested methods are not in any way prescriptive, but we hope that some or all may work for you and for your students.

Buzz groups

Typically, you would use this method (Figure 2.1) to obtain full and lively participation after a period of relative passivity, a lecture say, or other form of exposition. Divide the students quickly, and with minimal concern for group membership, into sets of four to six. Do not appoint leaders. Ask the groups to exchange views for ten minutes or so before returning to a large-group format for a question-and-answer session or further discussion. In this time, first impressions and opinions can be tried out and all students can become involved and can clarify their thinking before the more structured plenary session.

Another use of buzz groups is in tackling a task or question selected by you.

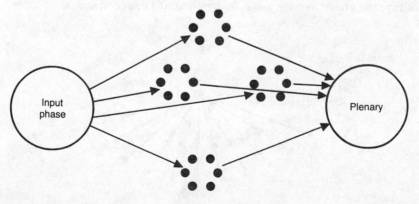

Figure 2.1   Buzz groups

It is important to select a topic that can be dealt with in the time available, usually no longer than fifteen minutes. You must also ensure that everybody understands the task or question before the groups begin work. It might be the same task or question for all the groups, or you might allocate related, complementary versions. If this is not done you may find yourself dashing from group to group, repeating the instructions and getting tired and irritated in the process. Sometimes a leader or recorder (or both) is appointed in each group. The job of the recorder is to summarize the group's discussion for a general session. It is up to you to decide whether or not to circulate and monitor progress. It is probably best to leave buzz groups alone to function in a spontaneous, uninhibited manner. You can direct the final session and obtain feedback there from all the groups.

When to use
- after a talk, film or other presentation
- when you want a task completed quickly
- when you want to pose a question for small-group consideration

When not to use
- at the end of a lesson when there's insufficient time to complete the task or to conduct the follow-up
- in a room where there is insufficient space for the groups to function effectively

Brainstorming
In this method (Figure 2.2) groups of up to twelve students offer spontaneous suggestions regarding a specific problem or topic. As with buzz groups, the time allowed for the activity is short, but there the similarity ends. In this set-up evaluation and criticism is taboo. All ideas are welcomed; you encourage the group to generate as many alternative suggestions as possible.

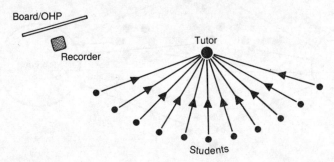

Figure 2.2   Brainstorming

You might well guide the group, and you should take time beforehand to ensure that all the students understand the rules and their purpose. Value judgements must be discouraged, as must any kind of audible or non-verbal negative reaction – groans, sighs, eyes raised upwards, and the like. The assessment, challenging and weighing of the ideas will be done later.

The brainstorming session will probably be used as the first stage of problem solving. You may follow it up with a detailed, careful balancing of alternatives. During the activity an energetic recorder should note all the suggestions – in their original form, not paraphrased – on a chalk board, overhead transparency, or flipchart. These suggestions can then be categorized and organized before the structured discussion.

You could of course combine buzz groups and brainstorming – each small buzz group could include a brainstorming session before discussing or evaluating a problem.

When to use
- before a focused and structured discussion of a problem
- to obtain first reactions to a film, video or similar presentation
- as the first stage of buzz-group work

When not to use
- after an organized, chaired discussion on the same theme
- in an insecure, uncooperative or unsupportive atmosphere

Pyramiding
Pyramiding (Figure 2.3) is sometimes referred to as *snowballing* or *pairs to fours*.

You can begin with task-centred buzz groups or with pairs. The groups combine in a doubling operation and at each stage a consensus is sought.

Set the task and warn your students that you will interrupt them after a given period (ten minutes, say) and that they will then form progressively larger groups to compare ideas and continue the discussion.

You will decide when the pyramiding should stop and full plenary session should begin. This might be after three or four combinations – you will probably make the decision according to the degree of fresh insight and interpretation being achieved.

The purposes of this method are to involve as many students as possible in the discussion, and to develop such skills as accommodation and negotiation. One potential problem is that the drive towards consensus may stifle individual and original interpretations and solutions. Another is that the stronger personalities may gradually swamp the quieter students.

When to use
- in a lesson which is wholly given over to the discussion of one problem, theory or topic

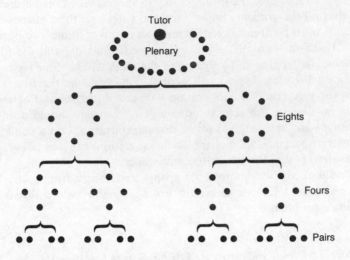

Figure 2.3   Pyramiding

- after your group has experienced other types of discussion and is ready to concentrate on the skills of negotiation and accommodation

When not to use
- when there is insufficient time to allow for enough combinations plus a plenary session
- with students who are unused to the art of discussion and who lack its basic skills
- with students who have not yet grasped the purpose of negotiation and accommodation to other peoples' views – they may destroy the procedure by sticking rigidly to their own initial points of view

Syndicates
This method (Figure 2.4) is sometimes called *task-centred groups*. It involves a number of small groups discussing the same or related problems and presenting their solutions through a spokesperson in a formal plenary session. It differs from some other methods in that research may be involved.

You provide each group with a starter pack of evidence and the group has to collect further information, using the library or even resources external to the school or college. In some versions the activity will require group members to assume and allocate roles and tasks among themselves. They will probably also have to decide upon procedure. You are likely to be a true facilitator here – acting as consultant only when directly approached.

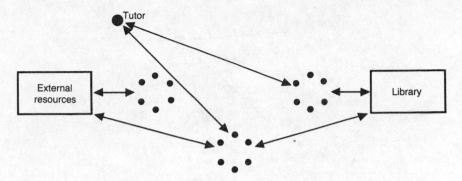

Figure 2.4 Syndicates

When to use
- while your students are working on projects
- as a means of introducing research methodology
- as part of a programme designed to influence attitudes through the collection and weighing of evidence
- in a study-skills course

When not to use
- with students who all lack the necessary literacy and information-retrieval skills
- in a short lesson that cannot incorporate movement between rooms.

Horseshoe groups
Horseshoe groups (Figure 2.5) are so called because of the physical arrangement of the seats. They are small task-orientated groups which are positioned so that you can be at the focal point for each one. Even when you have temporarily joined one of the groups to monitor progress, you can easily maintain eye contact with the other students. Once again the tasks or problems set may be the same for all groups, complementary or different.

It is possible to arrange buzz groups or syndicates in this way, although it is doubtful whether you would always wish to be either the focus or a participant. Sometimes you will deliberately avoid this seating pattern so that the groups can function unimpeded by your too-obvious presence.

When to use
- in lessons in which you wish to monitor all the groups' progress
- in the early stages of discussion and task-group work, when the students will need a lot of guidance and reassurance
- as one stage in the assessment and recording of student attainment and progress

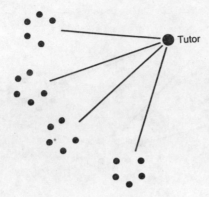

Figure 2.5   Horseshoe groups

When not to use
- when students need to function spontaneously, uninhibited by close observation
- during lessons designed partly to foster independence and self-reliance and/or co-operation and small-group cohesion

Fish bowl

Sometimes called a *double-ring exercise*, this is probably the most threatening and therefore dangerous of all the types of teaching group described. *You should consider carefully before employing the fish-bowl strategy.*

Arrange the seating in two concentric rings (Figure 2.6) and get the students to take up places in either the inner or outer circle. The inner circle represents

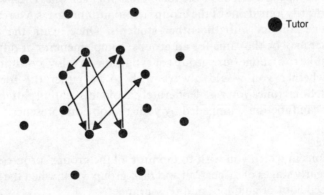

Figure 2.6   Fish bowl

fish inside the bowl; the outer constitutes observers who watch the fish.

The 'fish' are set a problem or task. (We are here concerned with discussion; in other contexts the task could be practical or a role play.) Each fish is observed by a counterpart, the person sitting directly behind in the outer ring. The observer notes the contributions of the fish to the discussion and to the inner ring's interaction as a whole.

At intervals, stop the discussion and ask some of the paired individuals in the two rings to change places. The fish will go to the outer ring and become the observer; the discussion will continue with the erstwhile observer, now the fish, taking up the thread. You may continue with this process of substitution until all the students have experienced membership of both rings. A variation is to make all the fish and observers exchange places simultaneously at appropriate moments during the discussion.

The exercise has value. You can check the ability of the students to concentrate and to adapt quickly to group membership. The students can develop confidence in expressing themselves in front of observers. Anxiety levels are likely to be high, however, and participants may be inhibited in their contributions. It is a method to be used only occasionally, and probably only after the students have experienced other discussion and group-teaching methods.

When to use
- after other discussion methods have been tried
- when you wish to develop concentration and listening skills
- when you wish to foster self-confidence and to help students become articulate and fast-thinking

When not to use
- with shy, nervous students
- in a group of very mixed attainment regarding speaking and listening skills

Assigned opinion
You can use this strategem in conjunction with several of the other methods described. Once the small groups are organized, a point of view is assigned to or chosen by each student. It is then up to him or her to explore and present that position, which is unlikely to correspond to his or her own current views. Thirty minutes might be an appropriate length of time for this activity.

The aim is to enable students to adopt different perspectives and as a result of that experience to see their own previous stance more objectively. The process requires a relatively high degree of sophistication and verbal skill, and you may feel that only the more articulate students should attempt the exercise. This would be a pity; the act of assuming a set of prescribed values can bring out some quieter students. It is possible that insecure group members might feel less intimidated while expressing views which are not seen to represent their own attitudes.

When to use
- at any stage of a lesson, probably after some of the other small-group methods have been introduced
- to encourage objectivity and a better understanding of other viewpoints
- to develop the ability to empathize
- when you are working to influence attitudes
- as a method that might help quieter students participate
- as an introduction to role-play

When not to use
- in a discussion that is highly charged emotionally or that is particularly provocative

Taking it further
This strategem can develop into role-play exercises. Have a look at section 4.2 for some more guidance.

Seminars
The term 'seminar' is associated with higher education and certainly it is the most common type of discussion group in universities and polytechnics. It could, however, be used to good effect with student on less academic courses.

The number of participants is probably best kept to twelve or below so that everybody can contribute. A leader – tutor or student – presents a topic in such a way that the rest of the group are stimulated to explore it. A short paper may be read or spoken to; an activity may be demonstrated; a situation may be acted out. It is very important that this introduction is kept to a quarter or less of the time available. You yourself have probably experienced at some stage a seminar where the leader spent three-quarters of the time reading a lengthy paper, only allowing time for a hurried and therefore frustrating interchange of views at the end. Students who are to lead seminars need to be warned against this, and a tutorial beforehand to help them plan could be invaluable.

When to use
- as a follow-up to individual research and projects, or to syndicate groups, to develop the skills of spoken presentation and listening
- in the first half of a long lesson as a presentation and discussion to be followed by buzz groups

When not to use
- at an early stage in the course before the students have practised less formal discussion

- in a short lesson where there will be too great a restriction on the general discussion

Encounter groups

This last group is included because there are those who advocate its use in teaching, particularly at the level that concerns us. This kind of activity approximates more nearly to a kind of therapy-group session than to other small-group teaching methods. You should therefore examine your objectives closely before selecting this method.

The original encounter groups developed in America as part of 'sensitivity training'. They are also sometimes referred to as *interaction groups, T-groups,* or *laboratory groups.*

Unlike the seminar and many of the other group methods described here, there is no statement of purpose at the beginning of the activity, and the leader does not attempt to structure the discussion. It is up to the group members to make the experience meaningful by deciding together the aims and structure.

The leader does have a role to play. She or he is there to help the group members identify and observe the social and personal dynamics at operation within the group. Normally an early stage of directionless, spontaneous contributions develops into an exploration of the usually hidden feelings of individuals in the group. *While this can be a rewarding experience it can also be destructive and hurtful.* Some hold that the baring of souls and the public exposure involved can bring a group of students to greater cohesiveness, supportiveness and mutual respect. This in turn can have a positive effect later on other types of group work. Others advise against the method on the grounds that the cost to individuals can be too high. Once again, as always, you as the tutor will decide. *If you do use this strategy, be careful; and be prepared to spend time picking up the pieces, or guiding the group as they attempt to do so.*

When to use
- once the students know each other reasonably well and appear to have sufficient strength to cope with the experience
- at a stage in the course when you feel the activity will improve group cohesion and mutual respect.

When not to use
- at any point if there is insufficient attention to the risks and possible outcomes
- in a group with insecure or over-aggressive members
- at any time if you feel at all uneasy or ill-equipped to deal with potential problems

2.4   Resources list

Tutors' background reading

Abercrombie, M.L.J. 1974 *Aims and techniques of group teaching*, 3rd edn (Society for Research into Higher Education)

Argyle, M. 1972 *The psychology of interpersonal behaviour* (Penguin)

Barnes, D. 1971 *Language, the learner and the school* (Penguin)

Barnes, D. and F. Todd, 1977 *Communication and learning in small groups* (Routledge and Kegan Paul)

Bligh, D.A. 1971 'Evaluation of teaching in groups by interaction analysis' in *Varieties of group discussion in university teaching* (University of London Institute of Education)

Bridges, D. 1979 *Education, democracy and discussion* (NFER)

Deutsch, M. 1949 'Experimental study of effects of co-operation and competition upon group processes' in *Human Relations* 3, 199–231

Gibb, J.R. 1951 'The effect of group size and threat reduction upon creativity in problem solving' in *Amer. Psych.* 6

Hare, A.P. 1962 *Handbook of small-group research* (Free Press)

Hill, W.F. 1977 *Learning through discussion*, 3rd edn (Sage)

Holt, J. 1964 *How children fail* (Pelican)

Illich, I. 1971 *Deschooling society* (Calder & Boyars)

Rogers, C. 1969 *Freedom to learn* (Charles Merrill)

Shaw, M.E. 1976 *Group Dynamics: the psychology of small-group behaviour*, 2nd edn (McGraw-Hill)

Stenhouse, L. 1972 'Teaching through small-group discussion: formality rules and authority' in *Cambridge Journal of Education* 2, 18–24

Yorke, D.M. 1981 *Patterns of teaching: a source book for teachers in further education* (Council for Educational Technology)

White, P.K. and R. Lippitt 1960 *Autocracy and democracy* (Hamish Hamilton)

3   Asking questions

3.1   The uses of questions

You may be puzzled to find 'asking questions' listed among strategies such as role-play and case studies. What needs saying about questions? Isn't question-and-answer a part of all teaching? Well, yes: certainly all teachers do use questions – but that doesn't mean that all teachers use them sensibly, effectively or even fairly. The questions you ask and the way you ask them can determine whether learning takes place and whether students feel secure in the environment you create.

Questions should always be asked for positive reasons. They should encourage students to explore ideas and to reason for themselves. Even when they are used as learning checks they can tease out understanding rather than confine themselves to factual recall. And it shouldn't always be you asking questions: in a lively and supportive atmosphere students will ask questions of you and of each other.

Why do tutors ask questions?

Starting a lesson

There are of course many different reasons why questions are asked. For example, you might use a few general questions to help a group relax and settle down. Social questions – such as 'Are you sorted out, happy with the seating arrangement . . .? Shall we open the windows a bit . . .?' – set the tone and confirm your role as tutor and theirs as students. It's all part of the creation of a specific world of teaching in which the rules and rituals differ slightly from those of the outside world. Carefully chosen, and delivered with the appropriate friendly non-verbal signals, questions like this can foster group cohesion and establish rapport. You ignore such apparent niceties at your peril; simply marching into a classroom and beginning a lesson without such a preamble will almost certainly lead to resentment, lack of motivation, inattention and possibly disruption.

Establishing content

Once the lesson has begun your first questions will probably be used to pinpoint and focus attention on the content. 'What do you know about . . .?' 'Have you heard/seen/read . . .?' This way you can check your students' current knowledge and understanding. There is a risk of course. Such seemingly open invitations can lead to lengthy, rambling contributions and to discussion that ranges much more widely than you expect or require. Experience leads to skill at handling discussion; you will soon become adept at using such contributions, keeping them sufficiently short and steering them towards the actual lesson topic. Before you introduce new knowledge or skills, you may also wish to check whether your students have remembered information and concepts covered in previous sessions.

Monitoring learning
As the lesson develops you will wish to integrate regular learning checks. Questions provide feedback on students' learning, particularly if you encourage the students to ask questions as well as answer them. Once a pattern of learning checks is set it should be possible to ensure that each stage has been understood before the next step is taken.

When your questions do uncover difficulties you will have to decide whether the majority of the group needs more help before you go on or whether only one or two students are struggling. In the latter situation a separate small-group session later in the lesson may be the most appropriate way of dealing with the problem.

Controlling progression
Each new phase of the lesson can be introduced by questions to identify the stage. Once the new information has been presented skilful questions can encourage creative and divergent thinking. Concepts can be presented in an *inductive* rather than deductive manner – you can use questions to coax students towards the new concept by helping them to narrow down the alternatives progressively at each stage. Eventually they should 'see' the meaning for themselves. This is usually more effective than *deductive* teaching in which you begin with a definition. Inductive methods may take longer, but students are more likely to remember things they discover for themselves. And if they are kept active in answering your questions you can be fairly confident that you have their attention.

Building confidence
Frequent question-and-answer phases can draw out shyer students. They should also increase motivation by providing positive feedback and reinforcement while signalling that answers are correct.

In lessons in which small-group discussion methods are used, you could set different questions for each group. This approach could be used in a wide range of learning activities, from problem solving to text analysis.

Controlling the lesson
Finally questions can also be used to establish and maintain control. Friendly

but firm direct personal addresses – 'Do you agree with that point . . .?' or 'Were you able to hear that . . .?' can discourage daydreaming. More serious disruption can sometimes be arrested in the early stages by carefully phrased and directed questions. You yourself have to be continuously alert and in touch with all your students in turn by eye contact or by verbal interaction.

When do tutors use questions?

Exposition lessons
In exposition lessons, in which you will tend to play a more obviously active role than your students, you will nevertheless use questions at regular intervals to encourage participation, to check learning and to focus on the individual steps in your presentation. You should also invite questions from your students. However well structured and delivered your presentation you should be willing to pause to allow time for the students to absorb the material. The most skilled and charismatic speaker will lose the audience's attention if there are no breaks in the flow of words. Visual stimuli will help but so will the questions. For most people the attention span is less than 20 minutes at a time so phase your questions accordingly.

Discussion lessons
In discussion lessons you will probably use questions as part of the stimulus; in whole-group discussions and in plenaries you will wish to direct the discussion by initial and follow-up questions. Skilled discussion-leading usually entails employing brief, well-chosen questions as prompts rather than delivering lengthy contributions. When you are setting up small-group discussions, role-plays, case studies and so on you will almost certainly set questions as stimuli.

Questions are also important in one-to-one tuition. As you work with a student to develop existing knowledge and to expose and treat weaknesses you may use questions to encourage active learning and to probe for possible causes of the difficulties experienced.

The guidance-and-counselling role often has tactful questioning as its base. Here it is also important to know when to *avoid* asking questions because they may be intimidating. When you sit with a student to complete part of a profile, to discuss a work-experience placement or the like, it will be by carefully chosen questions that you elicit whatever information, attitudes and feelings you need at that stage to identify and then explore with the student. For suggestions about the strategies for drawing students out, see the section on guidance and counselling (page 322).

It is probable that questioning should be a part of all teaching situations. Even a lecturer with a student audience of hundreds can pose questions, even if these are rhetorical ones, the answers to which have to be presented and considered as part of the performance.

3.2   Categories of questions

Writers on classroom language have analysed the discourse and have placed questions in a range of categories. The study by Barnes (1969) is well worth looking at.

The two main divisions are between 'open' and 'closed' and between 'factual' and 'reasoning' questions.

Open versus closed questions

Open questions

If you as a tutor ask a genuinely open question you are prepared to accept any answers: you are not trying to elicit a particular response. It's rather like brainstorming (page 42). At certain stages of the lesson you want students to feel free to offer their ideas without fear of rejection. You might ask, 'What did you think about that film?' If your question is really open you will welcome and probably receive a very wide range of answers from spontaneous emotional responses to carefully considered critical analyses.

Open questions are valuable. Used properly they can make students feel that their opinions are respected and needed. They can encourage and reward divergent thinking in problem solving. A drawback with them, however, is that used too often or at the wrong time they can lead to unstructured, messy and therefore tedious lessons. You need to know when and how to bring the wide-ranging discussion that an open question often stimulates back to your planned lesson topic. And you need to achieve this narrowing of focus without deflating or offending the students who are still plying you with answers.

Closed questions

The closed question tends to carry overtones of disapproval. It's as if lively, creative and warm teachers are seen as open questioners, whereas narrow, authoritarian and dull teachers are seen as closed questioners. In fact closed questions also are a necessary and valuable part of almost all teaching. If you have planned your lesson carefully you will have ensured a development from previous learning to new knowledge, from simpler to more complex concepts. And you will have estimated the time for each phase.

Flexibility is important and you should be prepared to depart from your plan either if the feedback you obtain indicates that most of the students are in difficulty or if one phase expands in so positive and useful a way that you feel it's worth postponing the planned later phases until another lesson. Generally speaking, however, you will need to steer each lesson phase and to manage the activities and learning so that your lesson objectives can be achieved in the time allowed. To do this you will need to employ closed questions: you will need to ask questions that are phrased to elicit particular answers that the current stage of the exposition lesson or discussion requires.

Sometimes you will need one particular word or phrase in answer;

sometimes an idea, which can be expressed in the students' own words but which will nonetheless need to adhere to your plan. Here the skill lies in asking the question in such a way that the students have little difficulty in perceiving and offering the answer you want. You can approach more complex concepts by asking a series of questions, the answers to which provide short interim steps towards the final concept.

Along the way you will receive 'wrong' answers. Do be careful not to reject these tactlessly, particularly if they are 'right' in every respect except that they're not whatever specific word or idea you require. It is possible to respond in a positive way – 'Yes, that's right . . . can you think of another way to say it?' or 'That's interesting, yes; what else could we say/use/include . . .?' – rather than in a negative one – 'no, that's not what I'm looking for!'

A danger with closed questions is that they may masquerade as open ones. Barnes (1969) calls these 'pseudo-questions'. They appear open but are treated by the tutor as closed. They lead to the 'guess what's in my mind' syndrome and students soon latch on to this. Instead of thinking about the lesson content in a reflective, reasoning manner, students in this situation can fire answer after answer at the unsuspecting tutor until one particular word triggers off the approval response. Imagine for example a tutor who wants the students to use the term 'relevant': in struggling to get that single word he may reject equally valid synonyms like 'pertinent'. If you do embark on one of these interchanges it is possible to get so caught up in the 'game' that you yourself lose sight of the educational objectives behind the question and concentrate solely on teasing out a particular word. Your students may actually derive pleasure from the exercise but it is doubtful whether they will learn much from it. And it can be very time-consuming.

Factual versus reasoning questions

Factual questions
Factual questions usually require specific information in answer. They are less concerned with students' thought-processes; more with their powers of recall. Although this suggests that their role in teaching should be carefully limited, Barnes found in his study that in the sample lessons observed there were more factual than reasoning questions.

One explanation for this might be that 'what' questions are more straightforward to plan and ask than are 'how' and 'why' questions. They are also less likely to lead to diversions. If you are anxious to continue with your planned presentation it is easier to insert a factual question such as 'What do we call this?' than a reasoning question such as 'Why does this happen?' And it's much easier to control the interaction that follows. Factual questions tend to lead to one-word or short-phrase answers; reasoning questions can lead to discussion with all the accompanying difficulties of control, focusing and timing.

Reasoning questions

Reasoning questions can themselves be further categorized as open or closed. You might set your students a problem, perhaps to consider how a certain process occurs and develops, and to offer suggestions. If your question is *open* you will welcome and accept many different possible solutions; if it is *closed* you will be hoping for a particular answer that you need before you can go on to the next phase of the lesson.

Closed reasoning questions, like other closed questions, can be useful in teaching. But you will have to decide in advance how much time you can give your students to come up with the required response. After a certain point you will have to find a way to give them the answer yourself without dampening their enthusiasm – there really is no point in dragging out what has become merely a questioning game.

Apart from these main categories we can describe questions in other ways – as social (appealing for attention, support and control), as providing encouragement ('Yes . . . do you mean . . .?'), as provoking follow-up ('In what way was . . .?'), or as inviting confirmation ('Don't you agree that . . .?').

It may seem a little artificial to apply such systems of categorization to what can appear natural, even spontaneous, classroom interaction, but it pays to give detailed consideration to why and how we use questions. With all these question types there are good and bad ways of asking and of dealing with the answers. If you get it wrong, the most meticulously planned lesson, even with the most adventurous and polished media-aids, can fall very flat.

3.3 Pointers to good practice

Whatever the specific purpose and category of your question, try to use it positively. Aim always to increase your students' understanding and to reinforce their learning. Don't ever use questions as a weapon to catch them out.

Formulate your questions carefully; keep them uncomplicated in structure; and think about why you are asking them. Plan them in advance as far as possible. Try to avoid questions to which students can answer simply 'yes' or 'no'. Give scope for the development of communication skills.

Ask one question at a time. If you ask several together your students won't know which to answer. Do not continually reformulate your questions: this will lead to confusion. Give time for students to think and to attempt an answer before you present a fresh question or rephrase the original one. Only answer your own questions when you are reasonably sure that the students are unable to do so.

Learn to cope with silence. Just smile, maintain eye contact, relax and *wait* for a student to answer. The pause will always seem longer to you than to them.

It's probably best to direct your questions to the whole group. After a sufficient pause you might name an individual if you believe she or he will benefit from some encouragement. If you say a student's name before you ask the question the rest of the group may relax instead of concentrating.

When students are offering contributions for you to write on a board, chart or overhead-projector transparency, try not to reformulate their answers; to do so can be very dispiriting for them. Modify their contributions only if there are real errors, and even then be careful and tactful. Give approval together with the correct answer: 'Good, yes – that's generally right – but let's say . . .'. Don't be negative or sarcastic. Recognize all contributions and give positive reinforcement throughout.

Encourage students to think aloud, to guess, and to improvise by asking lots of open and reasoning questions.

Gradually narrow down the focus, using a series of questions that demands increasing explicitness.

Avoid those pseudo-open 'guess what's in my mind' questions. Wherever possible give succinct answers to students' questions. Try to avoid over-long diversions, but establish a procedure whereby you can note any awkward queries during the lesson in order to pick them up later and so straighten out any deep confusions on an individual basis.

Finally, encourage as much active participation and dialogue as possible. It is a good idea to video- or audio-tape-record yourself in action so that you can analyse your questions to get a clearer understanding of your own reasons for using them.

3.4   The strategy

Asking questions

Why do tutors ask questions?

Social
- to create a relaxed atmosphere at the beginning
- to define tutor/student roles
- to establish rapport, to develop relationships and to foster group cohesion

Lesson introduction
- to set the tone and to sharpen the focus
- to check current knowledge and understanding

Lesson development
- to check understanding at each stage
- to provide feedback on learning, for student and teacher
- to prepare for and introduce each new phase
- to encourage student participation and active learning
- to foster creative and divergent thinking

- to teach inductively
- to encourage quieter students
- to increase greater motivation by feedback and encouragement
- to follow up contributions in developing discussions
- to set up small-group discussions and problem-solving exercises
- to prepare for the transition to the next lesson topic

Control
- to bring back wandering attention
- to discourage daydreaming and more serious disruption

When do tutors use questions?
- in exposition lessons at regular stages from introduction on
- in discussion lessons with whole groups, and in plenaries
- in small-group discussions, role-plays, case studies and so on, to stimulate the activity and to brief participants
- in one-to-one tuition
- in guidance, counselling and profiling tutorials

Categories of questions
- open/closed/pseudo-open
- factual/reasoning
- social/control/encouragement/confirmation
- initial exploratory/focusing/follow-up

Pointers to good practice
- use questions positively
- keep questions uncomplicated in structure
- avoid questions with yes/no answers
- avoid multiple questions and continuous reformulation
- wait sufficiently long before answering your own questions
- learn to cope with silence
- direct questions initially to the whole group, not to named individuals
- try not to rephrase students' responses
- give lots of positive reinforcement
- don't be negative or sarcastic
- don't ignore any answers
- do ask lots of open and reasoning questions
- use question series to narrow the focus progressively
- avoid pseudo-open 'guess what's in my mind' questions
- where possible give succinct answers to students' questions
- establish a procedure to pick up awkward questions and to overcome individuals' confusion later
- encourage as much participation as possible

3.5   Resources list

Tutors' background reading

Barnes, D., J. Britton, H. Rosen and the LATE 1969 *Language, the learner and the school* (Penguin)

Brown, G. 1975 'Questioning and answering', unit U1 in *Microteaching: a programme of teaching skills* (Methuen)

4 Using simulation

4.1 The different kinds of simulation

Role-play, simulation and gaming are frequently suggested as the most appropriate strategies for developing oral-communication skills and for fostering social confidence. Perhaps they are recommended too frequently. Certainly there is an assumption that all tutors are both eager and competent to incorporate such activities in their teaching, though this is unlikely to be the case. And unless you have had a training in the teaching of drama or, possibly, of English and communication, you will not have received any detailed guidance to help you.

We do not wish to imply that only 'specialists' should venture into this area. The likely rewards, in student motivation and learning, are such that we would recommend all tutors to use these strategies. What we wish to counter is the assumption that these activities are somehow easy to employ because they are fun. They can indeed be fun; but they are likely to be so only if the tutor has put a considerable amount of thought, time and energy into selection, preparation and classroom management. Few classroom activities are less entertaining than an ill-chosen, poorly presented and mismanaged role-play or simulation: such an experience can destroy the very confidence that it was designed to build up. And not just the students' confidence.

Some guidelines are offered here: if you are especially interested in this field, you should refer to some of the specialist books. There are some suggestions in the resources list (section 4.7).

Defining our terms
There can be no clear-cut distinction between role-play, simulation and gaming-simulation: the overlap is too great. A simulation game can, and probably will, incorporate role-play. The defining characteristics and differences should become clearer as we look at each in turn; for the moment, we may conceive a continuum, with simulation in the centre, and with role-play and gaming at opposite ends.

At the gaming end procedures are more formal and rule-governed; and the relationships between participants are more structured and less flexible. The setting is described in a detailed manner. The constraints on participants' behaviour may only be hinted at in a role-play; in a simulation game they are incorporated in the rules.

Games — shackled ↓ — more re social assertiveness
Simulations
role play   *4.1 The different kinds of simulation*   61

Moving towards the gaming end of the continuum from the role-play end, group participation will probably increase. Role-play may involve only a few students with the rest as audience; gaming involves everybody – there can be no observers. The degree of formal interaction also increases. In role-play it is possible, if not often recommended, for students to explore their own individually assigned or chosen roles with a degree of isolation from other participants. In gaming-simulation the individual roles are defined within a wider system. A dynamic model is created which depends on the formal interaction between roles, often marked by rewards and punishments. Much more is laid down in advance. In an open-ended, loosely structured role-play an individual can create a situation through his personal interpretation of a role. In a gaming-simulation, however, the consequences of some actions can be known to participants in advance because they are laid down in the model.

There are good reasons for these differences. Role-play, simulation and gaming, while sharing some general aims and purposes, each have their own individual objectives. The general aims draw on the learning theories developed by educationalists such as Bruner (1960 and 1967), and Barnes, Britten and Rosen (1969). These researchers all stress the need for participation and for active use of language – what is now termed 'experiential learning'. The specific objectives range from the demonstration of social assertiveness to awareness of the functioning of a complex social or scientific model. You the tutor need to be clear about your own aims and objectives before you select or design a particular role-play, simulation or gaming-simulation.

4.2 Role-play

Role-play as a teaching strategy draws on the assumption that we all play a number of roles in our social life – roles that depend on the context, on the audience and on our own experience, feelings and mood. This repertoire of social roles is sometimes referred to as our 'role set'. By simulating real-life situations under defined conditions in the classroom you can help students to enlarge their repertoire and to be more controlled and consequently more effective in the roles they choose or agree to adopt.

Structure in role-play
Advocates of role-play differ in the degree of structuring they recommend. Their choice depends largely upon the purpose they ascribe to the role-play. There are however some hard-and-fast general rules you must observe:

● Any role-play has three sections: the *briefing*, in which everyone should become absolutely clear, before the start, about the scope of his or her role; the actual *acting out*; and the *debriefing* session, in which everyone comes out of role and considers what happened.

- You can separate the sections into different lessons (for example, if the briefing has to contain a lot of information because the roles are outside students' experience and therefore unfamiliar), but this will cost you something in continuity and impetus.
- The acting-out section of the role-play cannot be 'carried over' to the next lesson: it has to be started and finished within one session.
- You can *never* afford to miss out a debriefing session. This is the time when the learning takes place, since students cannot at the same time be involved both in acting out and in objectively assessing events. If the debriefing session has to be done in a separate lesson you should try to have an audio- or video-taped record of what happened to help accurate recall.
- You as tutor must decide whether to join in or not; you must decide in advance and stick to your decision. Tutors with thwarted acting ambitions may find it hard to resist, but beware: you are always 'the tutor' (and thus an authority figure) even in a role-play, and if you take part you forfeit the right to take a controlling hand if necessary. On the whole, since there are risks involved, we suggest that you do *not* take part – you may be the only observer who will have seen everything at the end, as all your students will have become caught up in the action at one stage or another.

Role-reversal
Sometimes the main purpose of role-play is to help students empathize with others by asking them to adopt the roles of other people in society. Typical role-reversal exercises involve male students playing females, trainees playing supervisors, daughters playing mothers. Here the emphasis is on enlarging existing perspectives, on viewing situations from different standpoints, and on understanding the perspective of another person.

There may be little formal structure in a role-reversal exercise. You might simply ask the participants to take on different identities and to behave in as appropriate a manner as possible. The outcome would not be predicted: the students could create both the situation and the events without the formal constraint of rules. The role-play here would involve a spontaneous performance, with the students attempting to express views and opinions which would not necessarily be their own. Briefing could be minimal, taking the form either of oral instructions or of concisely written cues on cards. 'You are a sixteen-year-old girl. You wish to go camping with two boys. Try to persuade your father, who is reluctant to let you go.' A male student would take this role. 'You are the father and you would prefer your daughter not to go camping.' A female student would take this role.

The value of this type of role-play is in the interaction and the consequent awareness of others' feelings. It doesn't matter what 'happens' or who 'wins'. It *is* important however that the atmosphere is suitable and that everybody takes the activity seriously. Your role as tutor is to foster a supportive atmosphere and to lead the briefing and debriefing. The debriefing is an essential part of all role-plays, simulations and gaming-simulations. It is during this last phase of the lesson that the students reflect upon their experience, share their feelings and consolidate their learning. It is also here that any problem of hostility, aggression and insecurity can be tackled. Tactfully led discussion can defuse and take the pain out of role-plays that have ventured into emotionally charged areas.

Context-bound role-play

Where the purpose is to encourage role versatility, in order to help students become familiar with roles they may need to adopt, you will probably wish to introduce more structure.

Typical situations are job interviews and encounters with officialdom (including the law). Your students need to be able to relate their own situations, feelings and needs to the different situations of others. Empathy would be an aim, as would increasing self-knowledge and an awareness of the effects of one's own actions and words on others. Students involved in this type of role-play should learn to anticipate others' reactions and to steer the interaction towards their own chosen outcome. A positive experience can help increase the students' sense of power and control. This, in turn, should enhance their self-images. Confidence gained during a role-played job interview, for example, may be expected to transfer to the real thing.

Structure

How you structure the role-play depends, among other things, upon your resources (in particular how much time you have) and on the literacy level of your students.

As with role-play in general, it is obviously important that students share your understanding of the purpose and value of the exercise. Time must be given at the beginning to clarify the objectives and possibly to decide with the group the procedures to be followed.

Bearing in mind the specific context, classroom furniture should be arranged to simulate the real situation. You may decide to videotape the activity and students may take on that task.

Allocation of roles

Roles may be allocated by you, or chosen by the students, or picked out of a hat at random. You may wish students to take on particular roles because you believe they would be good at them or because you think they would benefit personally from that specific experience: if so you will wish to allocate the roles. On another occasion it might be best to let the students choose. A difficulty here is that the more forceful and articulate group members will tend to prevent the quieter students from securing their chosen roles. A way around this is to ensure that there is sufficient time to switch roles half way through the session.

Numbers involved

Another decision relates to numbers. You could have everybody involved, role-playing in twos or threes simultaneously while you circulate and monitor progress. Or you could ask one or two sets of students to play out their roles in front of the others as audience. There are obvious advantages in each approach. With everybody performing at the same time, quieter students may feel able to participate more confidently against the general background of noise. The same students might baulk at facing an audience of their peers. However, we have already stressed the importance of the debriefing session: it is much easier to note what is happening and to comment on performance if only one set of students presents at a time. Certainly video-taping is only feasible in the latter situation. Once again the choice will be dictated by other objectives. If a job interview is being role-played, you and the students will almost certainly want detailed feedback, with comments on non-verbal and verbal performance and with an analysis of feelings and impressions from the point of view of applicant and interviewer. Consecutive performances (involving different students) before an audience will therefore be required. If, on the other hand, the role-play is to develop confidence in self-assertion and in the control of hostility – it might, for example, concern a complaint about merchandise – simultaneous performances could be the best way. The catharsis involved in arguing a case might be best achieved in the comparative privacy of a noisy classroom rather than in the self-conscious arena of an observed performance.

Briefing

Another decision concerns the method of briefing. Do you merely tell the students who they are or is this information written on role cards? For some role-play situations an oral briefing will probably suffice. For other, more complex role-plays, detailed role descriptions can be written which might include pointers to character, personality, and likely behaviour in the given situation.

These more structured role-plays overlap with the type of simulation in which roles are described in detail and in which participants are asked to react to the situation according to their understanding of their assumed characters.

4.3 Simulation

The nature of simulation

Simulation involves role-play but it goes beyond the acting out of spontaneous interactions between pairs and groups of people to a representation of a complex social situation. Actions and reactions that in role-play may be looked at in a somewhat isolated manner are explored more fully in simulation. Participants, having assumed roles, have to make a series of decisions according to their understanding of the context; they then experience the simulated consequences of their own decisions. Typically a simulation might involve an environmental issue, such as a debate between planners and representatives of the local community and of industry concerning a proposed new motorway section. There are many published simulations: you might like to try some of these before designing your own.

Usually a large number of students is involved – between twelve and twenty perhaps. This means that the situation can be explored in more detail. With a greater number of participants, more factors can be introduced and the results of individuals' actions can be traced in all their complexity. As the situation develops participants need to interact with different sets of characters and they need to keep adjusting their strategies.

The main learning objective is the development of competence in coping with changing situations and in making decisions on complex issues. Communication skills generally should improve, along with the ability to work in groups. Divergent thinking is often encouraged because there is no danger if decisions do not lead to expected results.

The end result of the simulation is not decided in advance. The action unfolds gradually, influenced by the behaviour of all the participants. You, as tutor, may introduce additional information at stages through the simulation. The data bank can therefore be gradually increased. As well as playing roles and empathizing with others, the students have to cope with a continuous process of change. They have to understand the information they receive at intervals about the situation and environment and they have to predict the behaviour of others and the random effect of fate. They need to sift through the available data and to use what seems most relevant in order to invent strategies and to act. Another major aim of simulation is to develop students' ability to solve problems.

In most simulations the passage of time is artificially speeded up so that participants can observe the effect of time and change, and so that they can obtain feedback on the consequences of their actions. Sometimes time intervals are clearly stated – you may inform the students when, for example, six months has passed.

The real world is represented in a simplified yet dynamic model and the students become part of the simulated reality. The constraints and pressures of the real world are also present, embedded in the rules. Some advocates of simulation hold that participants should be allowed to change those rules by majority decision.

One of the major advantages of simulation is that in the *model* of the real world students can make decisions and act realistically but in a risk-free environment. Mistakes can be made and the lessons learned can be valuable later, perhaps when similar decisions have to be made away from the cushioned environment of the simulation. In the classroom there is no danger for the participants or for the resources they manipulate.

Conduct of a simulation

Choosing the simulation
The tutor's role is necessarily a complicated one. Take your time in choosing a simulation. Wait until you know your group and their abilities. Make sure that they will be able to cope with the model, the amount of information, the formal and knowledge aspects of the roles. It is no good simulating a debate in the House of Commons or a housing-squat confrontation with the council if the group has no idea what a Speaker is and does, or how the law affects squatters. Don't choose a simulation that has sacrificed verisimilitude in order to be entertaining.

Once you have selected or designed the simulation you have to introduce it in such a way that the students will be motivated to participate and sufficiently aware of its purpose and structure to be able to do so effectively.

It is best to try out a new simulation with friends before using it with students. Some of the more complicated and most interesting ones have clues and options kept hidden until part way through the activity.

Controlling the simulation
Usually you remain outside the action and assume the title of 'controller'. In a sense you act a role because you are a facilitator, the person responsible for feeding the information into the situation and for representing events in the outside world. Suppose, for example, that participants decide that a public enquiry will be held external to the proceedings they are simulating: it is up to you to report the decisions of this enquiry in so far as they affect the action. The participants have the power to influence events inside the simulation; you have the power to represent what happens outside it.

When you need to speak to the students you should refer to them 'in role' – as MPs or demonstrators or whatever. You may find it difficult to step out of your normal teaching role but you should try not to interrupt the simulation, even if you feel it is going off course. You should avoid giving even non-verbal signals, such as smiles or frowns. Once the simulation has begun it should remain under the control of the participants: if it does go wrong then the reason can be explored in the debriefing.

Occasionally you might experience disruption. If an individual or group does start to undermine the simulation, try to deal with them *within* the context: address them by their role names and if necessary remove them from their group for some invented reason that can be seen as part of the simulation.

Briefing

It is you, the controller, who are responsible for both the briefing and the debriefing. The former can be staged at intervals throughout the simulation. · (Most published simulations will guide you on this.) Try to make the initial briefing as concise and as interesting as possible. Often the role briefs will be written and these may confine themselves to factual descriptions regarding age, gender, marital status, and occupation; or they may include subjective references to temperament, taste, and attitudes. The understanding of participants often develops along with the action. You may need to present factual information: if so consider whether the board, an overhead projector or a handout will be the most effective. Include a brief exploration of the background to the simulation, its own specialized world.

Sometimes it helps if the links with other course work are made explicit. Ensure that the participants understand the learning objectives of the simulation – what in general you hope to achieve. Above all try to get the students interested and avoid information overload. When the action is under way you can continue the briefing: you can even combine it with group-teaching sessions at appropriate stages. Some simulations are designed to run over days or even weeks. It is, admittedly, a time-consuming activity.

Role allocation

Here the same dilemmas face you as in role-play and small-group discussion methods. Should you allow friends to stay together? Should you allocate roles or ask for volunteers? As always you must make the decision in the light of your knowledge of the particular students, of the simulation and of your resources. One thing worth mentioning is that it doesn't always pay to allocate roles on the basis of your knowledge of students' performance in other types of learning situation – occasionally a passive student can reveal unsuspected strengths in a new situation such as a simulation. Some roles require specialized knowledge and so you will have to allocate these yourself, or do some very careful individual briefing, or both.

If an important role falls vacant at any stage through student absence you may decide to take it on yourself but it is almost certainly better to stay as controller, even if you hide behind a more passive role, like caretaker or tea-person, that does not involve you in the dialogue. That way you can monitor much of what takes place. There will be times, however, when a group of students needs to hold a meeting in another room; you cannot expect to observe everything that takes place. Nor need you. As long as decisions are made and fed into the simulation when necessary you don't always need to know the route by which the discussion led up to them.

Management

Before you begin and while the simulation is under way you need to pay close attention to the environment. You certainly won't want to interrupt the proceedings to ask people to move tables around or to change rooms. Once the fantasy spell has been broken it is very difficult to cast it again. Have any documents, memos and the like ready for the appropriate stage. Memorize any essential information or be prepared to bluff to gain time during or after the simulation, to look it up. Be strict about deadlines. If a meeting is to begin at 3.00 p.m. then make sure it does, whether the students (and you) are ready or not! Remember that you are simulating the real world. This means a lot of skilful juggling before you begin to fit the simulation in with timetabled lessons and breaks.

Debriefing

Once the simulation has been concluded the debriefing begins. Try to ensure that this can take place in the same session as the final part (at least) of the action, while the participants are still in tune with their feelings and reactions.

Some people hold that the debriefing is the most important stage in the process. It is here that the links are made with the real situation on which the simulation has been based. When the participants are immersed in role-playing they may find it difficult to maintain an objective overview of the development of the simulation. It is in the debriefing that they can be helped to see this more clearly.

Usually this stage begins with each participant describing his or her role and explaining his or her decisions and actions. An open discussion can then follow, focusing on general principles which can be transferred to real-life decisions.

As with debriefing after less complex role-playing this is also the time to help individuals cope with any frustration, hostility or embarrassment which may be a by-product of the simulation.

Sometimes a questionnaire (to sample attitudes or knowledge or both) is completed at the beginning and end of a simulation so that the results can be compared.

You may also wish to lead on from the simulation to authentic or fictional case studies. This approach is looked at in Chapter 5.

Assessment

Most simulations are designed to be self-monitoring. Participants observe the results of their own actions and are usually faced with feedback on their progress. This, combined with discussion during the debriefing stage, is probably sufficient to inform both you and the students of their performance.

It may be that you or they will wish to record their progress on a profile. This is particularly likely where the simulation has been used partly to assess the achievement of aims such as those quoted at the beginning of this chapter. A questionnaire might help with this or you could ask the students to help you to phrase entries for profiles (page 327). The assessment should be individual;

it should be possible for students who are at differing levels of attainment and experience to work together in a simulation and for each to progress at his or her own rate. There should be no suggestion that a group or an individual has 'won'. Competition may have been involved but it is the process of decision making that needs to be highlighted.

Designing a simulation

Once you have experienced success in managing some published simulations you may feel ready to try your hand at designing one that would be tailor-made for your particular students. The advantages are obvious. You could choose a context that you know would be relevant and motivating and you could pitch the information and language at an appropriate level for your group.

It takes a long time to produce a simulation from initial idea, through piloting and revision, to a finished, workable state. There are several books that give useful, detailed advice. (Taylor and Walford, 1972, and Greenblat and Duke, 1981, are recommended.) The guidelines that Taylor and Walford offer can be summarized as follows:

- consider your aims and objectives
- choose your context and present a simplified abstraction of the situation which is free from 'background noise'
- highlight some of the relationships and aspects
- speed up the pace and passage of time so that the full implication of the dynamic situation can be observed
- ensure that students can feel the direct consequences of their decisions
- plan for collaborative learning, self-direction and learning from mistakes
- carry out a preliminary analysis to include identification of the problem, content and the isolation of the component parts
- employ operational modelling which involves resource manipulation and making the model work
- conduct refinement and testing which involves finalizing the rule system and piloting to tune the model

Taylor and Walford also give a very useful list of choices which they say are at the heart of the model-building process. This is worth reproducing:

1 Richness of detail v. manipulative simplicity
2 Complexity/accuracy v. playability
3 Logically structured learning sequences v. free player involvement
4 Immediacy (manual operation of choices) v. machine or computer calculation
5 Highly general objectives v. specific objectives
6 Closed system v. open system (anything may evolve)
   (Taylor & Walford 1978: *Learning and the simulation game*)

These guidelines also indicate many of the links between simulation and simulation-gaming.

An important decision that has to be made before the game starts is whether or not you join in and play with the students. If your aim is to break down barriers between yourself and your students then it may be a good idea. As a player, however, you forfeit the right to step in and take control if anything goes wrong. In common with role-play and simulation, a game can be a genuinely student-centred and dynamic strategem. However, in a group that has problems working together or that has split into segregated sub-groups, existing tensions can rise to the surface.

One potential problem with card and board games that are versions of games already known to the students is that the originals with which students are familiar (like snap, snakes-and-ladders, and Monopoly) are competitive. Your students may pick up this aspect and see winning as the prime object. You need to guide them to see that they are supposed to learn while playing and that the *outcome* is less important than the *process*. This may mean interrupting the game while it is in progress to make it clear that it is not a competition.

A final but possibly crucial point is that you must play the game yourself before you use it with your students. It should be a point of principle that you never ask students to do anything you are not prepared to do yourself. In any case you may discover that the game is not suitable for your group, or simply that it takes more time to play than you have available.

4.4   Gaming-simulation

Although the boundaries between simulation and games are blurred there are some features that can help pinpoint an activity as more one or the other.

Games usually include an element of competition; but occasionally, instead of competing with each other, the participants co-operate and work together towards a common goal. There are accepted rules which impose constraints and a context which limits the action. The players are faced with a series of decisions which will lead to success or failure in achieving their goals. There is usually a winner or a winning group. As with role-play and other types of simulation the mode of learning is experiential.

Gaming-simulations are games played in simulated contexts. The students learn through their own actions and discover for themselves the concepts and principles contained in the simulation model. This model reflects the *designer's* view of social reality; it may vary from the students' or from your own ideas and hypotheses. This is partly because each gaming-simulation is intended to clarify a complex situation. It attempts to do so by reducing complex interactions into a series of observable actions which can be controlled by explicit rules. Time is compressed, as in other simulations, to provide rapid feedback on the consequences of participants' decisions. Also, as with other simulations, there are no real risks involved. The simulation is not the real world.

The purposes of gaming-simulation

Gaming-simulations have many aims and objectives in common with other simulations. They can be used to help students acquire and consolidate knowledge and to apply it to fresh situations. Problem-solving and decision-making skills are developed. Oral – and sometimes written – communication skills are practised. Mathematical calculations may also be included. It should be possible to use these activities with students at different levels of ability and attainment.

Although it soon becomes clear to students that these gaming-simulations have a serious purpose, they are clearly associated with fun and increased motivation. Feedback and reinforcement are obtained at regular intervals through enforcement of rules, through team-mates' reactions or through information from the controller (or, increasingly, from a computer). The number of computer simulations and games that are suitable for vocational-preparation students is increasing, and with these there is often immediate feedback on the correctness of decisions.

Another good reason for using gaming-simulation is that it can foster the participants' control beliefs. It must benefit a young unemployed person to experience a sense of control over events and over a manageable environment. Such an experience can lead to the development of strategies to cope with the real world. Interpersonal skills are also practised as participants seek to persuade, to influence, and to reach compromises. Role-play and sometimes role-reversal within gaming-simulations may lead to the development of empathy and a growth in understanding.

Gaming-simulation models

Experts define three major categories of model (for example, Greenblat and Duke, 1981):

- *resource allocation model* – a model structured around concepts of competition for scarce resources;
- *group dynamics model* – a model emphasizing role-play and interpersonal skills;
- *system specific model* – a model entailing an explicit exploration of a complex system, which could be social, technical or economic.

Many gaming-simulations include aspects of all three models.

If you are interested in using this strategy it is probably worth reading about the theory in more depth and then experimenting with some of the gaming-simulations on the market. A large number have been produced for the business-studies and management fields in particular. At the end of the chapter there are some suggestions for reading together with references for the gaming-simulations that are recommended elsewhere in this manual.

Conduct of a gaming-simulation

Planning

The first act is one of selection. Choose the stage at which you introduce such an activity very carefully. The students have to be aware of the procedures and rules. They should also share your belief in gaming-simulations as strategies for learning. The 'end' of winning the game should not obscure the real purposes.

Careful management is needed. There are often detailed calculations and predictions to make. You (with a calculator or the instruction manual) or a computer must produce fast feedback to enable the action to continue after each set of decisions has been made.

You may need to work in a team with other tutors if the game is particularly complex or the number of students large.

As with other simulations the time schedule is crucial. Some games can be divided into sections and played over several days or even weeks. Others need a long continuous period. All of them reach stages at which play cannot be interrupted without ruining the effect.

Try to integrate the gaming-simulation with other coursework. There will usually be literacy, communication and numeracy links apart from social-education and vocational themes.

Your own role will again be that of controller.

Briefing

Briefing will include the initial discussion regarding the purpose of gaming-simulation in general as a learning strategy and your reasons for choosing the specific simulation in particular.

The rules will be introduced and the roles allocated. The students must be aware of the rules but they will be quickly and easily bored by a lengthy rule-reading session. Find a way to display the rules for quick checks, and you yourself should learn the most important and the most frequently used of them. There is likely to be a period of confusion to begin with: it is wise to mention this to the students in advance and to assure them that both the rules and their roles within the gaming-simulation should become clearer as the action develops. After a while it is probably best for you all to plunge in and sort out early confusions as you go along.

As with other simulations, some information and some additional rules may be introduced at intermediate stages.

Management

Your role as controller will vary. In some gaming-simulations you will have a series of tasks to complete as the simulation develops. In others you will be free to monitor the participants' progress. Do try not to interfere or let your feelings of approval or disapproval show. You may, however, need to give some assistance, particularly in the early stages. The calculations and the keeping to time deadlines will be your responsibility.

Debriefing
This will probably go through three stages. There will be an initial, probably noisy phase, with students releasing their emotions, and possibly arguing about results. Once this is over you can ask the group to focus on the experience and to analyse it in terms of what happened and how the simulation was perceived from the standpoints of the different roles. This phase should encourage students to enter into the feelings of others and to appreciate the relativity of reality. If there are divergent solutions, so much the better.

Finally you should help your students to make links between the simulation experience and the external world. What would have happened in the real world? Would the same decisions and subsequent courses of action have been successful? Would they have had the confidence to take the same risks? Occasionally a game model can distort reality. Behaviour can be rewarded or punished, chance can distribute opportunities in a very unreal way. Far from being damaging, this distortion in the hands of a skilled discussion leader can stimulate a useful exploration of what the situation and decisions facing the students really are.

As always the quality of the experience in gaming-simulation depends to a large extent on how you the tutor introduce, manage and use the strategy.

4.5   Games

Lack of resources and timetable constraints may make it difficult for you to introduce gaming-simulation in its full form. You may also feel that your students are not ready to cope with the organizational, linguistic, and social demands of the method.

Some games share some of the characteristics of role-play and simulation, but, because they concentrate on a narrower range of objectives, are more manageable and accessible. Card, board and group games are widely used with vocational-preparation students, partly on the grounds that an activity that is 'fun' will be accepted more easily than a formal 'lesson'. They are particularly useful at the beginning of the course because, used sensitively and constructively, they can help to foster group cohesion.

We can divide games into two main categories. The first type originates partly from research into the social psychology of groups, and these games are distant cousins of the encounter group (Chapter 2). They are related to role-play and simulation. The second type of game has a more structured format and imitates card or board games.

The aims of the first kind are personal development, increased confidence and assertiveness, and empathy with others. Used carefully and tactfully they can promote co-operation, tone down the dominating students and draw out the quieter ones. They can lead to heightened self-knowledge and personal growth in general.

But there are risks, so you should be very sure of your own objectives and of your willingness and ability to handle upsets and disturbances if things go wrong and if group exposure proves too much for individual students. You might like to look at Chapter 2, in which we refer to relevant aspects of group leadership and control.

You must be certain about the kind of learning you want to emerge from the exercise. If it is purely 'social' learning to promote cohesion, then the debriefing discussion can take up an entire session. Just five minutes spent as a feedback session at the end of the activity can produce enlightening comment on how it went and its effects on the group.

If your objective is to develop the students' power of self-observation, you may want the game played as a fishbowl exercise (page 46). This is one of the ways of using 'Personality' (page 81).

Some games are designed to make a point, to produce an outcome that can be discussed. *No bed, no job*, for example, is an activity that demonstrates the link between joblessness and homelessness. 'You're on your own' (from *Living in a city*) tests the usefulness of sources of information and advice. (Details are given in the resources list, section 4.7).

With games such as these the playing has to be finished before the discussion can start, so timing is important. 'What do I want my students to learn from playing this?' is of prime – and prior – importance.

4.6   The strategies

Role-play
● simulates real-life social encounters under controlled conditions
● can be loosely structured with participants interpreting roles personally, either acting in isolation from the rest of the role-players or, more usually, interacting with one or more of the others
● may have very few constraints or restrictions on performance, or
● may be context-bound with appropriate constraints (e.g. job interview; lobbying an MP)
● either full-group participation or separate 'performances' before an 'audience'

Aims
● to introduce experiential learning
● to enlarge the role set, the student's repertoire of social roles
● to develop social confidence, and a degree of assertiveness
● to develop empathy (probably through role-reversal)

- to increase ability to enter the feelings and understand the viewpoints of others

Structure
- varies in degree and detail
- can be loose

Requirements
- sufficiently large room
- movable, appropriate furniture
- written role cards (perhaps)
- suitable props, background information and stimuli – could be film, newspaper articles or fiction
- video-recording equipment (perhaps)

Timing
- anything from 20 minutes to 2 hours, depending on the purpose, integration with other lesson materials, and strategies

Tutor's role
- selecting contexts and roles suited to the interests, abilities and experience of the students
- classroom preparation – arrangement of seating, provision of any props
- conducting the initial briefing (with regard to the context and purpose of the role-play)
- fostering a supportive atmosphere
- supervising role allocation – by you directly, by random means or by students' choice (volunteering)
- managing the smooth running of the activity – circulating or being part of the audience
- conducting the debriefing
- assessment (perhaps) – negotiating profile entries, for example

When to use
- with mixed-attainment groups
- as part of a lesson, integrated by theme with other activities
- after the required background information has been communicated
- after a phase of passive learning

When not to use
- in a hostile, uncooperative atmosphere – unless you are experienced and confident in the use of role-play to develop cohesion
- in an insuitable room – a laboratory or home-economics room, etc.
- at the end of a lesson when there will be insufficient time for debriefing

Pointers to good practice
- be clear about your learning objectives, and make sure your students understand them too
- allow sufficient time for a full briefing and debriefing session
- complete the activity in one session
- be consistent in your degree of involvement – participate fully or observe: don't switch between the two roles
- try to foster a supportive atmosphere
- be prepared to intervene and stop the role-play if things get out of hand or too negative or threatening for individuals

Simulation
- uses role-play to represent a complex social situation
- explores relationships between a large (say 12–20) number of participant role-players
- is context-bound, often with constraints on role interpretation
- permits full group participation

Aims
- to introduce experiential learning
- to enlarge role sets, and to develop social confidence and empathy
- to practise decision-making in a risk-free environment and to experience the simulated consequences of own decisions

Structure
- usually highly structured, but the outcome is not decided in advance

Requirements
- simulation design and role briefs
- a sufficient number of students to fill the required roles
- a sufficiently large room or suite of rooms
- movable, appropriate furniture
- background information, props
- video-recording equipment (perhaps)

Timing
- there must be a sufficiently long period to complete the action – at least 2 hours, and possibly longer
- sometimes it is possible to split a simulation over two or three sessions

Tutor's role
- selecting or designing a simulation suited to the interests, ability and knowledge of students
- preparing the physical environment

- conducting the initial (and frequently intermediate) briefings
- inspiring enthusiasm and a suitably serious attitude
- supervising role allocation and conducting some individual briefing
- acting as controller to manage the simulation
- feeding in information; reporting back from the 'external' world
- staying on the outside – don't get directly involved in simulation; ensure strict keeping of time deadlines
- conducting the debriefing
- organizing any assessment – negotiating profile entries, for example, perhaps using questionnaires

When to use
- with mixed-attainment groups
- as the final stage of a series of lessons giving information about a specific social context, institution, etc.
- after you and your students have had a successful experience of role-play

When not to use
- before the students have acquired the background knowledge and information that will guide them in their role-playing
- with groups that are not cohesive, unless you feel confident that you can develop co-operation during the exercise
- in a short lesson

Pointers to good practice
- select the simulation very carefully
- make sure that it is not too complex and that the content is relevant and accessible
- allow plenty of time for the briefing and debriefing sessions
- avoid information overload, by staging the briefing
- know the material thoroughly yourself, and try to anticipate the stages at which you will need to give advice or more information
- address your students 'in role' during the simulation
- try the simulation out with friends first

Gaming-simulation
- is rule-governed, with rewards and punishments
- contains an element of competition
- is usually context-bound, with a detailed description of the setting
- requires structured relationships between the participants with individual roles functioning within the wider system
- permits full-group participation
- involves additional constraints when the consequences of some actions are already laid down in a manual

- exploits the compression of time
- reduces the complexity of the reality on which it is based
- needs feedback on performance and reinforcement at regular intervals

Aims
- to introduce experiential learning
- to enlarge the role set, and to develop social confidence and empathy
- to develop the ability to work in a team
- to develop awareness of the functioning of a complex and dynamic social, economic or scientific model
- to acquire and consolidate knowledge and to apply it to fresh situations
- to develop decision-making and problem-solving skills
- to foster control beliefs – participants should gain confidence in influencing events, and in having a degree of control over their environment and future

Models
- there are three major ones; the resource-allocation model; the group-dynamics model; and the system-specific model

Structure
- is highly structured and rule-governed, and has internal time deadlines
- usually very detailed manuals are provided with published gaming-simulations

Requirements
- the gaming-simulation and all information; props
- often a calculator or, increasingly, a computer
- a sufficient number of students
- a team of teachers (perhaps)
- a large room (or several rooms)
- suitable furniture for the simulated context

Timing
- usually laid down in the manual
- often several lengthy sessions, each of 2–3 hours

Tutor's role
- selecting or designing a gaming-simulation suited to the interests, level and knowledge of the group
- recruiting other tutors to team-teach (perhaps)
- preparing the classroom
- briefing (very carefully) with regard to the rules and purpose
- trying out the gaming-simulation first

- integrating the activity with other coursework
- briefing
- allocating roles
- acting as controller to manage the game
- conducting the debriefing

When to use
- when you are confident that your students have the required background knowledge and communication skills
- as an initial learning experience or in a consolidation stage
- after you have practised role-play and simulation successfully
- when you can set aside a lot of time – perhaps over 10 hours
- possibly during a residential period

When not to use
- in a short course in which it would take up far too much of your time
- with a group who have very limited attainment in both literacy and oral-communication skills

Pointers to good practice
- make sure your students understand the purposes of gaming-simulation as a learning strategy
- manage the activity meticulously
- treat all calculations and requests for information seriously and be as accurate as possible
- organize your time so that crucial phases won't be interrupted artificially by the timetable
- integrate the activity with other coursework
- conduct thorough briefing and debriefing sessions

Games

When to use
- as ice-breakers with new groups
- as a way of getting quiet or unsettled groups to work together
- when you want students to interact without going through you
- when you want to do something enjoyable with a group, particularly when you feel you do not get on well with them
- when you want students to discover some ideas or information for themselves, rather than be told

When not to use
- as time-fillers – this devalues the potential they offer as learning experiences
- with groups that are so unsettled that some students may seize the

opportunities presented for disruption, or to manipulate or make scapegoats of other students

Pointers to good practice
- try the game out first with friends, to test the design and the time necessary to play it properly
- decide in advance whether you want to join in or run the game
- once it starts, let things develop without too much overt interference from you: let the dynamics of the game take over
- don't let the noise level go past the level at which you can still talk to the whole group if you need to
- try to judge in advance whether any noise or movement is likely to cause real disruption to other classes

4.7   Resources list

Tutors' background reading

Alexander, T.A. 1978 'Simulation techniques' in *Guides for the improvement of instruction in higher education* **10** (Michigan State University)

Barnes, D., J. Britten and H. Rosen 1969 *Language, the learner and the school* (Penguin)

Bruner, J.S. 1960 *The process of education* (Harvard University Press)

Bruner, J.S. 1966 *Towards a theory of instruction* (Harvard University Press)

Dukes, R.L. and C.J. Seidner 1978 *Learning with simulations and games* (Sage)

Greenblat, C.S. and R.D. Duke 1981 *Principles and practices of gaming-simulation* (Sage)

Jones, K. 1980 *Simulations* – a handbook for teachers (Kogan Page)

Megarry, J. (ed.) 1977 *Aspects of simulation and gaming* – an anthology of SAGSET Journal, volumes 1–4 (Kogan Page)

Taylor, J. and R. Walford 1972 *Learning and the simulation game* (Open University Press, 1978 edn)

Classroom materials

Role-play
There are books solely on role-play, but you will find most information in sections in books that deal with simulation as well. Some have practical examples.

Ramsey, G. 1978 *Play your part* (Longman)

Simulation
There are many books describing simulation methods, although quite a few are based solely on American teaching experience and most are not specifically aimed at our level of student. It might however be worth looking at:

Alexander, L.T., S.L. Yelon and R.H. Davis 1978 'Simulation techniques' in: *Guides for the improvement of instruction in higher education* **10** (Michigan State University)

Jones K. 1980 *Simulations: a handbook for teachers* (Kogan Page)

Jones, K. 1984 *Nine graded simulations* (First published in 1974 by ILEA; now by Max Hueber Verlag, Ismaning, near Munich, and available from European Schoolbooks Ltd., 122 Bath Road, Cheltenham GL53 7LW) Individual titles: '1 Survival', '2 Front Page', '3 Radio Covingham', '4 Property Trial', '5 Appointments Board', '6 The Dolphin Project', '7 Airport Controversy', '8 The Azim Crisis', '9 Action for Libel'.

Shirts, R.G. 1969 *Starpower* (Simile II, Del Mar, California 92014)

Townsend, C. 1978 *Five simple business games* (CRAC)

Gaming-simulation

There are lots of books on gaming-simulation. Many are highly theoretical but if, for example, you would like to try your hand at designing you should read some, such as:

Dukes, R.L. and C.J. Seidner, 1978 *Learning with simulations and games* (Sage)

Greenblat, C.S. and R.D. Duke, 1981 *Principles and practices of gaming-simulation* (Sage)

Megarry, J. (Ed.) 1977 [details above]

Games

ALBSU *Games and simulations: a personal approach*

Careers Consultants Ltd. *Personality* (12–14 Hill Rise, Richmond Hill, Richmond, Surrey TW10 6HA)

Davison, A. and P. Gordon 1978 *Games and simulations in action* (Woburn)

Hopson, B. and P. Hough 1973 *Exercises in personal and career development* (CRAC)

Inner London Education Authority 'You're on your own' game in *Living in a city* (ILEA Learning Materials Service, Publishing Centre, Highbury Station Road, London W1 16D)
Workpack of students' materials with tutor's notes. Many useful communications assignments if you're working in an urban environment.

Kruper, K.R. 1973 *Communication games (participant's manual)* (Free Press, Collier Macmillan)

Mayblin, B. and G. Shaw 1978 *No bed, no job* (Community Service Volunteers, 237 Pentonville Road, London N1 9NJ)
Simulation game on young people and homelessness.

5   Experiential learning

5.1   Case studies

Case studies are often used to bring facets of the external world into the classroom. They may be required to simulate real situations because it is difficult or even impossible to arrange the actual experience. You won't be able to find or organize visits to all the situations with which your students need to be familiar. And you cannot usually make your students real bank managers, local councillors, works superintendents or college principals, even for one day. Even if you *can* arrange a visit, a case study may be needed first to help focus the students' minds and to prepare them for their observation and data-collection tasks during the visit. A further advantage of case studies compared with 'real life' is that too much risk might be involved if you enabled your students to make the decisions and carry out the actions involved in the real situations under study. There is an overlap with games and simulations. The latter are occasionally based on case studies, so it may be helpful to look now at sections 4.3–4.6, and at the guidance offered there with regard to preparation, briefing and debriefing.

Usually case studies are descriptions of imaginary contexts and situations which, though fictitious, mirror quite accurately the types of social or political organization, workplace or whatever on which they are based. Each may comprise a single sheet describing a problem situation, event or location. It may be based on a mock-up of a newspaper article or a description of people. Occasionally a pack of information is used which may include all of these, with additional background briefing details. Sometimes real newspaper articles, reports or statistics are used, and the case study is based on a description of actual practice. In either case the information can attempt to be factual or openly subjective. The material may be selected for its obvious bias or because it appears to present a balanced view.

The information that forms the basis of the case study may be as complex, detailed and ambiguous as in real life. Or you may decide to reduce the complexity in order to highlight the most significant aspects. This will depend upon your aims.

Aims
One overall aim is likely to be to acquaint the students with the situation

represented in the case study. You may for example wish them to use the material to answer the kind of question posed in ABC aim 1.6 (page 14) about management structure.

Some case studies demand a careful situational analysis. Students may have to take decisions by plotting possible outcomes. Your main aim may be to develop decision-making strategies, the ability to weigh options and decide on courses of action. Alternatively you may be concentrating on your students' ability to extract information from a text and to apply it to new situations. You may wish to concentrate on the language, to develop your students' powers to recognize emotive language and to distinguish fact from opinion. It may also be true that you wish your students to gain experience from a fictional case study which they can then apply in real-life contexts.

All these aims may involve a further one concerned with your students' ability to work in groups, to assume leadership, and to help one another while tackling a simulated problem.

Case studies are particularly useful when you are working with a group new to you or each other. Certain strategies, which require a high degree of mutual trust (e.g. role-play), may seem too risky at an early stage, whereas working on a case study is almost always a 'safe' activity. If this works well, then you can feel more confident about the more open-ended activities.

Preparation and presentation
Your decision as to how complex the case-study material should be will depend partly upon which of these aims are currently most important to you and your students.

Beware of bulky information packs with lengthy passages of text and complex statistical charts. Although you will wish to develop your students' comprehension skills, their general understanding and ability to solve problems should probably be highlighted. You may decide to rewrite the original texts in a simplified form; it is better to have less material, but a demanding set of questions to consider. These questions may be presented in written form with the case-study information or given to your students during the briefing stage.

You should know your material really well. Look for gaps and pitfalls; anticipate students' questions. Make sure that you have all the additional information you may need to answer such questions.

Writing your own case studies
The simplest kind of case study to use is one that you write yourself with your particular students in mind.

An example is a one-page handout which has a few paragraphs describing an incident at work, such as an argument between a trainee and a colleague or supervisor. Students read the brief outline of the event and then offer either their own solutions or suggestions for how the problem could be handled by the participants. An even easier format is to list possible solutions at the foot of the page and ask your students each to choose and justify one solution in discussion.

You will usually need to cue the students into the topic and context. Begin by asking them to contribute ideas and information from their own experience, either first-hand or, more likely, gained from reading and from the media. As always, progress from the known to the unknown. Make sure that they all know why they are looking at the materials before you give out the case studies. You will probably have to teach them how to learn from the activity. During this initial briefing discussion try to establish a common basis and to clear any early confusions.

Select some key questions that you think will inspire the group and get them started. For hints on organizing group work and for descriptions of various strategies, see section 2.3. The horseshoe arrangement might be the one best suited to case-study aims.

You will probably choose to be a facilitator, ready to join any group or pair but standing back as long as work appears to be progressing. Your role is similar to the one described in the section on role-play and simulation. As with all these strategies, leave time for a final reporting-back session in which to compare solutions, and to hear the ideas of the different groups.

Follow-up and related activities
Case-study work may involve, or develop into, role-play and simulation. For example, you may wish your students to practise their oral and written language skills. Letters and reports might be written, telephone calls made or simulated, interviews conducted. The situations presented in the case-study material might inspire creative writing – a narrative, short play, poem or video film script.

A small-scale investigation might be sparked off which could involve visits to similar contexts in the locality. A larger-scale survey or project might arise out of this work.

5.2   Visits

Visits are often recommended as the best, if not the only, way to introduce students to real (as against simulated) social situations. Case studies are said to be useful because they enable you to control the learning environment, to reduce complexity and to stage the gradual introduction of information about the context under study; visits, however, are the 'real thing'. On visits students can see for themselves how a place of work (Aim 1.2, 3, 4 and 8.2), a job centre (Aim 2.3), a local council or college academic board (Aim 9.3.4), a law court (Aim 9.15) or a social welfare centre (Aim 10.2) functions.

This argument seems sensible and irrefutable. However, unless you brief your students thoroughly and organize the visit carefully, they are unlikely to derive specific benefit from such an experience. They will probably enjoy the trip and will gain an overall impression of atmosphere. But the mass of impressions will probably overwhelm them and, unless you prepare them very carefully, they are more likely to remember the colour of the ceiling in the court or the hat worn by an old person in the day centre than the significant aspects you will wish to discuss with them after the visit. They certainly won't be able to collect information, conduct interviews, fill in questionnaires or write a report of the visit without help from you.

Organization

A few months before your chosen date, contact the places you intend to visit. This will give time for both sides to get organized. Find out how many students can be accommodated at any one time. There are often restrictions and you may have to consider staging a series of visits taking one group of students at a time. This, of course, will require careful organization to build the rest of your programme around staggered absences.

Check which days are likely to offer the most varied and appropriate experiences. Are there refreshments laid on? Ask the people you are negotiating with what they would suggest in the way of prior planning and briefing. They will probably be glad to be consulted and involved. Whenever possible try to visit by yourself first. Don't rely on telephone descriptions. You should also check whether any particular forms of insurance cover are necessary.

Make sure the people who will meet and talk to your students have an accurate idea of what will be needed and an understanding of the purpose of the visit. This is important as it should help them to select a suitable tone and level of language.

Consider carefully alternative means of travel and routes. Why not involve your students in this stage? This planning could incorporate communication, literacy, numeracy, and graphicacy work. Look at train and bus timetables and at local maps. Compare the costs of the alternatives and balance the results against gain in time and convenience. It might even be cheaper to hire a coach or to use several taxis. Decide together and make sure all your students are clear about the final choice, the money needed, and the time of departure. A whole visit can be spoiled if there is any hiccup in the travel arrangements.

Briefing

Introduce a general discussion on the type of place to be visited. Draw on your students' existing experience. Ask them to find out as much as they can on their own and to bring the information in to share during the lesson.

Be very clear about your own objectives. *Why* are you going to a magistrate's court? Or a Job Centre? Do you want your students to notice particular things? The procedure? The language? The physical surroundings?

Are they going to conduct interviews, fill in questionnaires, or write a report? Will they take part in a simulation and role-play afterwards?

Once you have decided, consider ways to cue them in, to help them focus on the significant aspects of the experience. It might be worth doing some limited role-play exercises before you go. You might show a short film or video, or photographs or diagrams of the kind of context involved. It is doubtful whether surprise or novelty will form part of the reasons for the visit, so you should probably give your students as clear a picture as possible before they go. If they are to interview people or to complete questionnaires, spend time practising. Section 5.4 might help here.

Discuss with them the forms of behaviour appropriate to the social context to be visited. Will it be all right for them to eat crisps? To take their portable hi-fi? If not, do they understand why not?

During the visit
You should almost always go with your students. The exceptions are when they are on placements and need to learn how to cope alone, and when your group is divided and students are visiting in small groups, week by week. Either travel with them or spend time checking that they are all clear about the meeting place. It is probably best to meet them outside the destination rather than inside.

During a long visit, draw your students together at intervals if possible, and go over what they've seen, heard and observed so far. Clearing up misunderstanding and filling in gaps as you go along can help prevent major confusions and wasted days.

Take with you a supply of extra copies of worksheets, questionnaires, pens, paper, and so on – some of your group are bound to have left theirs behind.

Debriefing
Hold this session as soon as possible after the visit, while the experience is fresh in your students' minds. Go back over the events and set questions and problems for large- or small-group discussion.

Bring in supplementary material to complement what they saw. It might be appropriate to work on a related case study, to lead on to a project, role-play or simulation. Some students may wish to write creatively about the experience and you may find literary extracts, poems or extracts from novels to continue the theme of the visit. It should be possible to find suitable writings concerned with the elderly which could be looked at after (or before) a visit to a residential home or a day centre or hospital.

5.3   Projects

A project is an effective way to integrate subject areas. It also provides a context in which to practise a range of skills and should help to develop your students' ability to work alone or in small groups. There will almost certainly be a product. This is often a written report describing the research, data collection and findings, but it could involve visual material and an oral presentation.

More important than this product, perhaps, is the process of conducting the research, analysing and presenting data, and working with others. Students working on a project learn to select material for themselves, to be responsible for their programme of work and to negotiate procedures with others. Your role will be that of facilitator rather than that of transmitter of knowledge. The skills acquired and practised in working on a project should be transferable to other tasks and contexts.

Many of the other strategies described in this manual can be linked with project work. Whole- and small-group discussion can precede the activity, as can role-play and simulation. Visits can be used as part of the project, to provide material or as an introduction or follow-up. Case studies are often used as the initial stimulus.

Aims

We can list many aims associated with project work. You will probably wish to weight them according to the priorities and aptitudes of your particular students. It is likely, however, that all will be relevant to some degree.

Projects can help to develop:

- personal attributes, such as self-reliance, independence and confidence
- the ability to work in groups, taking and sharing responsibilities
- planning and organizational skills
- information-retrieval and study skills; and the ability to select relevant data and to integrate data from different sources
- the ability to be critical and discriminating in weighing evidence
- problem-solving and decision-making skills
- oral and written comprehension and literacy skills
- creativity and the use of imagination

For the students, the end product of a project may be as important as the process. The booklet, folder of materials or whatever may well be the longest piece of work they have ever completed. They may feel pleased to keep it and possibly to mount a display for other students. This is in contrast to so much of their coursework which, being in the form of worksheets perhaps, is of no further interest to anyone else once it has been completed.

The communication skills are practical, and projects allow them to be developed in a framework in which language is used for real communication. Students will use language in their information search and in their oral and written reports. They will discuss and negotiate with others. They will have to synthesize information from notes, to revise and edit, and to decide the appropriate format for the final report.

Tutor's role

The tutor's role is that of facilitator. Unless you have already introduced regular group and individual work, your students will need help in adjusting to the shift of learning responsibility from you to them. Although your role may appear to be low-key, in fact you will need to give a lot of help to your students at the initiation stage. You could use individual and small-group tutorials to help your students decide upon the topic area and the methodology. You may need to stimulate initial ideas and then to help your students to shape these.

Try to ensure that your students select manageable tasks such that their chances of success are high. Without guidance they may choose to investigate global areas. Counsel them to shun over-ambitious projects that will take up too much time. They may also need advice concerning relevance. Tactful negotiation should ensure sensible, worthwhile choices.

Some courses stress project work as part of the continuous assessment. Students are encouraged to work in groups to carry out projects and to reflect on the process of group negotiation and effort. Their ideas, comments and analysis are recorded in a project log book. Your role here is to be in the background, helping but also assessing, with them, the contributions made by each member to the group project. This is not easy and calls for much tactful questioning and support. Done successfully, however, the gains in self-development can be enormous. Students come to realize, for example, that it is not always the noisiest, most assertive member who most helps the group. It might instead be a quieter student who encourages others to participate or who gets on with the task without needing a push to do so.

Preparation

Apart from acting as facilitator to help the students form groups and to decide their topics and ways of working, you will also need to transmit knowledge and develop some specific research and study skills. You may like to look at the section on survey methods (section 5.4) for some ideas on what kind of research skills your students might need.

They will probably need a lot of help in developing information-retrieval skills. Many a project has foundered because students have gone unaided to the library to find books on their chosen topic. Without help many will copy out chunks of reference books, only partly understanding the significance of what they are writing.

Develop their ability to obtain information from written sources by bringing a variety of books, magazines, journals and trade directories into the classroom and demonstrating the use of indexes and the techniques of skimming and scanning. Encourage them to practise telephoning for information; role-play visits to such sources as Citizens Advice Bureaux, law centres and libraries. Show them the various filing systems available – ring binders, envelope files, card indexes and the like. Then help them to develop their own system by attempting small tasks. There is a more detailed look at the study-skill area in section 15.2.

Presentation
Try to find time for a leisurely, enjoyable session when your students can talk about their projects and present the results to their peers. Encourage at least some of the groups of individuals to take photographs or make tape-recordings to chart the stages of the research. Displays of source material and supplementary evidence can help the students to learn from each other's work.

If a project has failed in the *product* sense, try to convince the students that the *process* is important and that they have gained knowledge and skills during the work even though they seem not to have much to show for their efforts. Their log books should document the reasons why the project 'failed'. It might have been too ambitious in scope, the students in the group may have failed to work well together, or perhaps the information needed was not available.

Overall try to ensure that there is a supportive, positive atmosphere and that all the students feel that their efforts are valued by you and by the group as a whole.

5.4 Surveys

It is unlikely that you will wish or need to prepare your students to carry out large-scale research projects involving sophisticated statistical procedures. However, projects often involve data collection, usually by questionnaire or interview schedule, and your students will probably welcome guidance in preparing a questionnaire and in processing the data gained from it.

Several ABC aims include references to this kind of activity. Students are to interpret and present graphs, pie-charts, bar-charts; to read and understand questionnaires; to express tabular or graphical data in written form or vice versa; to conduct surveys. Aim 8, in particular, refers to 'scientific method', variables, control, and correlation.

Introducing your students to such methodology may seem a formidable task. Unless you have a social-science or scientific background or have conducted research you will probably feel ill-equipped to perform the tasks yourself, let alone to help your students to do so. In practice, however, the number of concepts and procedures involved is very limited and there are many research manuals which will give you a basic grasp of these.

To help with projects and surveys the following concepts are useful:

- sampling
- data collection – by mailed questionnaire, interview schedule, or attitude scales
- validity
- reliability

- data processing – in terms of frequency counts, calculation of means, construction and interpretation of tables, pie-charts, histograms and graphs, and the use of microcomputer databases

You may well wish to add others to this list or to leave some of these out. It is meant only as a rough guide.

Sampling

You might like to discuss the question of bias and representativeness. Explain to the group that the 'survey population' refers to an overall class of people or objects. If the survey is into the take-up of nursery places in a particular town, village or borough, for example, the *population* would be all those households with children of nursery school age, or all the children themselves. The *sample* would then be those subjects actually approached – the households contacted, or the children investigated.

The difference between 'random' and 'given' samples could be explored. Your students could discuss ways of randomizing – picking names from a hat, using a computer, sticking pins in a list, taking every seventh name, using published charts of randomly generated numbers.

Although this is obviously a superficial approach, it is probably all that is needed at this stage. Your aims are likely to involve enabling your students to select a sample for a survey and encouraging them to consider the question of bias in surveys reported in the media and in advertising campaigns.

Data collection

A first requirement might be a consideration of what a 'fact' is. The difference between 'fact' and 'opinion' could be explored via newspaper articles and television documentaries. Next, questionnaires and interview schedules could be compared.

Questionnaires

The most straightforward way to introduce this would probably be by looking at a variety of question formats. You could include a tick-box form (e.g. 'yes ☐ no ☐ don't know ☐'), a free-answer or open-response one with a 'complete the sentence' format (e.g. 'Reading this book has . . .'), and an attitude scale. The Likert form of attitude scale is probably the best known. This has a statement and possible responses along a continuum, e.g. 'Reading this book has helped me in my teaching: strongly agrees/agrees/disagrees/strongly disagrees/undecided'. Students could devise different versions and formats to sample the same attitudes or to collect the same information, and try them out on each other. This could lead to the introduction of the concept of a 'pilot' survey, used to refine research instruments like questionnaires before the full-scale investigation.

Interviews
Here you could introduce the different ways of combining questionnaires with personal-contact interviews for data collection and attitude surveys.

Should tape-recordings be made? Should a tick-box question be answered during the interview by the researcher? Or should the actual words of the respondent be written down, or recorded, or both? Cards with a range of possible responses could be shown to the respondent and her or his selection recorded. The closed question with a tick box is often easier to deal with, but the open, free response leads to more spontaneous answers. Which is more genuine, and which more likely to lead to a biased view? Again your students could practise on each other.

Processing the data
You probably won't want to introduce many statistical terms. The mean, or average, could be explained and demonstrated using the students' ages, heights and so on. Frequency counts could be made, recording your students' favourite bands, cars, colours or whatever and then counting the number of votes for each category. These could then be used to make a graph, histogram (sometimes called a bar chart) and a pie chart. An overhead projector slide with colour coding and acetate overlays works well for this.

The concepts are not too difficult, but don't try to cover too much at once: it will probably take your students a while to absorb the information and get used to seeing data presented in different graphical ways. Practise translating from histograms to verbal descriptions and back. Advertisments often include this kind of graphical display. Compare different expressions of proportions, such as 'six out of fourteen students preferred red', '6/14', and 'just under half'.

A growing number of schools, colleges and training centres have access to microcomputers. There is probably a software package for the particular micro you have that will enable your students to set up a simple database in respect of which they can conduct frequency counts, evaluate averages and answer simple correlation questions (such as 'How many females chose engineering?').

Validity and reliability
These two concepts can be introduced, although your students could conduct a questionnaire survey without knowledge of them. Validity involves the question: does each test or question in the survey measure what it's supposed to measure? You could look at a questionnaire item and ask whether it is collecting information on more than one thing at once, or at a test item from a college or school exam and ask what it is measuring. Are there any other factors involved?

Reliability is concerned with consistency – with obtaining the same results on more than one test occasion. You might consider with your students whether they believe they would perform the same way in a test or in response to a question on two different days, weeks apart. You could get them to repeat a short questionnaire several weeks apart and then compare the results.

All of this may seem over-simplified and possibly a distortion of research method, but you have to be clear about your own objectives. An introductory programme such as is outlined here should enable your students to cope with simple graphical information and to carry out a survey as part of a project. Later on, if appropriate, they can develop a more sophisticated knowledge of survey methods.

Social skills and surveys

On the whole, *some* kind of survey, however badly it may measure up to any of the criteria outlined above, is better than no survey at all. Just getting your students out of the classroom and talking to strangers (or even friends) in a new context that makes them think more carefully about the encounter may be the most important thing you want to achieve with your students. If there are appointments to be fixed by letter or telephone call, let them make all the arrangements themselves. Try to avoid sending them unsupported into a situation where they might be rebuffed in a way that could shake their confidence too much, though how to cope with refusals may also be a useful thing for them to learn.

5.5   Residentials

A residential can benefit students in so many ways that it is well worth investigating the possibilities of funding and organizing one for your scheme. One or two weeks away from the normal educational, work and family environments can help students reflect on their learning and view the rest of their course and each other from a fresh perspective.

The overall theme of the residential can be outdoor activities, or drama and creative work, or an environmental or community project. The emphasis is on 'experiential' learning and social development. In other words the students learn social, communication, practical and other skills through their own activity and involvement. This means that the review and reflection aspects of the experience need to be structured and stressed. Your students will almost certainly need help in identifying the kind of learning that is taking place as they participate in the planned and impromptu activities.

Advantages to be gained

Residentials provide

- intense experiences of a new physical and social environment, away from home
- the opportunity to reflect on and interpret that experience
- the conditions for accelerated learning

- the conditions for faster development of social relationships between students, and between tutors and students
- the opportunity for young people to succeed in a tangible way so that they can recognize their achievements
- an environment in which the students can recognize their own and each other's potential and personal limits – they can achieve something on their own terms
- the opportunity for students to try out new roles and also to observe adults in different roles
- an environment in which students can develop self-awareness, self-confidence, self-control and self-sufficiency – they can develop a sense of individual and group responsibility as against dependence
- the opportunities to practise autonomous decision making, to become aware that choices often exist
- intense experience of working co-operatively in a group: students can develop trust in others and sensitive tolerance of each other's limitations
- the opportunity for students to become adaptable and to discover new interests
- the opportunity for students to identify their own skills through meeting new challenges

Possible difficulties
Detailed preparation and follow-up work is needed to prevent the residential from being seen as an isolated experience.

Individual students may fail to meet targets they have set themselves. This will obviously need careful handling because in the intense experience of a residential, failure, like success, can take on extra significance. Staff need to be committed and prepared to work very long hours.

The tutor's role
The key role is that of mediator, for the students, between their experience and their learning. You will be required to bridge the gap between the two. While fostering group respect for individual achievement, you will need to organize and occasionally lead small- and large-group discussions to reflect on each day's activities and to draw out the learning. Some of the strategies described in Chapter 2 may be useful. A brainstorming session could lead to a large sheet of paper on which are recorded students' thoughts, observations, personal and group targets. This could be put up on a wall and students could add to it as and when they felt moved to do so. Later, photographs could be added to provide a more permanent record.

It is the whole experience of being and working together that is important but students may not recognize specific points of learning unless you help them to identify these.

The planning and preparation before the residential can be a shared responsibility between you and the students. Make sure you begin early enough. Some centres need over six months' booking notice.

You will have to decide between self-catering and catered-for centres. The former can lead to useful practice in communications and numeracy and in organizational and practical skills, but the latter will leave more time for the other activities and for reflection. Whichever you choose, your role will be that of supporter and facilitator. Try to give the students as much responsibility as possible.

During the briefing and preparatory sessions stress the integrated aspects of the courses. Make sure that your students don't see the residential as a separate, isolated holiday. The work covered during the residential should follow on from the rest of the course.

Similarly, on their return, students should use the experience gained as a basis for further work. This need not be a tedious essay entitled 'What I did on the residential'! It could be a project to find out more about an idea or skill newly acquired.

A well organized and successful residential can bring about permanent changes in the attitudes, interests and ambitions of the participants.

5.6   The strategies

Case studies

When to use
- when your students need to study a social, vocational or political context and you are unable to arrange a visit
- as a means of preparation before a visit to the real setting, or as an aid to reflection and analysis after such a visit has been made
- as material to develop decision-making skills
- as a basis for discussion, reflection, comprehension and analysis
- as a means for developing the ability to work in groups
- as a stage in role-play or simulation

When not to use
- as a soft-option substitute for a real visit and survey
- with a group whose level of literacy prevents them from reading the information pack with understanding (although in that situation an oral approach might work well)
- whenever you have insufficient time for a full briefing

Pointers to good practice
- avoid over-long text extracts, which can cause information overload
- know the material well yourself and have additional information to hand
- anticipate students' queries

- cue the group in, and teach them how to learn from case studies
- give thought to the organization of the group activity
- act as facilitator – only participate in small-group discussion when you are needed
- find ways to explore the material fully
- encourage individuals to find their own preferred ways of taking the ideas further

Taking it further
- extend into role-play and simulation
- conduct a fuller survey or project
- arrange visits to similar situations

Visits .

When to use
- as part of a systematic study of a vocational, social or political context
- before and/or after detailed classroom discussion and analysis of similar contexts

When not to use
- on the spur of the moment, because you feel it might vaguely interest students
- at the very beginning or end of a topic, when there is insufficient time for preparation or follow up

Pointers to good practice
- arrange the visit well in advance and in detail
- involve your students in planning the travel
- brief the group carefully and cue them in, to help their observation skills
- go on the visit yourself; on a long visit, hold interim briefing meetings
- conduct the debriefing session as soon as possible after the visit
- follow up with supplementary materials and assignments

Taking it further
- use as a basis for role-play and simulation
- look at case studies based on the same context
- use the information gained to begin a project
- encourage creative responses to the experience

Projects

When to use
- once the students are accustomed to individual and group work
- as a follow-up to a visit or to case studies
- in conjunction with role-play and simulation

When not to use
- too early in a course, before students are able to work together
- before students have developed the necessary information-retrieval, research and study skills

Pointers to good practice
- check that your students have the required study and research skills
- act as facilitator
- ensure that your students understand the purpose of the project
- help your students select viable projects such that there is a good chance of success
- encourage the use of log books and regular reflection on individual and group progress and cohesion
- incorporate a presentation sesson with sufficient time and resources to do justice to the projects
- make a realistic time-scale and help students stick to it: groups need to finish more or less at the same time, not too soon to produce anything worthwhile, nor too late to sustain interest.

Surveys

When to use
- as part of a project that will take your students outside the classroom to collect data
- during media studies, using data presented in newspapers or on film

When not to use
- in asking students to construct tables or charts from data that they do not understand or perceive as relevant
- in setting up surveys that involve complicated statistical procedures or over-long interview schedules (which are likely to increase the likelihood of failure to complete the planned work)

Pointers to good practice
- plan the procedure in detail before introducing the activity
- involve your students in the choice of subject
- give sufficient initial briefing in subsidiary skills (like questionnaire design) but then let them draft the final version
- try not to simulate interviews without progressing to the real thing: get out and involve local people, but prepare your students first by role-play and simulation
- encourage group project work and let your students negotiate individual tasks
- show them how to keep a log book recording the survey's progress

- if necessary, incorporate individual help with communication and numeracy skills
- help your students to plan manageable surveys and to practise a range of techniques
- encourage them to present their results in a professional manner

Residentials

When to use
- in the induction phase, to help integration and to foster group cohesion
- later in the course, as an opportunity for reflection on learning progress and possibly to work on lengthy group projects

When not to use
- too near to the end of the course when there will be insufficient time to evaluate the experience or to conduct follow-up course work
- at times when your students have too many relevant commitments to want to go

Pointers to good practice
- provide plenty of time for your students to prepare for the residential
- involve them in the detailed planning (budgets, itinerary, menus, etc.)
- integrate the period with the rest of the course
- be prepared for heightened emotions and possible upsets as your students adjust to living together and to testing themselves in a new environment
- make sure the staff who go expect to work long hours
- hold regular discussions to reflect on the experience and to develop the learning
- take photographs or make a film, collect material to exhibit on your return, and let the students set up the display
- plan lengthy follow-up sessions to reinforce the learning and to transfer newly acquired skills to other learning situations

5.7 Resources list

Tutor's background reading
Despite their reference to an outdated scheme, the advice given in the two publications about YOP is still relevant and valuable.

Further Education Unit 1978 *Experience, reflection, learning* (FEU)
Manpower Services Commission *Using residential experience in YOP* (MSC)
National Youth Bureau *Residentials in YOP* – alternative learning settings and strategies (NYB)

6 Lecture and exposition lessons

6.1 Lectures

The label 'lecture' conjures up a stereotypic image of an authority figure (usually male) standing on a raised platform in front of rows of attentive students with pens poised over notebooks.

And this is the concept of post-secondary education that most people would recognize. It is not a valid description of the kind of teaching done most often by the further-education or adult-education tutor or lecturer, or by the YTS trainer or tutor.

This is just as well: research indicates that lecturing is not the best method of developing thinking, reflection, and other 'higher order' skills (Bligh, 1975). Formal exposition, the almost continuous verbal delivery of information, needs to be supplemented by discussion and by the types of active student participation described in section 2.3.

In a lecture the flow of information is too steadily in one direction, from tutor to student. Although students can interrupt to ask for clarification, in practice they seldom do. So it is very difficult to obtain feedback. At its worst a lecture can involve a tutor jogging at an ever-increasing rate along paths she or he regards as thoroughly familiar, while the students drop out one by one as each turn is made. Even those who stay the course may be unable to navigate the route alone. Little information is retained and it is likely to be the unusual landmarks, the anecdotes and jokes, that are remembered.

This is of course an extreme example. Planned and delivered well a lecture can be an efficient and an appropriate way to present new information to a group of students who would have little from previous knowledge or experience to contribute to the topic at that introductory stage. A lecture can promote factual learning and comprehension. But it has to be done well.

Planning
It is not enough to know your material thoroughly and to write it out as coherent lecture notes. You have to think of ways of conveying to your students the information that is already so clear to you. And your students are unlikely to share your own accumulation of knowledge and experience. You have to relate the new information to their own current understanding.

This task is often made even more difficult by the lack of homogeneity within your student group. They almost certainly differ from each other in their social, educational and personal experiences. They will know different things, be interested in different things, and their ability to take on and make sense of new information and ideas will vary. All this points to a need for *individualized* learning. Yet before that stage is reached, you still might like to present some information to the whole group – to give a short lecture.

Although you will wish to plan carefully and in detail you will also need to be flexible. You will need to alter the pace, to re-order the material, possibly even to change the content if you realize during the lecture that your students aren't following.

The first step is to make sure that you know your subject matter really well. You need to be sufficiently confident to talk while maintaining eye contact with the students. They will soon lose interest if you keep looking down at your notes.

Some lecturers prefer to write out a lecture script in full. This is all very well, but it can lead to a determination to cover the ground exactly as you have planned, regardless of students' reactions. Anyway, if all you intend doing is to read it out you might as well give the script as a hand-out.

It is much better to note down the key points, the order of sub-topics, and the examples you intend to incorporate. Writing lecture notes this way forces you to think of the *structure* of the material, and of the internal organization of the content.

Structure

Educational theorists (amongst them Bruner, 1966, and Ausubel *et al.*, 1978) have stressed the need to pay attention to the hierachical relationship between concepts. Some things have to be learned and understood before other things can be introduced. Numeracy and language teachers are amongst those who are particularly aware of this, but it affects all teaching. You the tutor must be aware of the underlying structure of your subject and of the topic you are presenting. It is largely this structure that will determine the order in which you present the information.

There are at least two types of structure. These are sometimes referred to as the 'discipline-logical' and the 'psychological' sequencing of content. What this means is that although you, thoroughly immersed in your own subject or the topic you are covering, can see a certain *logical* ordering of material, this ordering may not be the best way to get the material across to your students. It might be more fruitful to introduce steps in a slightly unusual, even illogical, way – if by doing so you can relate each new piece of information to the students' existing knowledge, interests and experience. Suppose, for example, that you want to convey information about the rights of individuals in encounters with police. You could draw up an ordered logical sequence of information. But it would be much better to deal first with those aspects of the topic that affect your group most closely – leading on to other information once you have captured interest, established motivation and promoted some understanding.

By making the topic, whatever it is, relevant to your students, you help them fit the jigsaw bits of subject matter together. Without help they won't automatically see the connections between the subject parts that are probably self-evident to you. Always try to empathize and to start from the students' viewpoint. A good way is to elicit information from a group first, before you even plan your presentation. Tell them that you intend to look at a particular topic with them on a later occasion, and invite their contributions and help in assessing their current experience and understanding. A drawback is that this invitation might spark off a lively discussion which anticipates too much of what you plan to cover in a more formal way. Experience will help you to elicit just sufficient information to whet the group's appetite without encouraging too much on-the-spot exploration. Once you have assessed your students' starting points, plan your lecture around the material. Don't try to present more information than they can cope with. Beware the dreaded 'information overload'.

Write out a flowchart of points to be introduced. Jot down any facts you need to refer to, rather than trying to memorize everything. A few suitable anecdotes and analogies are usually helpful. Make sure that you have an inspiring introduction that will create interest, focus attention and help to establish rapport; and a planned conclusion to recap and reinforce the main points. Think how you are going to obtain feedback and evaluate the learning. Look at the sections on questioning (Chapter 3) and on small-group discussion methods (section 2.3) if you would like some ideas for follow-up activities.

Presentation

Yorke (1981), drawing in turn on the work of Bligh (1972 & 1975) and Brown (1978 & 1979), refers to four different types of presentation. There are:

- linear presentations, which take a title theme and develop it through a series of clearly defined stages
- comparative presentations, which explore the relationship between two aspects within one topic
- step-by-step presentations, which divide the lecture into separate phases and evaluate learning after each step with questions and answers
- problem-centred presentations, which present a problem at the beginning, elicit possible solutions from the group, and develop into a combination of exposition and discussion.

Yorke points out that the fourth type of lecture can be seen as an exposition lesson.

Whichever type of presentation you select, try to monitor your students' progress – indicated by their attention, interest and note-taking – as you go along.

Delivery

Speak loudly enough to be audible from any seat in the room. And speak slowly. Don't be frightened of slowing your usual conversational rate of delivery right down. Leave lots of pauses. Punctuate with your voice. Emphasize using voice inflexions. Vary the pitch and intensity to avoid monotony. If you haven't taught much before you will probably be reluctant to slow down your delivery too much. Your own voice will sound artificial and strange. Try to arrange to have video- or audio-recordings of a few of your lessons. You will soon realize that what sounds embarrassingly slow to you is a suitable, comfortable delivery pace for your students. In one-to-one and small-group work you can often use your normal conversational versational pace, but the larger the group, the slower the pace and the more exaggerated the tone shifts and emphases should be. It's very like acting in a theatre.

The main points need to be delivered emphatically, repeated and probably written – on a board, overhead-projector transparency or incomplete handout. Sometimes a summary can be built up in this way or presented later as a handout.

The illustrations and anecdotes can be offered in a quicker, more conversational tone. And do try to avoid too many meaningless syllables like 'er . . . ah . . . um . . . uh . . . er . . .harrumph'.

Gesture

Don't be too wildly emphatic. Arm waving and rapid pacing can distract if it's overdone. But your students will also be distracted if you stifle all your natural gestures and present an artificially static image. Again it really is worth recording yourself at least once on video. If you can't manage this in a real teaching situation, get a group of colleagues and friends to join you and present a 'micro-lesson'. Then look carefully at your body language. Do you smile? Do you look at as many students as possible? Do your hand gestures accompany the emphasis in your voice? Have you any irritating or amusing gestures which you could, and perhaps should, stifle? Frenzied twisting of hair, regular tossing of chalk, anxious leg swinging when perched on a table can get in the way of your students' learning in a way that varied and emphatic use of your hands and facial expression will not.

Student study skills

Your students will need particular skills if they are to derive value from a lecture. Note-taking is a highly complex information-processing task.

They will need to

- listen with understanding
- sort main from subsidiary points
- sort factual information from illustration and opinion

- write notes in an organized and sufficiently fast manner
- synthesize, to build up these notes into coherent information after the lecture

Many factors will affect your students' ability to listen with understanding. Their previous knowledge and experience, and their attitude towards both you and the subject matter, will influence their success in coping with the information. Your speed of delivery will need to match your students' thinking speed.

You can help your students identify the internal structure of your lecture by using certain phrases to introduce points and by connecting these phrases in a sequence. Yorke (1981) refers to Brown's work in identifying four types of structuring moves. He includes a helpful table which is reproduced here (Table 6.1). If you can introduce your own versions of these verbal cues you will help your students to structure their own note-taking. With practice they will learn to respond to the cues and to use them as a guide to distinguish main from subsidiary points, and facts from opinion.

There are ideas for helping your students develop their written note-taking skills in Chapter 15. To begin with, at least, you could provide a handout or incomplete worksheet with just the main points listed and with gaps where your

Table 6.1 Structuring moves (adapted from Brown, 1979)

Structuring move	Purpose	Examples
Signpost	To describe the range of structure of an exposition.	'. . . we will cover the basic rules of committee procedure' '. . . I shall describe the Wheatstone Bridge and show how it can be used to determine an unknown resistance'
Frame	To indicate the beginnings and ends of topics.	'To begin with . . .' 'And now we'll look at . . .' 'I'll finish this section by saying . . .'
Focus	To emphasize important points and examples.	'The key point is . . .' 'The best example is . . .' 'You should remember . . .'
Link	To indicate relationships within the subject matter and, perhaps reservations as to the extent of application of a principle or relationship.	'Because . . .' 'Therefore . . .' 'It follows that . . .' 'Now you can see how X links with Y' 'The relationship only holds as far as . . .'

students can add their own notes. You can take these in and check them at regular intervals.

Visual aids
It is difficult for anybody to absorb information from the spoken word alone. Think how much harder you have to concentrate when you are taking in information from the radio as against the television. Your students will have your facial expressions and gestures to help them but additional visual cues will help.

If you can incorporate pictures, photographs, charts, maps, tables, films or computer printouts these will help all your students to make sense of the lecture. And some of the students will be 'visiles' as against 'audiles' – they will consistently learn better from visual rather than audio cues.

The overhead projector is particularly useful as it enables you to build up diagrams and charts in stages, to use overlays and to write additional information on the acetate as you talk. Students' contributions can also be added, although this is more likely to happen in other exposition lessons than in lectures.

6.2 Exposition lessons

The lecture is itself a type of exposition. Exposition skills are the teaching skills of communicating, of getting a message across. Almost everything we have said about effective lecturing applies to other types of exposition teaching.

The difference between a lesson and a lecture is in the degree of interaction between you and your students. In a lecture the students are less active and make fewer contributions than in other types of teaching situation. At the other extreme some of the small-group discussion activities, role-plays, simulations and projects may involve very little formal exposition from you, the tutor. The students may be responsible for almost all of the classroom activity. You will be the facilitator. For more detail about these strategies, please read the relevant sections of this handbook.

When you are presenting information during an exposition phase in your lesson, you need to introduce as much variety as possible. If you skim through the strategies described in this handbook you will see how many different ways there are to get your message across to your students.

Introduction
The interest aroused by a novel, successful introduction to a topic can motivate your students and carry them through the succeeding stages of your presentation.

This opening phase is sometimes described as 'set'. It refers to the process of capturing your students' attention and helping them to focus on the lesson objectives and content. You need to help your group by creating a frame of reference into which students can slot the new information.

There are various ways of achieving this. Sometimes you will want to tell your students what your purpose is: you may describe the objectives and explain what you hope you and they will achieve by the end of the lesson. At other times you will prefer to keep them guessing so that you can introduce an element of surprise. If you are using the second approach it's probably best to warn them that you don't expect them to understand at once what's happening; they will then remain intrigued as the lesson gradually unfolds, rather than feel anxious and insecure.

Some tutors are adept at the use of unusual stimuli. Some take a particular object into class – a potted plant, a bicycle, a pair of tights – and let the students stare at it for a while before revealing the 'meaning' behind it. Others wear unusual dress or behave in a planned 'unexpected' manner at the beginning of a class to stimulate their students' interest and lead into the lesson content. Such an approach is fine, and well worth trying occasionally. Used too often, though, it loses its appeal and becomes as 'normal' as the set of class textbooks students were used to in school.

Development

Exposition does not necessarily mean you talking and the students listening. After your introduction you can use many different means to continue.

As you describe a process or outline factual information you can pause at regular intervals and obtain feedback by question and answer (see section 3.1). Points can be revealed at appropriate levels, already written on overhead-projector acetate or on a flip chart. Contributions from the class can be added or written on a board. You can use film or video clips, slides or sets of photographs. A practical demonstration or activity might be appropriate. If you are describing a historical event or a social situation you might read a poem or an extract from a novel, to introduce a more personal perspective.

As in lecturing, vary your pace of delivery and use voice inflexions – change your stress, tone and emphasis. Be enthusiastic. Use gestures and facial expressions to convey mood and to engage the group's attention and interest. After ten or fifteen minutes with you in control of the whole group, you may feel that it is time for a change of pace. Divide the students into pairs or small groups and invite them to consider questions related to the topic. (Section 2.3 describes various types of small discussion groups.) This will give you the opportunity to circulate and monitor the progress of individuals.

Whatever you do, keep your purpose in mind. Try to make all the different activities, your talk, and the various exchanges – between you and the students, and among the students – integrate and flow back to the lesson topic. If the structure is apparent to the students it is more likely that they will remember the experience and learn from it.

The conclusion

The end of the lesson is as important as the beginning. There is often a temptation to keep going until time runs out. This should be resisted: it is better to leave an activity or a set of handouts until a later session than to rush through a new item in the last few minutes.

We can distinguish between 'cognitive' and 'social' closure. *Cognitive* closure refers to the consolidation that can take place at the end of a lesson, the summarizing of ground covered. It is equivalent to the establishment of the learning set at the beginning. It focuses the students' mind on the points raised during the lesson, and can also prepare them for the next lesson.

Social closure means giving the students a sense of achievement and well-being at the end of the lesson. Let them know what they have learned. Although you yourself may sometimes feel that very little ground has been covered, you can almost always point to some progress that the students will be able to perceive. And if the lesson has been such an obvious fiasco that you and the students *all* recognize a lack of achievement, use the last phase to discuss the reasons for this. Always try to turn any classroom situation to a learning advantage. Students are usually perceptive and able to pinpoint the problems. And they usually appreciate being part of a co-operative process. If they can perceive and analyse the problem, be these the result of information overload, group dynamics, or unsettling events outside the classroom, you will all have established a good basis for work in the next lesson. In most cases, though, the lesson will have gone well in the main, and you can all use the last few minutes to agree upon the ground covered and upon any further work, class or individual, that is needed.

This stage is even more important if the students are recording their own progress on a profile or checklist. They will need to translate the lesson content and their performance into the achievement of learning objectives and the mastery of specific skills.

6.3   The strategies

Lecture

When to use
- in the interests of efficiency, when your group is too large to convey all the required information by other means
- when your students are unable to contribute much to the topic because of their current levels of understanding and experience

When not to use
- in situations in which you can make use of experiential learning role-play, games, or small group-discussions
- when you wish to develop thinking and reflective skills

- whenever your group is sufficiently small to allow for individual and small-group tuition

Pointers to good practice
- know your material thoroughly, so that you're not over-dependent on a lecture script
- make a clear note of key points, organized so that you can see them at a glance
- maintain eye contact with the group
- structure the material carefully so that it makes psychological sense to your students
- vary pitch and intonation
- be enthusiastic and expressive
- don't wave your arms around too wildly, but do use gestures to accompany your verbal delivery
- remain flexible: vary the pace, order, and even content if the group appears to be floundering
- try to monitor your group's progress throughout by picking up non-verbal clues
- present some information visually
- help your students to develop their study skills (note-taking in particular)
- incorporate some question-and-answer sessions, to provide feedback
- always try to follow up with a more active learning phase

Exposition

When to use
- as a lesson phase when information needs to be presented to the whole group
- in association with other strategies

When not to use
- - whenever learning could be better achieved by *doing* as against *listening* (but even then, a short exposition phase might be included)

Pointers to good practice
- be clear about your objectives and the relationship of the exposition phase to the other lesson stages
- use a clear introduction to create a frame of reference for your students
- introduce variety; present your material in many different ways
- be lively, and use stress and intonation to keep the students' attention
- try to include phases of activity and full participation
- incorporate visual and multi-media aids
- conclude with a summary of points covered, and some indication of the next stage

6.4 Resources list

Tutor's background reading

Ausubel, D.P., J.D. Novak, and Hanesian 1978 *Educational psychology: a cognitive view*, 2nd edn (Holt, Rinehart and Winston)

Bligh, D.A. 1972 *What's the use of lectures?* (Penguin)

Bligh, D.A. 1975 *Teaching students* (Exeter University Services)

Bruner, J.S. 1967 *Towards a theory of instruction* (Harvard University Press)

Yorke, D.M. 1981 *Patterns of teaching* (Council for Educational Technology)

7 Creative writing, literature, and the media

7.1 Students' needs

As your students are on fairly short courses with a vocational flavour, your main aims for the development of social and communication skills will reflect the functional bias of the overall syllabus. You will be concerned to foster self-reliance and personal effectiveness.

Your students will need a basic command of a reasonably standard form of spoken English, and to a lesser extent written English, in order to survive. They will need to develop the ability to make themselves understood and to receive and correctly interpret the messages relayed to them by others. What is needed is practice in selecting a suitable level of formality and tone: it isn't really a question of correct grammar. More important is the ability to detect the hidden messages that signal the speaker's attitude. When should your students appear assertive and when submissive? We all play these games whenever we communicate with each other but your students will probably need help in recognizing the rules and acting in accord with them. Ways of developing this awareness in your students and suggestions for helping them to become more skilled in communicating are included in Chapter 14.

7.2 Creative writing

This section concerns another dimension of language use – the creative, imaginative and reflective uses. This area is often missing from 'Communication' course syllabuses, and there are some valid reasons for this. Traditional English courses sometimes neglected the functional role of language; oral skills were not practised and students, though they were taught to respond to poems and to write imaginative stories, were not taught to write letters or fill in forms or to make telephone calls. Basic communication courses redressed the balance, but in doing so they left out an important area, that of fantasy. Your students will need to learn how to write standard, conventional letters and how to present themselves to a prospective employer or DHSS official; but they will also benefit from the opportunity to explore the world of the imagination, to respond in a creative way to their experiences, to make personal statements, and to interpret the experience of others in their own terms.

Responding to other peoples' writing is helpful in this, but it is the losing of inhibitions about expressing one's own feelings, emotions and attitudes that is crucial. Many of the topics dealt with in a 'Social Education and Communication' course are provocative and potentially disturbing to students. They may feel their own self-images are threatened. They will be asked to explore their own attitudes towards themselves, each other and their families, and towards those in authority over them. They will consider where they stand in relation to society and its current preoccupations – unemployment law and order, the peace movement, the position of women, issues of race. Writing and speaking in a free manner, uninhibited by too great a concern for conventional standards, can help them come to terms with new ideas and controversial issues. They can make their own personal statements. Not all your students will want to do so; but if you encourage them and provide this opportunity, you will probably be rewarded with sensitive, imaginative and original contributions.

Contexts for creative writing

We do not suggest that you set aside a period and label it 'creative writing', although this was and possibly still is common practice in most lower-school English courses. A more fruitful approach is to offer some type of creative task – and the end product could be visual, musical or oral, not necessarily written – within the context of other work.

For example, you could suggest to your students that they might like to write something from the perspective of an old person seen in a visit to a residential home. Such writing could take the format of a poem, a diary entry or a letter. Or they could try to see themselves in the situation of a defendant in a magistrate's court, of a police officer on duty during a demonstration, of a woman or man alone at home with young children, of a politician in parliament, or of a footballer or musician. It could become accepted practice to write an imaginative piece as part of the course work. In particular, case studies, role-play and simulations, projects, visits and residentials could all include periods of personal reflection and response.

Your students will benefit from comparing this poetic and expressive style of writing with the transactional, functional style of official letters, curricula vitae and telephone memos. Discursive writing in a persuasive mode is also important. Your students should practise arguing in a lucid manner, balancing different viewpoints and summarizing the alternatives before presenting their own conclusions. Although you may justifiably shy away from organizing a formal debate, discussion will assume an important role in your teaching. Why not get your students to respond in writing to the content of a discussion? It is probably best to do this occasionally rather than to make it a routine occurrence: students might find a regular 'writing up the discussion' slot tedious, and some discussions lead on more naturally to other tasks and activities. Films and videos are often shown to students and usually lead to discussion on the central issues of the 'Social Education' syllabus. Once again, you can encourage the occasional creative response – an imaginative article for a newsletter or a script for a video, a poem or a short play.

You will soon discover which students want to seize the opportunities you give them and which are reluctant. A workshop type of organization (section 8.1) would enable you to set different tasks and activities to suit everybody.

Ways of developing the skill

Creative responses are seen as spontaneous, but as any experienced writer would stress, writing is a craft that entails careful, systematic effort and the application of technique. Occasional stream-of-consciousness writing is fine, but there are ways in which you can help your students to order and develop their ideas more effectively.

The first few times you suggest this type of activity, you might help the group produce a joint effort. Suppose for example you had all visited a day centre for the elderly. You could show your group photographs of old people and invite each student to select one particular person with whom to identify – the person from whose perspective he or she will later write. The next step would be to choose a photograph for the whole group to consider as an example. First brainstorm ideas in the full group or in buzz groups (section 2.3): What kind of life had the person had? What are his or her present thoughts, wishes, and preoccupations? Imagine the family and friends, the likes and dislikes regarding food, entertainment, clothes, politicians . . . Then draw the ideas together in a large-group session. Organize the suggestions under headings on a board, flip chart or overhead projector-transparency. What would make a compelling introduction? How many paragraphs would it occupy if the whole text is an article or essay? Would it be best to have a single idea per paragraph or verse? If the text is a narrative, would flash-back be useful?

After the group experience your students could be expected to write more confidently and effectively about their own, individually chosen, photographs.

Allow complete freedom for any kind of creation – narrative, poem, short story, words, pictures or music. This kind of activity could culminate in a media project such as the preparation of a tape-slide sequence.

Newspaper articles can also be used to provide the basic situation and context. Students can choose to identify with particular characters in the story, and to see events from their individual perspectives.

As long as you create a safe, relaxed atmosphere in which your students don't feel too pressured to perform, they should enjoy the exercise. Their work could then be photocopied or displayed for the whole group or added to their own folder work, with the other communication assignments.

If you have access to a microcomputer or word processor, small groups could write together, entering the product via the keyboard. Revisions and editing can be fun once the word-processing package is sufficiently familiar. There are some software packages for the micro that allow students to work on branching stories. This could be a useful and entertaining group activity. There are also many computer-based adventure games on the market which could lead to some interesting written assignments.

Closely linked to this kind of activity is the introduction of other peoples' creative writing into the course.

7.3 Literature

We have talked elsewhere about the need to empathize with the position of others in communication situations. Role-play can help with this (section 4.2), as can work on case studies (section 5.1). But one of the most effective means is through literature. You can use extracts from novels, plays, poems, in conjunction with other source material, to help students appreciate, and sometimes identify with, other people's perspectives.

As with creative production this strategy can be linked with other activities – role-reversal exercises, for example (section 4.2). Before getting your students to assume the identity, attitudes and experience of other people, you could read them appropriate extracts to help them to develop alternative perspectives and adjust to their roles.

If they are undertaking a project (section 5.3) they might like to sift through poetry and short-story anthologies to find suitable extracts and quotations which could be used to cue the audience into the subject matter. They will obviously need a lot of help with this. It is a type of information-retrieval and study-skill exercise: you might like to look at section 15.2 for some ideas on helping them to skim and select material.

Select literature extracts linked to social-education themes. Do remember to include writing from different cultures. This doesn't just mean extracts from West Indian, African, Asian writers, for example; look at contemporary writing from the British Black community, and from Ireland, Scotland and Wales. Many community centres and literacy schemes have local publishing ventures from which you can obtain small-circulation publications that include local writing.

Try to avoid examples of overtly sexist writing unless your task is to identify sexist language characteristics. Look also at the content and illustrations. If the pictures all show white people or gender-typed occupational roles, try to find examples that have a healthier balance. If you cannot find examples then get your students to produce illustrations themselves. Try to find story lines in which black people and in which women succeed and are in positions of authority – otherwise you may be helping to reinforce negative self-images, the kind of attitudes that can lead your students to feel they have no chance of social success in any context.

Although this is particularly relevant if you teach in an urban multi-racial area, you shouldn't assume that it doesn't apply to you if you happen to live in a rural, predominantly white area. Society in general is multi-racial, and in any case your students may not always live where they now live: education should work as a positive force to combat such prejudices as racism and sexism.

So far we have considered using literature as a support for other communications and social-education work. It also has value in itself. Just as you aim to make your students literate in a reading-and-writing sense, you should help them to become *culturally* literate. To enter fully into their culture they should read more than just application forms, soap packets, or newspapers; they should enjoy reading literature, watching films, listening to music and going to the theatre. Although functional communication will and should remain your first aim, creative literacy is a very important secondary one.

Introducing literature

It is easiest to begin by saying how *not* to do it. *Don't* give out copies of the text and 'read around the class' – that is, get student after student each to read a section. Nothing kills literature more quickly than a range of faltering, bored, monotonous voices struggling over the pronunciation and completely missing the rhythm, tone shifts and pauses. If you know you have skilled, willing readers in the group, by all means use them. If not, read it yourself.

One way to proceed is to let your students follow while you read. But it is usually better to read the extract yourself while they listen, and to give out the text afterwards. You might cue them in first or give an initial reading, then lead a discussion; in the light of this discussion they can listen during the subsequent reading for particular content, moods, feelings and so on. Only then might they receive their own copy. Buzz groups (section 2.3) can also be used for the first readings, with students coming back together to contribute their reactions and interpretations.

Another possibility is to transfer the text onto OHP acetate and reveal it to the group section by section. This ensures a progressive staging of their reactions. You can lead discussion and decide when to move on to the next section. A refinement of this approach is to use overlay acetate sheets, each with a verse or paragraph. You can then reveal them in any order you choose; with some extracts, it is most effective to reveal the final section first.

Whichever way you select, leave sufficient time for your students to react to the material in their own ways and to make their own connections with the overall theme under consideration.

7.4   The media

First we need to distinguish between media studies and using the media as a method of learning. Here we are concerned with the latter, the strategies.

Chapter 15 includes some suggestions for teaching the former. By 'media' we mean newspapers, journals, magazines, television and radio; we could also include theatre, music and the arts.

In the classroom you can use the media actively, as a creative strategy. Your students can produce tape-slide sequences, make video films, publish a newsletter. Or you can use it as a support, a stimulus for communication, using newspaper articles as a case study for role-play, perhaps, or as a starter for a written task. Either way you will be developing your students' communication and social skills.

Objectives

Communication skills

Any type of media work should enable you to emphasize oral and listening skills. And the importance of *visual* communication is often highlighted. Non-verbal communication modes, like gesture, movement and sound, are stressed. This is particularly valuable if you have students who are weak as regards literacy skills but who excel in the areas of vision and sound.

Some projects will further allow you to explore with your students the effect of using a number of these modes together. Pictures will communicate different messages if they are combined with words or sound. Students are more likely to recognize the need to communicate clearly, precisely and convincingly if they have to consider a range of media and to select their own combinations of images, words, sounds and movements. They should also learn to discriminate between richness of detail and the confusion which comes from the inclusion of irrelevant material.

Projects will often involve them in a search for material to support an argument. Here again they will find themselves considering which medium is the most appropriate for their message. Would a moving or a still image make their point best? Should there be silence, a commentary or music?

If you use media extracts as a support or stimulus, you may find that your students relate to one mode rather than another. A student who has difficulty unravelling the message from a written passage may respond immediately to a film extract or to a piece of music or a picture. For most people in Britain television is the most familiar communication channel, and sound and vision predominate over the written word.

During these activities there will be opportunities to practise giving and following instructions. The kind of communication James Britton (1970) describes as 'the expressive use of language' will be highlighted: students should develop their abilities to use language in sorting, categorizing and generally making sense of the information and ideas being considered by the group. Abstract ideas or themes, such as 'poverty' or 'friendship', will need to be linked with specific, concrete examples and illustrations if a film or tape-slide sequence is to be the end product.

Information-retrieval and study skills will be called upon (section 15.2). Ideas will need to be summarized and notes taken during discussion; occasionally, group scripts and narratives will be produced.

Most media work will involve group activities. Planning together should help students to learn how to modify their own ideas to accommodate the suggestions of others. They will need to argue persuasively and tactfully in order to get others to take up their own ideas. And they should also learn to deal sensitively with the contributions of their peers.

Social skills

Students working in groups to plan, design and carry out media projects are likely to be practising collaboration and developing decision-making skills. They will be assuming roles and negotiating the allocation of tasks. (If you haven't already looked at section 2.2 on small-group discussion methods, it might be worth doing so now.) It is likely that you will need to help your students get used to group work and that your role as facilitator will involve you in a lot of behind-the-scenes prompting and guiding work in the initial stages.

Your students may need help in recognizing the need for gentle coaxing and tactful bargaining as they seek to impress the other members of their group with the value of their ideas. They will have to learn to cope if the group modifies these ideas or rejects them. Majority decisions will have to be accepted and adhered to. Ideally you will be able to guide them to appreciate the worth of the contributions made by the quieter, more passive group members. It is not always the most talkative and assertive member who contributes most. A more passive student who gets on with a task or who helps an even quieter colleague to participate may well be contributing more. It will probably be during the briefing, presentation and plenary stages that you will be able to foster this kind of awareness. Ultimately, though, each group should develop its own leadership style and way of proceeding. While students are working, you will be circulating – to troubleshoot, and to monitor the progress of individuals working within a group. The end product, of course, will be a shared one in which the individual contributions of students should be co-ordinated and merged into a balanced, internally consistent whole. It would be an unsatisfactory project if the individualism and different working standards of the group members were glaringly obvious in the result.

Ideas for media projects

Tape-slide sequences

A tape-slide show may be developed as an isolated activity: if so, you will probably need to spend time eliciting ideas for topics and themes from your students. A tape-slide show may also be used at the presentation stage of a project or as a record of a residential or visit (section 5.5).

As a presentation or record

In either of these situations it is likely that most of the slides will already have been taken. The first task for your student groups will be to sort, select and sequence the slides – this will involve decisions of selection and rejection to avoid repetition or confusing disjointedness. There are at least two ways of setting about this. A script sequence could be brainstormed (section 2.3) and roughed out: the slides could then be considered in the light of that. Or the slides could first be chosen and a script drafted around them. The first method is more likely to lead to a coherent and logically sequenced whole. If the latter approach is adopted slides may be chosen for comparatively unsuitable reasons, like the identities of the students who appear in them or the 'prettiness' of a view.

Once the script has been roughed out and the slides chosen, visual and sound gaps must be identified. Additional slides will probably be needed – shots of still photos, or of written comments or drawings, perhaps. Musical extracts and sound effects might be included, along with any narrative and commentary.

You might like to encourage your students to produce story boards with roughly drawn representations of the slides alongside the words or cues for sound effects. Only after such careful planning and rough drafts should the scripts be finalized and the tapes made to synchronize with the slides.

As an isolated activity

If the tape-slide sequence is *not* to be a record or presentation of another activity, the first stage is the selection of a theme. Extracts from stories, poems or plays, video clips, newspaper cuttings, case studies or role-play can all help your students focus their ideas and select a particular theme that interests them.

Once each group has its initial theme students will need to work in brainstorming or buzz groups (section 2.3) to develop their ideas and to decide how they will interpret the theme and collect their material. A general concept like 'community relations' or 'peace' will need to be translated into concrete images and specific examples. Should they choose one aspect, one locality? Will they include a historical perspective and conduct research into past practice, or will they concentrate on the present? Above all, what kind of slides do they need? What are they trying to communicate? They may well need a lot of help from you at this stage. It is usually best to talk things over thoroughly in the classroom before going out with a camera.

There is, however, an alternative approach. It might be interesting and certainly creative simply to 'find' images and pictures, without determining the perspective and overall context in advance. It probably depends on how much film and time you have available.

Once the slides have been taken and developed, the procedure is the same as that described above for a tape-slide sequence used as a report of another activity. The script has to be written, possibly using story boards, and the tape has to be made.

Students will need a lot of practice and dry runs to get the timing and pauses between frames right, unless you have the knowledge, skill and resources to teach them tape-splicing and tape-editing.

Once the tape-slide sequences have been made, do allow plenty of time for showing them and for students to comment on each other's. Although the *process* is often seen as the most significant and valuable part of the learning, your students will probably have been motivated largely by the existence of a tangible end *product* of which they can be proud.

Video film

In introducing students to video film-making, you may well wish to begin by making a video of a tape-slide sequence – this uses the video equipment without venturing into a totally new area. This will obviously depend upon whether your base has the necessary hardware, expertise and support staff. In any case it is best to start with a relatively modest enterprise while you and your students learn to operate the camera and monitor, and to move on to more complex and challenging projects later. There are plenty of specialist manuals and books on film-making to help you develop your own knowledge and expertise: we will concentrate on the teaching ideas rather than the technicalities.

Story-board narrative or documentary

One fairly simple way of making a film is to attach finished artwork and photos to a polished version of the story-board. Intersperse these with carefully produced written cues and film them in sequence. Music and voice-overs can give the story line.

The narrator will set the scene and link the pictures in a continuous narrative, or, if you wish your students to practise reflective and discursive writing, there could be an interpretative commentary, comparing the pictures and presenting a reasoned argument in documentary form.

Dramatized film

Once a simple audio-visual approach has been tried, you and your students may wish to progress to a more complex pastiche of studio live improvised inserts and location interviews.

Remembering that for the field of social and communication skills it is, as always, the process that is more important than the product at this level, you shouldn't worry too much if you feel that technique or acting skills, or both, are lacking. Your aims differ from those of a film or media-studies teacher, particularly from one teaching on examination courses; and as long as the experience is rewarding and the planning and production stages lead to gains in communication and social skills, it won't matter too much if there are occasional out-of-focus shots and ham acting. Your students will set their own quality standards.

The first stage will be the planning, the selection of a theme, the rough drafting of a script and the choice of visual images. There may be improvised sections or live filmed discussion, or the whole script may be carefully written in a final form and learned in advance by the participants.

A rough type of story-board might be used – not one to be filmed with finished artwork, photographs and so on, but one that drafts out the film, using outline drawings and notes of the type of shots and the accompanying sound effects and dialogue.

Film vocabulary

● You could teach your students a limited film vocabulary, with terms like:

  ★ Shot: ELS — extreme long shot
         ES — establishing shot
         LS — long shot
         FLS — full-length shot
         MS — medium shot
         CU — close-up
         ECU — extreme close-up
  ★ Camera angle: LA — low angle
               HA — high angle
               S — straight
  ★ Camera movements: pan, tilt, track, zoom

These could be incorporated in a chart with script headings and columns for detailed entries (figure 7.1). If you do go into this amount of detail it is probably best to go through at least one sequence filling in a chart with the group as a whole. One way would be to analyse a video film with the group and break it down into these elements as a practice session.

There is no need to include this type of planning. You will decide given the interests, motivation and skills of your group and the time and resources you have available.

Shot	Camera angle	Vision	Speech	Sound effects
ELS	straight	distant view of shopping centre	It is 11.00 a.m.	traffic noise

Figure 7.1 Sample chart for a filming session

News programme
One way of combining the use of media – as a strategy – with media studies is to get your students to make a news programme. You may like to look at section 15.3 for some background ideas and suggestions regarding the aims of media studies.

Following on from a project (section 5.3), survey (section 5.4), case study (section 5.1), or role-play (section 4.2), you might like to get your students to write news items that draw on related areas. The news could be fictitious, to carry a message and overall perspective perhaps, or real. The catchment area of the programme could simulate national or local community coverage. Or you could aim your programme at the specific student audience in your centre.

Small groups could work on different items and the whole group come together to decide the running order, headlines, and summaries of main points at the beginning and end. Studio interviews could also be incorporated. During the process students could acquire and practise the specific language of news broadcasts. You could ask them to watch the news the night before you begin the activity and to collect appropriate phrases like 'We have just heard . . .' or 'News is just coming in . . .'

A full range of communication and social skills will be developed and practised during the exercise.

Integrated projects using the media
You will have noticed that we have linked these media activities to other strategies like case studies and visits. If you can organize your time and teaching resources sufficiently, it might be worth trying to establish a theme that can run through a range of strategies leading up to a final tape-slide sequence or video presentation.

You could begin with a small- and large-group discussion in the chosen theme. Some of the students' contributions could be audio-taped and then pictures be chosen to accompany their comments. Short stories, poems or plays could be written, and then improvised dramas could be videotaped. Case studies on the same theme could be undertaken and then used as a basis for a role-play and simulation which could also be videotaped. A visit could be made to a relevant location and photographs taken, or an outside video or a sound recording could be made if you have suitable equipment. Finally a video or tape-slide sequence could be produced, drawing on all the experiences gained and material gathered.

Using media extracts
Instead of or as well as producing a film or set of slides, you may well use film, television or press extracts in the same way as literary extracts – as source material to stimulate different types of writing.

You may also wish to study extracts with the students to help them distinguish between fact and opinion, to recognize bias and the difference between objectivity and subjectivity. Your purpose might be to develop their awareness of the ways in which the media can both reflect and shape society's thinking in general. Or you might wish to look at media extracts during an exploration of a specific theme – sexist and racist bias in language, for example. There are some ideas for this kind of activity in Chapters 14 and 15.

Newspaper articles and film clips are also useful as an initial stimulus leading to role-play and simulation (sections 4.2 and 4.3) or as background material for case-study and project work (sections 5.1 and 5.3).

7.5 The strategies

Creative writing

When to use
- as an additional activity in conjunction with other strategies (role-play, case studies, visits and projects)
- as a means of helping your students empathize (enter into the feelings of others)
- after your students have developed some skill in more functional, transactional writing
- to encourage the use of fantasy as a positive means of expressing experience and imagination and of developing the self-image
- as a means of distancing the students from disturbing topics and helping them come to terms with their own feelings

When not to use
- as a free-standing lesson, unconnected with the themes and activities of the rest of the course
- as a hurried final activity at the end of a lesson, when there is no time for the sharing of the creative output

Literature

When to use
- as source and support material to help students identify with other peoples' viewpoints
- as supplementary material for case-study and project work
- as a stimulus for role-play and simulation
- as a means of helping students to become culturally literate
- as part of a programme to promote an awareness of cultural diversity

When not to use
- as an isolated literary-appreciation activity, in which there is no obvious link with the rest of the course

- as a vehicle for analysing material that is racist, sexist or in any way socially biased unless your specific aim is to identify and discuss the problem

Media

When to use
- as a means of developing oral and listening skills
- as part of a programme to develop an awareness of the importance of visual and non-verbal communication
- as source and background materials for case studies, projects, role-plays and simulations
- as stimulus material for creative and discursive writing
- as base material for a study of bias and emotive language
- as creative group activities to integrate different modes of communication
- as a group activity to develop social and decision-making skills

When not to use
- whenever you have insufficient time to carry projects through to fruition
- if you have insufficient resources – of time, equipment, or staff expertise

7.6   Resources list

See also the resources lists in Chapters 14 and 15.

Tutor's background reading
Britton, J. 1970 *Language and learning* (Pelican)

Classroom materials
Adams, E. and K. Baynes 1982 *Art and the built environment: study activities* (Longman Resources Unit)
Lorac, C. and M. Weiss 1981 *Communication and social skills* (Schools Council Project/Wheaton)

8 Communication workshops

8.1 The need for workshops

Most of the strategies described in this manual require your students to work together on identical or related tasks, using the same source materials. This is fine; it encourages co-operation and helps to develop group organizational skills. It also means that you can brief your students together and lead full presentation, plenary and debriefing stages. The materials you produce are likely to be suitable for all the students and so you have time to circulate, to participate where feasible, and to monitor progress.

Your students, however, will also need individual help. Their attainment and ability levels will vary. They will need practice in different types of skills and on materials which differ in their complexity and general level of difficulty. They will also be interested in different things. It wouldn't do, therefore, for them always to be working in a large – or even small – group. They will require individual tasks and related tuition on a fairly regular basis. This is the main justification for a communication workshop.

The workshop strategy encourages your students to proceed at their own pace, using materials suited to their individual levels and interests. Sometimes pairs or small groups will work together, but in any one session a range of activities and materials will be in evidence.

There should be the opportunity to develop oracy (speaking and listening skills) as well as literacy. Individual and group assignments may well involve a range of activities, including oral tasks, probably incorporating the use of a tape recorder.

Communication skills, often developed within a social-education context, may be integrated with numeracy and manipulatory skills. Wherever possible, communication and social-education tutors should liaise with numeracy and vocational-skills tutors to ensure that assignments are developed that encourage students to see the links between these areas and that reinforce skills taught in different parts of the course. This should encourage the transfer of abilities from one context to another.

In some workshops double staffing is possible, with tutors from different specialist areas working in the same room, and with students choosing between, say, communication and numeracy or social-education and vocational-skills follow-up work.

Practical communication skills are usually stressed, with an emphasis on getting the message across and receiving it in a range of modes designed to suit the purpose, audience and content. Chapter 14 explores this area in more detail. It is important that the kind of writing, speaking, reading and listening tasks are acknowledged as relevant by the students – relevant to their personal lives, their courses of study and to their developing vocational skills and interests. This in itself would result in students working on different assignments, as what is relevant at any one time to one student may not be so to another.

8.2   Running workshops

Your role in a workshop is one of supervisor, organizer and helper. You will probably find that you need to be in several places at once. Workshop sessions require patience, calmness, boundless energy, constant vigilance and tight organization on the part of the tutor.

Organization
The following represent the conditions and materials that, in an ideal situation, you should secure. We recognize that in practice you may have to struggle along with a great deal less.

- large room, as a base
- extensive shelves and/or box filing system
- filing cabinets
- movable tables or desks, and chairs
- tape-recording booths, in a separate area
- comfortable chairs, in a reading corner
- journal racks
- room dividers
- display boards
- means of blacking out the room
- overhead projector
- slide projector
- video (on trolley)
- microcomputer (on trolley)

The large-room base should have plenty of shelves or a box-file system on racks and sufficient filing cabinets.

The shelves and boxes are for the mass of worksheets and learning packs with which a workshop needs to be stocked. If each student is to work at his or her own pace and on assignments that are relevant for his or her level and interests, you will need to have a vast supply available. If you're setting up for the first time, get in touch with your Regional Curriculum Base and with local colleges and other centres. There are many materials freely available to start you off. They will probably need adapting, but you can do that from week to week as you get to know your students.

You will decide upon the filing and indexing system. Some workshops have separate box-file areas for basic literacy, numeracy, spelling and listening tasks, for multi-skill and integrated assignments, for media projects, for case studies, and so on. As long as you, your colleagues and the students all understand the system, the layout is unimportant. What *is* important is that you keep the boxes stocked and that you file the originals somewhere safe. An efficient reprographics service is vital.

If possible, a separate area should be set aside for tape work. Booths, a converted cupboard, or a system of screens are all possibilities. Try to avoid tape-recording in corridors or in the middle of a busy workshop.

As well as boxes of worksheets you will need adequate shelves and tables to display published packs and books, journals, newspapers, telephone directories, maps, travel timetables, trade directories, dictionaries and other reference works. A supply of short stories, novels, poetry and short plays could be available in a separate area.

Change the display of posters and pictures on the walls regularly. One student assignment could consist in groups or individuals taking turns in presenting visual and written material on topical themes.

The tables or desks and chairs need to be movable – you will probably want to change the layout to suit different types of group and individual work. And although we have stressed that a communication workshop is a place for students to work on different activities, there will be times when you wish to draw the group together to introduce a theme or present some materials.

If you can scrounge some comfortable, easy chairs, these could be arranged in a corner near the magazine and newspaper rack. Room dividers are useful, particularly if they can also function as display boards. Blackout facilities would also help: you may well wish to show slides or films. Finally, if you have the resources, an overhead projector would help, as would two equipment trolleys, one to provide video recording and playback facilities, the other to hold a microcomputer.

We do recognize that you may be teaching in unsuitable, cramped rooms, and that the kind of communication workshop described here is not available to you. If that is the case, try to adapt some of the ideas to incorporate in your room layout. This is not easy, of course, but whatever you *can* achieve will be a step in the right direction.

Staff development

This kind of teaching requires close liaison and co-operation between tutors. You will need regular meetings to explore and share your ideas on the function of the workshop. This is particularly important when it comes to the diagnosis and assessment of students, but it is also needed earlier, at the stage when you plan both the course and the materials needed for it. If possible, arrange to visit communication workshops in other centres. There are many different ways of organizing such aspects as student access to materials and the keeping of records. You should shop around before you decide on your own way of working.

Look also at the way craft workshops are organized. These provided the original model on which communication workshops were based. A further, more recent development is the multi-skill workshop, in which a range of technical craft skills can be developed and practised in one area, with attention being drawn to the common, transferable, skills acquired.

Diagnosis and assessment
Some centres give students a specially designed entry test, usually with written exercises stressing reading for understanding and knowledge of grammar. It is probably best, however, to stay with the spirit of workshops from the initial diagnosis through to assessment: that is, make them individual and informal.

If your course includes an early induction phase (see section A.1) this would be the ideal time to explore each of your students' needs and competencies. Otherwise set aside plenty of time in the first few teaching sessions so that you can interview each student separately.

Student self-assessment
Your first task will be to discover your students' own perceptions of their needs, strengths and weaknesses.

During a first interview, encourage each student to talk about his or her strengths, and to pinpoint, with your assistance, the areas where help is needed. There are a number of frameworks you can use for this. You might have a checklist of competencies which you could go through with the students, getting them to tick those which they feel they have. Suggested areas are:

- following written instructions
- following a diagram
- filling in an application form
- making a telephone call in answer to an advertisement
- taking down a telephone message
- asking questions of a tutor

Many more will occur to you as you plan. If you like, you can work from the objectives laid down for a course like the City and Guilds 772 'Communication skills' course.

Some tutors like to combine this self-assessment activity with their own assessment and diagnosis. Suppose for example that a student is deciding whether or not she or he can follow verbal instructions. You could help by having a variety of tasks available which can each involve the receiving and following of instructions. The results could be entered on a chart after the

Competence	Level	Students' names
Communications		
Reading a narrative text	1	
	2	
	3	
Reading and following instructions for a practical task	1	
	2	
	3	
Listening to and following oral instructions	1	
	2	
	3	
Giving oral instructions for a task	1	
	2	
	3	
Interpreting graphs and charts	1	
	2	
	3	
Explaining a process in written form	1	
	2	
	3	
Giving a verbal explanation of a process	1	
	2	
	3	

Figure 8.1 A self-assessment chart

students have tested themselves with your help (Figure 8.1). You will no doubt perceive the difficulty with this kind of record sheet. What precisely do 'level 1' or 'level 2' mean? How do you select passages and instructions that will seem relevant for all your students?

In any case you may feel strongly that this phase should encourage students to express their own feelings and judgments, unthreatened by any testing, however tactful and informal. A lot depends upon how you intend to use this self-assessment. Will it determine the kind of coursework your students will do? If so you have a problem to consider: what if a student states clearly and unequivocally that he or she can take down a telephone message accurately, but you discover that this is not the case? How can you counsel and persuade that student to let you help with the development of that skill if he or she feels that no help is required? How can you prevent loss of face while giving the tuition you feel is needed?

The ILEA FHE Curriculum Development Project team has devised a 'Self-assessment pack' based on cards. (You can obtain a copy from your Regional Curriculum Base or the ILEA project team.) The team stresses that this pack should *not* be used for diagnosis. At an early stage in the course students read through cards that specify abilities like 'use a public or private telephone' and 'talk to people you have not met before'. They then sort them into two piles, one labelled 'abilities you feel you already have' and the other labelled 'abilities you would still like some help to gain'. They also add two ideas of their own on to two blank cards, one for each pile. After that they put the cards in order of priority: you keep a record of the result on a chart provided.

You may like to try this kind of activity, but if you do, think very carefully about the kinds of abilities you describe on your cards. Will it be clear to the students what you mean by 'good with your hands'? Some students may not be able to read the cards: you will need to put aside plenty of time for lengthy individual interviews in which to mediate the materials. You might like to look at section A.4 on profiling – some of the suggestions given there are also relevant here.

Assessment by tutors

It is very unlikely that you will be able to find published, standardized tests in communications or literacy that are suitable for your own assessment purposes. Your students will almost certainly be a very mixed group with differing previous educational and life experiences, differing first languages or dialects, and differing current needs. You will however wish to obtain some kind of picture of their current attainment in English and of their understanding of written texts and oral communication before you can plan a suitable course.

This is not to say that you should expect to pigeon-hole them once and for all at the beginning of your course. Assessment should be truly continuous: each assignment or project you do with them will yield information on their progress and their needs. All you require at the beginning is a general picture of their various starting points.

One way to achieve this is by means of a variety of written texts and visual material. This might include:

- local newspaper cuttings
- cassette and LP sleeves
- food packets
- various hobby and vocational journals
- car and bike service manuals
- short stories and poems
- photographs of local street scenes
- picture-strip magazines
- advertisements

Show your students the materials and ask them to select something to read. Do this on an individual basis. As they read, note their fluency, hesitations, degree of accuracy. If they read smoothly and well, urge them to try a more difficult text. You could perhaps select it yourself. If they find their choice too difficult, suggest a simpler extract. This does not give a highly structured technical diagnosis, but it is an effective way of obtaining a very general overall picture of current performance.

Tell your students what you're writing down; show them your records. There is no need to keep these confidential. You will be entering a negotiated contract with your students (see section A.1 concerning the induction phase). They need to know the basis on which you make your teaching decisions.

Next ask them to choose some visual material and to talk about it. Then ask them to write up to half a page about it. Look at their writing for general accuracy and fluency. Is it legible? Does it make sense? What's their spelling like? How about the punctuation? Is their written English in a standard form?

Next get them to follow short written, and then oral, instructions – instructions on how to fold paper or wire, perhaps.

Finally ask them if they would like to write anything else for you, to show what they can do.

The next stage is to go through the notes you have made and tell them your immediate reactions concerning the kind of help in communication you think you might be able to give them. Explain that as they progress through the course their needs may change. They will probably reveal new strengths and abilities as they tackle different assignments. They may also reveal weaknesses, points where they need help.

If you have chosen not to use the kind of student self-assessment pack described on page 125, you may now like to ask them to talk about what they hope to gain from the course. In which communication and social-education areas would they particularly welcome help? They will probably need you to describe what 'communication' and 'social education' mean – these labels have become familiar to tutors, but not yet to most students.

The information that you gain from this kind of individual interview will be far more use than the measure of reading age that a standardized reading test would yield or the catalogue of errors that a language test would give. Such a procedure is time-consuming, however, and you may well find it difficult to get round all the members of your group. Perhaps you could organize your lessons at the beginning of the course so that there is always a workshop period or a lesson phase where your students work in groups or individually. You could then work gradually through the individual interviews.

Planning and record keeping
The type of lesson plan that is useful for large-group sessions is usually not appropriate for a workshop. What you will need to assemble is a file of fairly detailed notes on each student. These notes will include a session-by-session record of work done, together with comments on any difficulties encountered or reports of particular achievements. You might like to make separate lists of

Date	Assignment worksheet	Reading for understanding	Information retrieval	Following instructions

Figure 8.2   A simple record chart

topics covered, worksheets used, words misspelled, and so on – this will depend upon your own interpretation of the priorities, both for your teaching and their learning. Then, on the basis of progress made and work covered in each session, you can identify the next stage for each student. This might mean recommending a particular assignment or worksheet.

There are lots of ways of organizing this kind of teaching. You might give each student a folder containing his or her record, with suggestions for the next task on a sheet attached to the inside cover. These folders could be kept in an unlocked filing cabinet in the workshop. After each session you could go through the folders, bring the notes up to date and place inside them the worksheets for the next session.

This is a particularly useful way of organizing the workshop if several tutors are involved: everyone is kept fully up to date. Where profile assessment is involved it becomes vital (Appendix 4). Alternatively you might like to keep your notes on each student separate, though accessible to students. A simple chart (Figure 8.2) in each folder could then record, by ticks, assignments completed; and these could be cross-referenced with the skills and competencies involved. A large version of this chart could be pinned to the wall with each student's progress recorded. Although this is fairly common practice in workshops, there are dangers: a public chart would be saddening and disturbing for an individual student whose progress through the assignments and skills lagged far behind other group members.

Whatever combination of methods you select, don't let the organization take over and rule your teaching. There will be times when you will wish to regroup your students and set them assignments that involve several skill areas. It would obviously not be possible to match such an assignment to the precise level of attainment for each student in each skill. Your intention may be to foster group spirit and co-operation or to introduce a theme that will be worked on elsewhere in the course. At times, therefore, you will override the individual records and introduce material for everybody to use. A compromise is to have all your students working on the same theme but with worksheets written at different levels.

Worksheets
The materials-storage boxes in a communication workshop are likely to be stocked with an enormous variety of worksheets. Here are some possibilities:

- *formfilling* – actual blank forms; student help sheets; closure (fill-in-the-gap) exercises
- *sequencing* – sentence sequence (putting them in the right order); picture sequencing (to show a logical process or narrative); diagram stage sequencing
- *proof-reading* – correcting texts or pictures for logical, grammatical, or spelling errors
- *comprehension* – reading for understanding, and answering questions on texts, graphs, or pictures
- *note-taking* – passages to reduce
- *closure* – fill-in-the-gap exercises concerning spelling patterns, grammar, or confused pairs of words: sometimes multiple-choice options are given
- *information retrieval* – exercises on the telephone, using trade directories, and testing the use of alphabetical order
- *library search* – quizzes and project-suggestion sheets
- *travel comprehension* – exercises on using street plans, road maps, train-timetables, and underground maps
- *model patterns* – letters and memos, either given in full or with closure gaps or separate points to synthesize
- *visual/text linking* – pictures and text; to give practice in translating between modes or putting them together to make a narrative or report
- *dictionary exercises* – sometimes isolated words to check, more often a passage with underlined words to research
- *vocational vocabulary* – lists of words related to particular vocational areas; to be used in context, to group, or to define
- *graphical display* – tables, pie charts and histograms: to interpret and analyse, and to convert to written text
- *conversion* – from one mode to another, e.g. from flowchart to written instructions, or from room plan to room description
- *literacy* – closure exercises to learn vocabulary (days of the week, months, etc.); phonic patterns and spelling exercises; short stories in jumbo typeface, with or without closure and comprehension questions
- *paragraphing and punctuation* – passages of text to rewrite or to paragraph and to punctuate; punctuation closure exercises
- *essay and report writing* – hints on organizing ideas and note-taking; skeleton plans
- *quizzes* – on popular themes (like sport, music, or driving), involving reading and comprehension skills
- *multi-skill assignments* – usually a context provided as a narrative passage followed by speaking, listening and writing tasks; often for groups of students, and often requiring a tape recorder
- *integrated assignments* – like the multi-skill ones, but involving work in other fields, such as numeracy and the vocational areas

- *project assignments* – comprising a variety of tasks requiring additional source materials (such as newspaper and video)

As you will have noted, some of these can be worked on by individual students and others are for groups.

In almost all cases students should be guided by you as to which worksheets to select. If you leave your students to go haphazardly – or even carefully – through the boxes so as to choose their own, you are abdicating from your role as facilitator and guide. They will almost always need your help before they can make a sensible selection.

Try to foster an atmosphere such that your students understand that they all need to develop and practise different skills and that materials that are useful for one student may not suit another. Discourage competition and the desire to work on the same tasks, otherwise some of your students may choose worksheets only because they are attractively presented or because they notice friends working on them.

Worksheets should be used as part of an overall series of strategies. Try to integrate their use with other types of teaching. You could organize a simulation (section 4.3) or give a short exposition lesson (section 6.2) and follow it up with worksheets on the same theme.

Worksheets at different levels

We need to consider the question of worksheets at different levels. Suppose you had visited a Citizens Advice Bureau or a magistrate's court with a group of very mixed attainment in literacy and oracy, and you wanted to conduct some follow-up work. It would be possible to devise a range of worksheets which, while using the visit as context, provided practice in different skills appropriate for different attainment levels. These could be targeted at specific students or groups of students or they could cover a series of stages, becoming progressively more complex and difficult. Your students could then begin with the easiest and work through as far as they could go. Another alternative would be to design a core of worksheets for everybody to tackle, with supplementary ones, on the same topics, covering separate skills to provide further practice for those individuals who needed them.

This can be an effective way of working provided that your students all feel secure, and not threatened by comparisons between different attainment levels. If there is any hostility or unpleasant competitiveness in the group, it would be better to use the same worksheets and to provide extra help for those who need it, via the normal process of individual workshop tuition.

Student assessment

Worksheets can include a guide for students to assess their own progress. This could be an answer key for multiple-choice or closure exercises, or a detailed description of what the objectives are and what the students should have included in their answers. It is a good idea, anyway, to state the objectives in a form that your students will understand, even if you do not include a self-assessment aspect.

Layout and typography

Worksheets must be legible, readable and, preferably, attractively presented. Where you have options, pay attention to the colour of the paper. Lay the text out so there is plenty of blank space. Use double-spaced typing and clear black type. Don't imagine that your students will struggle to decipher unclear text: they won't. In any case, reading partially eroded and fuzzy letters is a difficult task – they might not be able to do it. If you have access to a bold-face or 'jumbo' typewriter, experiment with upper- and lower-case layouts. You will be surprised at how few words you can get comfortably on a page. Be particularly careful about the spacing. Because of the size of jumbo typefaces you need to leave extra spaces between words and between lines, or the text runs together and is *more* difficult to read than normal-sized type.

Try to include diagrams and pictures, and arrange the text in blocks so that there is not too much continuous prose to take in at once. You will pick up ideas from other people's worksheets and from published materials.

Learning and study packs

Learning and study packs share the characteristics of individual worksheets but are specifically designed so that students can work alone and unassisted. Typically they comprise a set of learning objectives, a list of required additional resources and information, a series of worksheets and suggestions to help research a topic (for a project, for example), and a self-assessment schedule.

Some are more open-ended than others. These consist of materials and resources loosely assembled and organized around a central theme. The precise tasks are left to the student or tutor to determine. Most, however, are fairly prescriptive; the objectives and tasks are described in detail.

You might like to get your students to design study packs as part of their work on projects or case studies. Other students could then work on them.

Integrated assignments

Integrated assignments combine work in several skill areas in one context or theme area. The FEU publication *ABC in action* gives a breakdown of skills within the overall context of decorating a room (Figure 8.3).

Ideally you should work with colleagues from other areas, numeracy and vocational skills perhaps, to design such projects. Other ideas include building an adventure playground for local children, giving a lunch party for senior citizens, or organizing a fund-raising event for a local concern.

Once you have your topic, your students might be able to help you identify the constituent skills. A residential (section 5.5) might be an ideal opportunity for planning and carrying out one of these integrated projects.

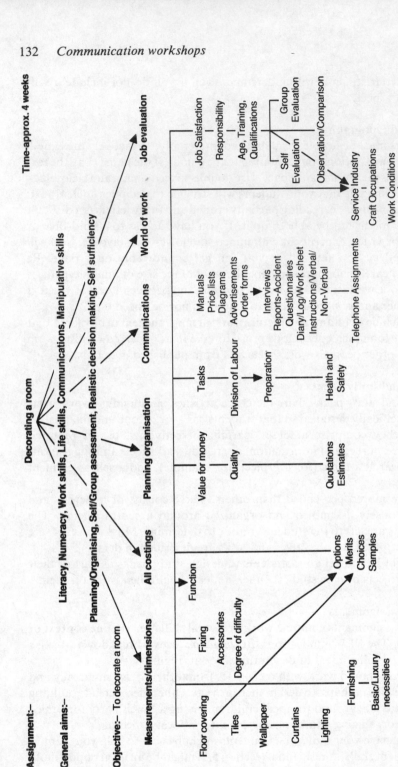

Figure 8.3   An example of an integrated assignment

Integrated Assignment: Decorating a Room

'This assignment would help to improve the students' ability in various ways;
a.   *Literacy and Communication*
To read and understand data in a variety of forms (eg manual, safety regulations, catalogues, bus time-tables, telephone directory, street directory, diagrams, graphs, tables);
To compile notes (eg observations from visits);
To complete order forms;
To understand work sheets;
To compile a diary, log work carried out;
To convey written and verbal instructions;
To discuss recommendations, evaluate advice, distinguish fact from opinion;
To write letters;
To devise a questionnaire and evaluate the answers;
To appreciate the effectiveness of various mediums of expression;
To undertake interviews (if possible, of employees carrying out this task in industry).

b.   *Numeracy*
To undertake basic calculations;
To use standard units of measurement and make conversions;
To make estimates of size, cost, time, quantities required;
To calculate perimeters, area, volume;
To use rulers, calculators;
To understand simple discount system;
To calculate wages, bonus;
To understand a percentage (VAT, discount, tax).

c.   *Manipulative and Physical Skills*
To use basic tools (tape-measure, paint-brush);
To perform various manual tasks (cutting, joining, pouring, mixing);
To experience the need for physical stamina, eg standing for long periods, working for set time with limited breaks;
To use ladders;
To experience lifting, carrying in the work situation;
To perform a manual task requiring attention to detail (eg painting intricate woodwork);
To make judgements relating to shape, size, colour;
To adapt working methods according to the properties of the materials used.

d.   *Planning and Organisation*
To understand how to plan methodically;
To organise a task in relation to time and manpower;
To work within external restraints;
To plan resources to complete a task;
To divide a task into component parts;
To decide on order in which elements of the task should be carried out;
To experience the system of division of labour in operation

e.   *Vocational Studies and Knowledge of the World of Work*
To understand the job structure of one example of a service industry;

To formulate job profiles of a number of jobs within the industry;

To understand the working conditions in a particular industry;

To appreciate the importance of Health and Safety regulations at work places;

To understand the economic organisation of a firm, the role of capital, cheques, banking etc in relation to an undertaking;

To describe the role of trade unions within a firm;

To understand the entry requirements for particular jobs within the industry;

To be aware of the systems of recruitment and training within the industry;

To assess the impact of technological change on the industry and future prospects in relation to numbers of employees and need for adaptability

f.   *Social Skills: Personal Development, Self-Awareness etc.*

To experience responsibility and working on one's own;

To measure how one relates to others working in a team;

To develop confidence from achieving a set task;

To develop self-awareness of strengths and weaknesses;

To understand the importance of unfailing concentration;

To make a group decision;

To assess own feelings towards the task carried out.

8.3   The strategy

Communication workshops

When to use

- at regular intervals to provide the opportunity for individual tasks and tuition
- when you wish to integrate communications with social education, numeracy, and vocational options
- when you want to encourage students to work on their own, at their own rate
- when you wish students to use the tape recorder and video, to develop oracy
- on occasions when you are particularly keen for students to work on separate assignments which are relevant to their individual needs and interests

When not to use

- for regular whole-group activities that do not exploit the workshop resources
- as a dumping ground for students, leaving them to work unsupported and unassisted

Taking it further

- contact your nearest Regional Curriculum Base, ILEA FE/HE Curriculum Development Project

● visit local centres with communication workshops

8.4 Resources list

Tutor's background reading
Cuerdon, G. 1983 *A communication skills workshop* (London College of Printing)

Part II

Topics

9   Introduction to Part II

Each of the chapters in this part of the book explores a different theme. Taken together they could constitute the material for a social and communication skills curriculum. Each topic included is also necessary for achieving some of the aims of the influential core curricula (*A Basis for Choice*, and City & Guilds 365) now being used widely in schools and further education.

A core curriculum is not a course. It can only identify aims that should be included. Such an outline list of aims and objectives does not provide you with a syllabus: the tutor is still left the central tasks of selecting the angle or angles from which the topic is to be presented, and of organizing the strategies that are to be used in the classroom.

The advantage of the core-curriculum approach is that guidelines presented in this form recognize that teaching is fundamentally a creative activity. The disadvantage is that it can produce a series of lessons that lack coherence or direction and which therefore do not have a pattern that is clear to the students.

Each of the chapters in this part of the book consists of those elements that we hope can provide the kind of support tutors need in turning a core-curriculum aim into a series of lessons, namely:

- a brief exploration of the theoretical background relevant to the topic
- ideas for teaching activities
- a sample outline plan for a lesson
- a resources list containing both a bibliography of source books and a list of associated classroom materials

10   What is an adult?

10.1   Perspectives on adulthood

'Perspectives on adulthood' has been chosen as the initial theme because the issues thus raised are fundamental to the themes of all later chapters in this book. Teachers differ widely in their working philosophies and political attitudes regarding the purposes of social education, and in their intentions for their students. Despite this, certain topics recur: they include getting (or not getting) a first job, acquiring a basic knowledge of legal and political rights and understanding one's own personal development and important relationships. These form the themes of later chapters in this book. The connection between these topics is that they are all aspects of being recognized *as an adult*. If social education attempts anything distinctive, it should be concerned to develop a critical awareness of how adult status is achieved and to identify the factors that affect the students' control over this.

We have no intention of offering a simple answer to the question posed by the title. Arriving – or failing to arrive – at an answer that satisfies you is a task for both you and your students. This chapter deals with prior issues: why should 'What is an adult?' be so difficult to answer? Who defines the line that marks the end of childhood or the state of dependence? How differently were these boundaries drawn in the past? What, if anything, is distinctively different about 'young people'? Are the problems of adolescents caused by the young people themselves or by older people they come up against?

Rather than providing a general discussion, four separate viewpoints on the question of adulthood are taken in what follows: historical, sociological, psychological, and legal. There are two reasons for this: first, different teaching strategies are used within each perspective; second, you may be expert in one of these but unfamiliar with the others, yet you may wish to widen the range of your own teaching to take in new areas and try out new strategies.

10.2   The historical view of children

Why is the beginning of adulthood so difficult to pinpoint in our society? Legal definitions do not provide a simple answer – the legal boundaries dividing childhood from the responsibilities of adulthood have shifted continually and rarely seem to have been more confusing than they are now.

(This is dealt with in more detail in the section on legal status.) The beginning of economic independence is not always a sure dividing line either, since the school-leaving age varies through time and between social classes. To take economic independence as the dividing line would also mean that the unemployed would have their 'childhood' extended far into the period when they have 'adult' legal rights, such as enlisting, voting, and marrying.

The idea of 'childhood'
The concept of childhood as a separate period of life between infancy and adulthood developed during the 17th and 18th centuries. The child came to be seen as someone whose moral development needed careful monitoring. The educational theories that subsequently developed fostered the idea that schools were the proper place for this carefully supervised period of growth. This pushed the boundaries of childhood forward to school-leaving age.

Two important groups were not affected by these developments during the first half of the 19th century. Girls, it was thought, needed domestic training and preparation for motherhood rather than a planned education; and extended schooling was a luxury that working-class families could not afford for their children.

Even allowing for these exceptions, the idea that the 'child' was a special individual who needed to be separated from adults and cared for in a specialized institution continued to gain ground throughout the 19th century. By the end of the century their segregation from adult society was nearly complete, and the boundaries that are familiar today had been firmly established.

Contemporary assumptions
● You can use historical material for comparative work. Your aim will be to encourage students to examine and question contemporary assumptions:
   ★ What should a child's 'place' be?
   ★ What would it be like if this segregation had not taken place in the way that it did?
   ★ Are children better or worse off today?

Historical continuities
Providing state education for all children in the late 19th century was also seen as a solution to the growing problem of social disruption caused by the army of rootless children and young people in cities. Elementary education for all did seem to deal successfully with this problem. By the end of the century, complaints about unruly street behaviour were directed at youths rather than children. For the first time, working-class young men had leisure and money at their disposal, and the growth of commercialized leisure (such as professional football) was accompanied by complaints about the anti-social

behaviour associated with it. In just the same way that is familiar today, 'youth' was focused on as a problem group in society. The theories that were developed to explain this phenomenon are dealt with in the next two sections.

It is important to stress again that this aspect of the social history of youth virtually excludes girls. The continuing contrast could form the starting point for a series of lessons.

Girls in society

● Discussion topics:
  ★ Why have historians ignored the activities of girls?
  ★ Did girls have no activities outside the home?
  ★ Do girls have no historical record of anti-social behaviour?
  ★ Is this due to lack of opportunity or motivation?
  ★ Have things changed?

Related reading

Two principal sources for a historical view of the development of childhood are Ariès (1973) and Walvin (1982). There is also a useful summary in Hoyle's own chapter, 'Childhood in historical perspective', in *Changing childhood* (1979), Ariès traces the history of the child in France from medieval times. In the 15th and 16th centuries babies and toddlers were coddled as entertaining playthings, and weaned late (between the ages of five and seven). After this the child entered the adult world of pursuits and activities: Chaucer's Wife of Bath married at twelve, Shakespeare's Juliet at fourteen. Before the late 18th century, boys of 14 and even 11 were in the French army. A period of military service came to be accepted as a formal sign that adolescence had begun. (This connection has not disappeared today: some schools still encourage boys to join 'cadet' forces.)

The family and the school were the two main institutions that removed the child from the wider adult world. Walvin also describes the ethos that developed in the British public schools of the 19th century. His account follows the development of childhood and youth from the 19th into the 20th century.

The middle-class family and the public-school system kept a close watch on their young. Working-class children presented a different kind of problem. Government, supported by influential middle-class philanthropists, saw mass education as one way of keeping this army off the streets. Their numbers were very high. From 1801–1901 England's population grew from under 10 million to 32 million, and throughout this period the proportion aged 14 and under was never less than 30 per cent, and was frequently nearer 40 per cent. (A detailed table is provided in Walvin, p. 19.) By contrast, in the 1960s this proportion had halved to about 20 per cent.

When a third of society is under 14, and a great proportion of those in cities are living on the streets either permanently or for most of their day, the control problem becomes obvious. Walvin argues that much of the behaviour that was drilled into the young in elementary schools (punctuality, cleanliness and obedience) aimed to produce a workforce suitably disciplined for the 'machine age'.

Once the younger working-class children had been taken care of in this way, attention was turned to the disruptive behaviour of those older ones who had a great deal more independence. Walvin shows that by 1914 'teenagers' or 'adolescents' had come to be seen as a distinct age group with its own peculiar problems. New sciences (paediatrics, psychoanalysis and psychology) grew up to explain the causes of these problems. As adult society has gradually adopted more successful strategies in coping with the social threat posed by the young (by institutionalizing and segregating them), paradoxically adults have also been persuaded to see the young as much more complex and troubled creatures. As a result adults perceive more in the behaviour of young people to justify their fear and mistrust.

Young people in society

● Ask students to imagine what it would be like if such a situation existed now, with half the population under 14.
  ★ What would the unemployment problem be like?
  ★ What would the teenage consumer market look like?
  ★ What law-and-order issues would the media be taking up?
  ★ What would family life be like?
  ★ Would politicians take the interests of young people more seriously?
● Small groups could produce a television news bulletin or newspaper on one of these topics.

Pearson's splendid social history (1983) of youthful disorder and 'hooligans' has a wealth of material which could be adapted for classroom use. It contains illustrations and examples of misbehaviour with extracts from law and press reports which support a wide-ranging and comprehensive reassessment of the 'Law-and-Order' myth.

Teaching suggestions
The books suggested as sources contain plenty of illustrative material as evidence. All have extensive bibliographies listing other source material. Historical evidence can be used for comparative studies, both between periods (by comparing historical with current evidence) and across cultures (by comparing contemporary Western childhood with the Third World version, for example). Both the groups mentioned as exceptions – girls and working-class children – merit special attention. A selection of ideas is listed below.

Comparative studies

- 'Then and now' case studies can be compiled from sources and used as the basis for discussion, e.g. accounts of children at work in the 19th century and now. Issues focused on can include comparison of wages and conditions. How is each better or worse off?
- You can use historical evidence to explore past ideas about how girls should be educated, as the basis for a comparison with current attitudes to the education of girls.

Discussion topics

- How does the age-segregation that has occurred show itself in different areas of the students' lives (e.g. schools, work, leisure)?
  - ★ What activities do the different generations share?
  - ★ Do these affect their views of each other?
- What would it be like if this process had not happened in the way it did? For example, supposing schools and colleges belonged to the children or students instead of vice versa? (This notion has much in common with A.S. Neill's approach to the running of Summerhill.) What would students think was worth studying? What rules would they have? What would the timetable look like – if there was one? (This idea is used as the basis of the model lesson plan at the end of the chapter.)
- Suppose many of the major transitions happened at the same time, as often was the case for Victorian children. What would it be like to leave school, start work and set up home independently at 16?
  - ★ What would the legal rights and restrictions be?
  - ★ What practical knowledge and abilities would students need?
- Consider the argument that schooling was also used as a form of social control to render young children more malleable, and more suitable as material for the 'machine age'.
  - ★ What are the similarities between school and work?
  - ★ Is schooling still used in this way?
- Are children natural anarchists or a threat to social order if left to roam around in groups? (*Lord of the Flies* is an obvious source for illustration.)
  - ★ Imagine the possible scenario that might result if some present trends (such as truancy, or youth unemployment) continue. Give students a starting point – the government raises the school leaving age to 18; masses of students refuse to go to school – and ask them to continue the story.

Sentence completion

- Take different points of view (father, grandmother, politician, etc.) and complete: 'The trouble with young people today is . . .' Collect contributions and discuss them. How much notice do students take of these different opinions?

Literature as a stimulus for role-play
● Cross-cultural comparisons can focus on particular conflicts experienced by children in some second-generation immigrant families from cultures whose ideas about child-rearing have more in common with the ideas of earlier historical periods. Conflicts usually centre on discipline, sexual relationships, and the limits parents feel it is right to put on their children's personal freedom.

10.3 Who defines youth?

Social history shows that the age selected as the boundary between childhood and adulthood has varied widely. Different ages – or stages of growth – have been chosen at different historical periods, for different purposes and by different sections of society.

Currently the 'growing' period is being extended still further. Because of the fear of unemployment, many young people are choosing to stay in educational institutions for longer; and unemployment, if they suffer it, denies them adult status for a further period. The large range of labels for the young indicates how many institutions oversee this extended dependence – 'pupil', 'student', 'trainee', 'apprentice' and 'young adult' are just examples.

Labels
● Compile a list of such labels. (Groups can compete to produce the longest list.)
  ★ Who uses the different terms?
  ★ What associations do the names have? (Students can play a free-association game to collect ideas about these.)
  ★ Ask groups to draw cartoons or do mimes to illustrate the differences. Other groups can play 'spot the label' to identify the one being illustrated.
● Discuss the sources of disapproval approbation connected with the words.
● Press reports often use such terms in a value-loaded way. Collect examples from the local press (e.g. 'Teenager steals bike', 'Young man wins award').

Whereas social history describes the development through this century of the concept of 'adolescence', sociology seeks rather to identify the section of society from which a given definition originates, the precise group at whom it is aimed, and the people whose interests are served by the definition.

Adolescence in the twentieth century

The word 'adolescence' has been used to describe the period between childhood and maturity. During the 20th century its use has been closely connected with the reactions of certain influential sections of society to social changes, particularly the growth of population in cities that accompanied continuing industrialization. The activities of the young have been differentiated more sharply by the divisions of social class. Middle-class adolescents largely conform to adult expectations. 'Adolescence' lasts longer for a middle-class child than it does for a working-class child. Middle-class children's extended education denies them independent economic status and erodes their potential political power.

Working-class children present the opposite face of adolescence. Many stay on in education or training to become skilled workers. Do they perceive their continued dependence on adults as acceptable, or as a price that must be paid for their eventual rise in social status? The majority leave school at the earliest opportunity to become wage-earners. They relish their earlier financial independence, though this is only a short-term advantage and is rarely enough to enable them to live independently, away from the family home. They marry and have children at an earlier age than do their middle-class contemporaries. Some working-class young men behave in a way that is defined officially as 'juvenile delinquency' and punished by the law. The misbehaviour of middle-class young does not so readily incur legal penalties; indeed, middle-class young people are allowed certain lapses into anti-social behaviour. Such lapses are tolerated if they can be defined as 'student pranks' or 'student unrest', and are acceptable as a proof of the young people's youthful irresponsibility.

Sociologists seem to have given juvenile delinquency and deviancy more than their fair share of attention. There are far more young people who are rarely if ever involved in the extremes of behaviour that attract public attention.

Invisible groups

● The 'invisibility' of some groups of young people is worth exploring with your students. The activities of girls, of the rural young, and indeed of the majority of young people never make the headlines. How representative therefore are those groups that *are* in the news? Who singles out these groups as 'newsworthy'?

★ To test this assertion, organize a month-long analysis of local press, radio and television stories about young people.

The child savers in the early twentieth century

The title 'child savers' has been given to those influential members of the professional middle classes whose activities in the early 20th century helped spread ideas of the 'right' and the 'wrong' ways in which adolescents 'should' develop. The child savers used ideas taken from the new psychological theories of growth to explain and justify their attempts to protect youthful innocence from the corruption of its urban industrial surroundings. Adolescence was a vulnerable period for the young person: carefully supervised, it could produce adults fit to be the carriers of civilized society. Thus rejuvenated, society would be stable enough to resist political unrest from within, and military threats from overseas. Clubs and movements such as the Boy Scouts and the Boys' Brigade exemplified the child savers' view of the ideal of youthful behaviour. Their meetings were marked by militaristic discipline and their leaders emphasized the importance of selfless service to others.

Once this definition of 'normal' behaviour became common, it is easy to see how many aspects of the behaviour of working-class youth were inevitably defined as abnormal or deviant. Since conformist young people were idealized as one indication of a healthy society, the next stage was to draw the conclusion that the inadequacies or faults of youth were the cause of unwelcome social developments.

The link between youth and social problems is still frequently made today. (This is another area worth exploring with students.) Public discussion of widespread youth unemployment has produced its own crop of explanations which link this particular social trend to the individual characteristics (or lack of them) of young people. One such explanation asserts that more young people are out of work because standards of literacy and numeracy have declined. From other sources comes the view that today's young people lack motivation, show the wrong attitudes to work, and possess inadequate social skills. Such explanations are less commonly offered by official sources now than in the late 1970s, but the views certainly persist. Yet there is nothing new about such views – precisely the same causal connections were made during earlier periods of economic difficulty and decline. The qualities of young men were seen as causes of the 'Boy Labour' problem before the First World War, and resurrected for criticism during the 1930s.

Two stereotypes of youth

The model adolescent

The 'correct' kind of adolescent development, leading to a mature and socially useful adult, was largely demonstrated by those middle-class young people who were kept under adult supervision for longest. Paul Goodman, writing in America in the 1970s, objected passionately to the oppressive aura of conformity surrounding the majority of American college students. He compared them to the stereotype of the 'organization man'.

Linked to the critical view of middle-class youth is the scepticism that questions the value of extended education. School can have a disabling effect. This challenge to the view that education is largely beneficial could be made the basis for a critical reassessment of their education by students, particularly those who accept the values of an academic education.

Staying at school
● What are the benefits of staying on, as opposed to leaving as soon as possible?
  ★ What are the personal costs to the individual at such an important stage of their lives?
  ★ Is it financially worthwhile in the long run?
  ★ Are educational institutions run in such a way that conformity is valued above individualism?

The deviant adolescent

Children who grew up too fast in terms of the adult standards represented by the 'model' adolescent were seen as potential deviants. 'Precocious' was a word frequently used by writers on youth in the early 20th century to describe problem adolescents. The case that historians make is that certain aspects of youthful behaviour that could be tolerated or accommodated by pre-industrial society – aspects such as earlier marriage, sexual relations, certain kinds of licensed disorder – were seen as much more threatening to social order when the youth population was both more numerous and more concentrated.

Social historians can show how youth has become a 'social problem' in the 20th century. Sociologists studying deviance document the process by which much of the behaviour of working-class young men has moved from being unacceptable to being classed as 'criminal' and therefore subject to legal punishment. The main thrust of much of the sociological view is that many of these examples of 'anti-social' behaviour can be seen as a non-political form of protest. The protest is seen as being made against pressures or constraints that many working-class young people feel are set on their freedom of action or choice. John Holt called childhood a 'walled garden', around which the boundaries are set not for the protection of the inmates but for the benefit of those outside the walls. The model adolescent may rebel against these constrictions too; but, as current unemployment is demonstrating most clearly, it is working-class young people who suffer most.

The value of this critical approach is that it offers you an alternative viewpoint to explore with your students in opposition to the ones that they are presented with from more popular sources of opinion. The 'model' and the 'deviant' adolescent are both stereotypes – the descriptions are exaggerated and selective. They are derived from descriptions based on factual examples, however, and this evidence can be useful if your aim is to counteract the selective and partial images of youth that are offered by the press and television.

The invisible adolescent

Studies of sub-cultures and deviance have concentrated on boys and young men and virtually excluded all mention of girls. Explanations of why this is so are largely based on the view that family socialization (indirectly reinforced at school) emphasizes that the principal future role for girls lies in marriage and child-rearing. Girls' activities are mostly seen as rehearsals and preparation for this rather than presenting them as free to try out a wide range of possible future identities.

Both marriage and having children represent, in the short term at least, evidence of maturity; they are therefore a passport to adult status. There is evidence that early marriage and motherhood is on the increase as youth unemployment rises.

Girls' choices

- Explore your students' views on these issues.
  - ★ Do girls' leisure pursuits direct them towards domesticity?
- Consider the implications of courses of action.
  - ★ Is marriage and child-rearing a real alternative to unemployment or a dead-end job?

Related reading

Gillis (1975) has written a social history of youth that links in detail the demographic and economic changes in the early 20th century with the rise of the idea of adolescence as a crucial and troubled period of life. Once the economy no longer needed a pool of child labour, the idea of adolescence was 'democratized' and middle-class norms of behaviour were presented as universal standards by which all children's growth should be judged. Middle-class development became 'normal' development.

The theory was firmly founded in developmental psychology in 1904, when G. Stanley Hall's work *Adolescence* was published. Armed with these ideas, the activities of the child savers accelerated. There are some telling quotations from contemporary social reformers in *Consciousness of class and consciousness of generation*, by Murdock and McCron (1976). Their paper argues that this period was the beginning of a movement that replaced the coercive control that one social class exercised over another with control by ideology. The ideology that identifies youth as a problematic phase avoids explaining social friction as the result of class divisions. This is the underlying argument of all the papers in *Resistance through rituals*, by Hall and Jefferson, which takes various aspects of the sociology of youth subcultures and interprets them as expressions of class divisions and antagonisms.

Section 10.2 suggests that the critical viewpoint presented by social historians and sociologists may provide you with a way of identifying issues worth exploring with students. One recent example chosen for illustration was the link often made between school-leaver unemployment and declining educational standards. Reeder provides evidence that similar judgements were made in the 1930s when working-class school leavers were again suffering the effects of recession.

The whole area of how young people get into trouble with police provides many more examples of ways in which the behaviour of young people is seen as the *cause* of a social problem rather than as the *result* of social forces that may originate elsewhere. Gillis shows historically how street behaviour that had been tolerated as part of 'juvenile sociability' became criminalized as legal sanctions increased. Contemporary sociologists of deviance (e.g. Cohen, 1980) show the same process still at work in relation to delinquency and working-class young people.

Few formal accounts of the activities of girls exist. Brake (1980, in a chapter on 'The invisible girl') and McRobbie and Garber (1976) link the activities of girls to other accounts of male-dominated gangs and cults (such as Rockers and Skins) in which girls are allowed to act in a subordinate role.

Teaching suggestions
The interpretations provided by these perspectives challenge assumptions in many areas: about 'normal' as opposed to 'abnormal' growth; about how and why young people earn the approval and disapproval of adults; about the 'natural' advantages of extended education. These topics and others are suggested below as lesson ideas.

The ideas for topics are not accompanied by any detailed descriptions of possible teaching strategies, though many of those described in the section on discussion and small-group teaching (section 2.3) may be appropriate. Any activities that involve the examination of factual evidence are suitable for these topics. Students can collect factual material by survey, select media extracts or compile case studies. Their intention should be to expose the particular points of view or assumptions contained in the material.

Assuming responsibility
- Examine varying attitudes about the right ages at which to make certain transitions: to get married, to have a child, to get a job, etc. How do these vary with age, and with social class?
- Discuss the advantages and disadvantages of staying on in education (or training) until 16, 18 or 21, bearing in mind the loss of money, rights and status that this entails.
- What does it cost (in personal and economic terms) to stay dependent on your family for longer?
- Are marriage and bringing up children satisfactory alternatives to paid work, for girls who face unemployment?
- How do girls' friendships differ from boys? The picture presented by some sources is that of girls who 'pair off' rather than join large

groups or gangs. Do girls *never* lead groups? How is their acceptance of a subordinate role connected to their 'family-centred' socialization? What different rules do parents impose on the behaviour of their sons and daughters?

● What reasons do older people have for disapproving of young people? Are young people being used as scapegoats for any other social, political or economic problems? Issues taken up besides the one mentioned – youth unemployment – might include truancy and drug-abuse. The latter would have to take adults' use of tobacco, alcohol and tranquillizers into account; and consider this use accompanied by the view that adults can use these but young people can't.

10.4 The adolescent as an individual

The view of youth taken by psychologists has been criticized both by social historians and by sociologists. They have shown that psychology was one of the new sciences that served useful purposes for certain influential sections of society. Theories of the psychology of adolescence were used to justify the extended institutionalization of the young and to identify the approved social purpose for these institutions. Psychology was also used to justify opinions about 'normal' and 'abnormal' growth in such a way that many aspects of working-class childhood and youth became 'abnormal'.

To see psychology as the villain of the piece would be unjustified, however. The previous sections have described the social background against which changes in the status of youth have occurred. Not all the elements of the complicated picture that emerges of the relations between adults and young people can be explained within the frameworks of sociology and history. Some aspects of these relationships have a strong emotional colouring that is not accounted for by the factual evidence.

Frequently commentators remark on the fact that adults have shown more hostility to the young than the young display in return. The inevitable conclusion seems to be that adults fear the independence of young people on a personal level as much as anything else. They are afraid of their physical and sexual energy and of their potential power. Although adults themselves have contributed to the segregation of the young, they resent signs or demands from the young that they be recognized as a distinctive group. Why do adolescents present such a threat? Psychology provides another set of answers to this question.

The relevance of these ideas in the classroom is that they can be offered to your students as support in developing a reflective understanding of their own relationships as well as to add depth to the critical discussion of social trends.

The stages of adolescence

Early, middle and late adolescence are described in the literature as distinctive phases, each of which provides a major task for the individual. Although generally the age span of these phases is assumed to be somewhere between eleven and sixteen, there can be considerable variation in the pace of development. It is one of the main criticisms of separating schoolchildren into classes on the basis of age that within one class of 14–15-year-olds there may be individuals who together span all the stages. The variations even out after a time, but the timing of the earlier stages can vary greatly with age.

Early adolescence

The first and most obvious stage is marked by the physical changes associated with puberty. Understanding and coming to terms with these changes is the main task of this phase.

Mid-adolescence

Initially the young person relies on parents and other adults to explain these changes which mark the end of childhood. Progress to the next stage is marked by a growing desire in the young person to be left alone to develop in his or her own way: separation from the parents is the next major task of adolescence.

The adults most closely involved in this have a difficult balance to negotiate. They must respect the young person's need for privacy and greater independence, keep some overall watch on the process, and recognize their own reluctance to 'let go' of a child they knew intimately. They must also relinquish their own centre-stage place as models, and be replaced by others chosen – by the young person – as more desirable.

Late adolescence

The young person moves on to the task of trying out different identities, and in the process becomes preoccupied with his or her own appearance, and intensely concerned with his or her own emotions and reactions, and with making the right kind of impression on others.

Alternative lifestyles and identities may be one of the areas you want to look at with students. Often tutors want to broaden the students' range of choice and to challenge ideas that they feel to be limiting or conformist. This happens most often in relation to ideas about sex roles, frequently because there is a clash between the students' values about these and those of the teacher.

Young people often seem to want to cling stubbornly to stereotyped models rather than to modify them, even when presented with factual evidence that shows that people they know are not like this. You may well be sensitive to the fact that it is not right to try to impose your own values on students, but still want to challenge their resistance to changing their inconsistent views. It may help to see this in the context of the psychological interpretation of what young people are trying to achieve during this phase. During this time, at which establishing their own sexual identity is their most important concern, young people are attracted to stereotypes precisely because these present exaggerated but consistent sexual types. Attempting to discredit such types by saying that they are unrealistic is not going to meet with much success.

Work roles
Work provides – or used to provide – a major opportunity to assume a new identity. It is important to spend some time with students considering their job choices in the light of the psychological needs that work can satisfy as well as the obvious economic needs. It is equally vital that they appreciate why unemployment can be psychologically (as well as financially) damaging, in order to appreciate the importance of strategies to cope with this.

What jobs are worth
- Give students a list of different jobs and ask them to write by each the wage they think it deserves. (They can do this in pairs or threes.)
  - ★ Ask them to spell out the criteria they used to justify their decision (e.g. social usefulness/what the market will bear/scarcity of labour/unsocial hours/dirty work).
  - ★ Now ask them to form larger groups and to agree on a final wages list.

Work satisfactions
- Ask students to discuss their work experience or part-time jobs. What is it about such work that makes students feel they are accepted on a more equal footing by adults? Is it the work task? The satisfaction of their customers? The friendship of older people? Coping with 'real' problems?
  - ★ Ask groups to make a list of the various jobs that would most satisfy the same needs. (Give them a list to choose from as a prompt, if necessary.)
- If there is no chance of work in the immediate future, what other activities might satisfy the same needs?
  - ★ Pool ideas to compile a list. Give groups the task of finding out how to gain access to these activities.

The importance of friendships
Another principal means whereby people test and confirm identities is through their close relationships with friends – both friends of the same sex and those of the opposite sex. Friendships reflect different aspects of one's self-image, and consideration of these often very contrasting friendships provides students with an opportunity to study various aspects of their personality. Students can approach all these issues by discussing the qualities,

values and characteristics they expect of all the people involved: parents, best friends, boyfriends or girlfriends.

Classroom discussion of personal issues

As with other topics suggested by this approach (how parents should deal with adolescents, for example), these are all very personal areas in which disclosure may feel threatening to students.

There are several teaching strategies that can be used to avoid the need for personal disclosure. The use of case-study examples, improvised dialogue or role-play all allow students to project their own ideas without directly revealing their own experiences. Literature is a rich source of illustrations that can be a stimulus for discussion. Asking students to reverse roles serves the same purpose; considering issues such as the way they intend to bring up their *own* children is 'safer' as a classroom activity than is asking them to analyse their relations with the adults with whom they live; it is also more appropriate. Students may well volunteer information about themselves if they trust the teacher and feel safe in the group. For this reason there may be an overlap between social-education and counselling approaches, but the two activities have distinctive differences in the aims they hope to achieve.

The needs of the adolescent

Besides models the adolescent needs heroes: one set of figures acts in a role complementary to the other. Following on the realization that their parents are not infallible comes the need to feel that those who do enjoy fame or success genuinely deserve it. Connected with this is the need to criticize adult society, to expose its failures and challenge its hypocrisy. Opposing adults and asserting one's own right to take over is one part of this challenge: developing a system of personal ethics is also an important product of this stage. Late adolescence is marked by a high degree of rivalry with parents. This is all part of the process of asserting that parents are past it; that their views, ideas and skills are out of date. In one very obvious way the young are right, of course. Social, medical and technological changes happen so rapidly that they do indeed face choices and constraints that are beyond the experience of their parents. Challenges and disagreements between the generations may not be about issues at this general level, though, but about personal power and rights that are in all senses much closer to home. Families fight on more personal battlegrounds.

The needs of adults

It is easy to see why the emotional tone of these challenges can be so intense, but is important to encourage students to consider the points of view of the adults involved. Parents of adolescents have to renegotiate the relationship with their children, and cope with their own emotional reactions to these changes. They need to feel that their children's dependence has altered but not ended, and they need to feel a sense of achievement as the period of dependence comes to an end, rather than a sense of failure. Memories of their own adolescence form an important part of all this. If their own experience of these challenges was that they resulted in failure and rejection then they may be unable to overcome all the negative emotions that will assault them as parents: envy, fear, guilt and hostility.

Adolescents as the 'outsiders'

It is easy to see how these potent ingredients can colour not only family relationships but also the way adolescents are seen by society at large. Just as their challenges can, if unsuccessfully handled, shake the stability of the family, so as a group they are often represented as the barbarian hordes who threaten the stability of society. This understanding links directly with the earlier points made by social historians and sociologists about the ambiguous nature of the adult view of childhood. The general impulse to prolong dependence can be justified as a desire to protect the vulnerable young, prompted by altruistic motives. It is possible, however, to interpret it as a hostile wish to maintain power, prompted by envy and fear.

Related reading

In some of the sources already mentioned, there are suggestions that these psychological factors may be important. Gillis (1974) describes how the child-saving movement gave rise to two contradictory images of youth: the 'innocent adolescent' and the 'predatory delinquent'. He interprets these images as embodying adult fears about threats to their own sense of security. The papers on girls and subcultures (Brake, 1980; McRobbie and Garber, 1976) refer to the way in which adults assume that non-conformist behaviour is necessarily linked with sexual promiscuity. This causes particular problems for girls, who are subject to double standards that label them as 'slags' or 'whores' if they imitate the rebellious behaviour of the boys.

There is a straightforward account of the developmental stages of adolescence by Hyatt-Williams in *Adolescence and the crisis of adjustment* (Meyerson, 1975). Gosling's foreword to Meyerson's book explains how the distinctive aspects of these changes interact with the changing politics of the family to produce the strong emotional reactions often seen in the adults involved. (See also Upson's paper in the same collection.)

Probably the most useful descriptions of this phase are those which show how psychological factors can have effects that reach far beyond the individual level. Rogers (1961) and Erikson (1977) both write from a psychotherapeutic viewpoint which allows them to interpret and give weight to adult reactions to young people. Rogers' comment on the applications of this perspective to education (in Chapter 14, 'Significant learning: in therapy and education') show why the efforts of adults to control the young may spring from a desire to limit their power rather than from a desire to protect them.

Erikson gives a detailed and illuminating account of the successive changes (in Chapter 2, 'Eight ages of man'). His book was first published in Britain in 1951, when youth unemployment on the present scale was undreamt of. He was able to emphasize the way in which work could offer the chance to assume a new identity, without having to consider the implications of unemployment. His comments about the needs of adults during this process are sympathetic and enlightening, and could provide plenty of starting points for the development of lessons.

Making choices
● Students should assess and reflect on their own criteria for the selection of friends, boyfriends or girlfriends, and heroes. Ask small groups to list a limited number of the men and women they most admire; and to compare and justify these choices. Alternatively, give them a list of names to rank in order of importance. What qualities do these people have in common?

Parents and young people
● What are the major sources of disagreement and conflict between parents (and other authority figures) and the young people they have responsibility for? Group-work strategies are probably most suitable for the task of eliciting these and comparing experiences. The aim is not merely to identify common problems, however, but also to explore the emotions and attitudes of those involved, both adults and young people. These first activities should be complemented by a dynamic strategy such as role-play which aims to develop some kind of empathetic understanding in the 'victims' of these arguments (i.e. the young people) of the feelings of the adults involved. Role-reversal case studies can also be used, e.g. 'Imagine that your parents have suddenly taken to wearing extreme clothes and staying out until all hours with friends that they never allow you to meet. How would you feel about this?'

Being part of a community
● Ask the students to imagine that they live in a community of people of their own age – sharing a house without adults. Ask them to draw up a list of the 'house rules' they would impose.
● Which 'house rules' exist in their own homes regarding space, equipment, meals, shopping, noise and privacy?

Reasons for working
● The significance of 'work' as a place to develop one's identity has been mentioned already. A comparison of the functions work fulfils for people at different stages of their life would underline to young people

why the first job is so important. Ask students to interview people of different ages to discover their reasons for working.

10.5   The legal status of young people

Previous sections concentrated on the conflicting views of young people that adults hold. It is reasonable to assume that these contradictions will also result in anomalies in the ways in which young people are treated by adults in the various formal roles which they occupy. Institutions have rules by which they control the admission of the young to new statuses, rights, and responsiblities. This section examines some of the contradictions in one particular area: the legal status of the young adult.

Any legal system reflects values and beliefs held in that society, though these need not be either currently or generally held. Since adults find it difficult to hand over responsibility to the young, we can expect that the way the law reflects this will also be confused. Certainly it does not seem any easier for the law to decide when someone becomes an adult than for parents or others.

The topics chosen for closer examination in this section are taken from a recently published and comprehensive resource pack that examines legal status and limits in many areas. Its title, *Enfranchisement* (National Youth Bureau, 1981) echoes the situation presented by the historical picture of youth in the 20th century: that there has been a gradual disenfranchisement of young people. In respect of their political and economic status, their mobility, their opportunities to hold positions of public responsibility and others, young people's rights have had greater limits set on them. The authors of *Enfranchisement* identify the giving of up-to-date facts about legal rights and statuses as one way in which teachers, youth workers and others can help clear up confusion and begin to counteract these disadvantages. The giving of information is certainly a necessary part of this, but it should be complemented by activities that encourage students to *use* the information in ways that will develop their awareness of their position.

Two aspects of the law and young people have been selected for discussion here.

Alcohol

Alcohol is our society's legal drug. It is presented as something that is desirable but that is only made available, under certain conditions, to responsible adults. Young people are made aware of the messages that manufacturers convey about alcohol long before they are legally entitled to use it. Advertising links alcohol use with many desirable goals – social and material success, friendships, and sexual attractiveness. The effect of this widespread advertising of alcohol is something that students should explore, to see what associations they already make between drinking and the kind of social life they would like to lead. Even before they have an established pattern of drinking in the way that most adults do (though they are likely to be experimenting) they will already have attitudes about which desirable adult activities drinking will admit them to.

As well as the images conveyed by advertising, there are cultural values that non-users (or apprentice users) already associate with drinking. There are strong associations that link masculinity and drinking in a positive way, whereas women's drinking habits are more circumscribed – certain types of drinks and a certain degree of intoxication only are acceptable. There are social values that require you to 'stand your round'. Students should recognize these, too: they underline the extent to which adult society endorses regular drinking not only as a desirable but as a normal part of adult life.

A short quiz such as the one given below serves not only to test students' factual knowledge about the law, but to expose anomalies which can then form the basis for further work and discussion. This particular quiz can be copied for use as a 'starter' to a series of lessons on the topic of alcohol, or it could form part of an extended quiz on age limits.

Finance

The change from being given pocket-money to earning a wage is probably the most important sign of adult status for most young people. Although this move is possible for the 16-year-old who gets a job, they are not completely free to spend their money as they choose. A 16- or 17-year-old can marry and leave home to set up one of their own, but there are still considerable limitations on their rights to use credit facilities and make contracts. These limits may exist as safeguards to protect them from getting into debt, but they may also prevent them from learning to be responsible about money and even in extreme cases allow some young people to be unscrupulous and escape any liability for some of the debts they may incur.

Family budgets
- Present students with the argument that protection by the law may actually prevent them from learning to handle money responsibly. (This could be by formal discussion or debate.)
- How far do parents also prevent their children from seeing financial matters realistically? Should older children have more say in organizing the family budget?

Those who have had regular pocket money or allowances before leaving school probably have a spending pattern that does not include any contribution to the family budget. Their money will go on 'inessentials' (though they do not see them as such) marketed specially for their age group. They are probably totally ignorant about a large area of basic family finances – rent, food, fuel, clothing costs, and parents' wages. There is a gap between their experience of using money to buy 'extras' and their knowledge about the financial

Age limits and alcohol

● Below is a series of statements about young people and the alcohol laws. Underline the answer or answers you think correct.

1   No young person under the age of 14/16/18
    is allowed in a bar during
    licensing hours. (N.B. Certain
    exceptions are listed in the
    Enfranchisement alcohol table.)

2   A young person over the age of 14/16/17
    may buy .... spirits/beer/cider/wine/porter/perry
    with a sit-down meal in a part of
    the premises where meals are
    served and which is not a bar.

3   A young person under the age of 14/16/18
    may go into a bar with older
    friends as long as he or she does
    not buy intoxicating liquor, nor
    have it bought for himself or
    herself.

4   An assistant in an off-licence is
    breaking the law if he or she sells
    intoxicating liquor to anyone
    under the age of 16/17/18

5   An adult who buys intoxicating
    liquor and gives it to a young
    person aged 14–18 is not breaking
    the law as long as this does not
    happen in a bar .... true/false

6   Young people under 14 are not
    allowed in pubs but may go into
    registered clubs .... true/false

7   The law does not prevent under-
    18s from drinking or buying
    alcohol in registered clubs (unless
    the club has specific rules banning
    this) .... true/false

● *Answers*: 1 — 14   4 — 18
              2 — 16, beer, cider,   5 — true
                     porter, perry   6 — true
              3 — 16, 18   7 — true

Table 10.1   Sources of financial support at age 16+

Option	Own money from official sources	Parents' money from official sources
staying at school	none	child benefit (£6.50)
full-time futher education	possible grant	child benefit (£6.50)
on 21-hour course	supplementary benefit (£17.30 — if you are still available for work)	none
on YTS scheme	MSC allowance £26.25	none
after YTS	supplementary benefit	none
at work	wage	none
on dole	supplementary benefit (£17.30 for 16–17-year-olds and £22.45 for 18-year-olds at home and unemployed; £28.05 for those with own flat)	none

realities of independent living. This makes the possibility (if it exists) of their moving into a place of their own or shared accommodation even more difficult to manage.

Financial support for young people
Another current area of confusion and inequality is the variety of funding (or lack of it) available to support young people over the age of 16 (Table 10.1).

Financial limitations
● Table 10.1 can be used as a stimulus for discussion of several issues, such as
  ★ Are the amounts fair?
  ★ Who is actually better off?
  ★ How often is money the main factor that decides which course of action a 16-year-old (or his or her family) can afford to follow?
● If students add in money from pocket-money or part-time earnings, does this make much difference to their total weekly incomes?
● Each student can review (privately) his or her own situations. Results can be discussed if the students are willing. What limits are there on spending power in relation to these things:
  ★ essentials?
  ★ leisure activities?

★   saving?
★   any intentions to live on one's own at some stage?
●   Compare this with the circumstances of an imaginary person in
another category.

Banking

In practice you must be over 16 and at work before you can open a current
account. Even if you satisfy these conditions, however, a bank will not issue
you with a cheque card until you are 18. As most shops will not accept cheques
without cards, this means that in practice your spending power is severely
limited. Sometimes extreme examples of how unreasonable this can seem
make the newspapers. Consider the following extract from *The Daily
Telegraph:*

CHEQUE CARD FOR £35,000 BOY

A bank has finally given a cheque-card to a 16-year-old boy with the Midas touch,
to help him part with some of his £35,000-a-year salary. The young man had been
refused a cheque-card by every bank he tried when they learned his age.

The boy, who designs computer games, said three banks finally rang him up to
say they would give him a cheque-card. 'But Lloyds were the most helpful. They
even promised to give me a credit card which the others wouldn't,' he said.

Credit

In general, minors (young people aged under 18) are not bound by contracts.
Exceptions to this are contracts relating to employment and apprenticeship
and those that affect the supply of essentials for independent living. Minors
are bound by contracts that refer to food, clothing and rent, and if they do not
pay gas or electricity bills the services can be cut off.

These restrictions mean that in practice traders are reluctant to open credit
agreements or make hire-purchase arrangements with minors because they
cannot recover any debts. (They can recover the goods, and without any
obligation to repay money already paid, but only if the goods have not already
been sold to some third person.)

A detailed account of these and other legal conditions relating to credit or
contracts is given in *Enfranchisement*.

Money and the law

As far as the law is concerned, you are not ready for full financial responsibility
until you are 18. If you are under 18 and a wage-earner, however, you cannot
escape the standard deductions from your wage-packet. The restrictions on
your freedom to spend means that, although you are legally able to marry and
set up a home of your own, in practice you either probably have to pay cash for
everything or find someone who is over 18 who will buy things on your behalf.

It has already been suggested that these restrictions, although protective in one way, may be obstacles to learning to handle money responsibly.

Controlling your money
- Those who stay on in full-time education until they are 18 do not have to go through this period of financial 'apprenticeship'.
  - ★ Do your students think they would be ready to try living away from their parents' home at 16 or 17?
  - ★ Are 16- and 17-year-old wage earners being penalised unfairly by these legal restrictions on how they spend their wages?

Using alcohol
- Find out students' attitudes to alcohol. (This can be done in conjunction with the study of other drugs.) Is it seen as desirable or dangerous or neutral? What are their own patterns of use at this stage? How does alcohol compare with other drugs? What effects does it have? How are these produced? What do they understand by alcohol abuse? If the laws did not exist at all, could people be left to themselves to establish reasonable habits? Should children of all ages be allowed in pubs? Should there be licensing hours at all?

Budgeting
- What are the spending habits of 'pocket-money' students? What exactly is this spent on? Make a list. Ask students: 'If you had to give up one of the items on your list, which would it be? What proportion of any money you get after 16 should be paid for keep?' (Table 10.1 can be used.)

Organizing finances
- Carry out a case study of two 18-year-olds sharing accommodation. Joint incomes total £x p.w. Estimate standard deductions. What proportion of the remainder goes on rent/fares/light/heat/fuel/food/clothes/entertainment/savings? Arrange these items in descending order of priority. (To find out wages for 18-year-olds in jobs in your own area contact your local wages inspector. Addresses and telephone numbers are available from the Wages Inspectorate at Hanway House, Red Lion Square, London, WC1H 4NR.)
- Discussion of the inequalities of financial provision (Table 10.1). If the government had a Department of Youth, what changes should it make? (This could also be done as a role-play or simulation, or by formal presentation of a case.)

Rights
- Make a chronology of access to rights. *First Rights* (NCCL) and *Enfranchisement* (NYB) both have details.
  - ★ What changes would students make in this? (This could be done as combination of task-based group activities, with each small group being given a different topic to research.)
  - ★ Set students the task of writing a charter of rights for people of their own age.

10.6 Sample lesson plan

Length of session: 45 minutes. Group size: 30.

Resources
- OHP, board or wallchart.
- 3 large sheets of blank paper; felt pens.

Aims
- To encourage students to consider formal education.

Objectives
- To elicit as many answers as possible to the question posed in phase 1.
- To organize these into categories relevant to solving the problem in phase 2.
- To help students to produce a revised list that will serve as a description of the features of their 'ideal' school or college.

Method

Phase 1: Brainstorming (10 minutes)
a Divide your students into three groups each of 9 students plus 1 recorder.
b Pose this question (written on an OHT or wallchart): 'Supposing from next Monday you were given the responsibility for the running of the school/college/centre, what would you like to see happen?'
c Get the groups to brainstorm, recording their ideas on OHTs or wallcharts.

Phase 2: General feedback session (15 minutes)
a Reform into one group. The three recorders now read or show the ideas on their OHTs or charts.
b Pose the second question: 'Can you identify any common ideas that could be listed under the same headings, or any unique contributions worth headings of their own?'
c Guide discussion towards an organization of the ideas into categories, listing these on an OHT or a chart.

d   At an appropriate moment reveal your own chart, divided into columns with headings similar to the categories being elicited from the group. These could be: community involvement; resources; subjects worth studying; timetable if any; type of teachers; any other staff; rules of entry and selection; rules of institution, and sanctions if these are broken; who governs (i.e. decides finances and budget, hires staff, etc.)?; assessment. You may have to negotiate with your students regarding any glaring omissions or obvious discrepancies between your list and those of the groups.

Phase 3: Buzz groups (20 minutes)
a   Divide into six groups each of 5 students.
b   Give each group a sheet with the columns and headings (altered if necessary). A recorder is again appointed.
c   Give the groups the task of listing their comments under the appropriate headings. This should produce a description of the school/college/ centre the students would like to run or participate in.

Follow-up
●   Invite the students to write up the results of the group discussion as a paper or to give a personal version.
    Complete the City & Guilds assignment, at Level 1, 772; *Setting up a common room.*
●   Read and discuss extracts from sources such as *Summerhill* (A.S. Neill) and *Deschooling society* (Illich). Look at relevant films or videos.

10.7   Resources list

Tutors' background reading
Aries, P. 1973 *Centuries of childhood* (Penguin)
Brake, M. 1980 *The sociology of youth culture and youth subcultures* (Routledge and Kegan Paul)
Cohen, S. 1980 *Folk devils and moral panics*, 2nd edn (MacGibbon & Kee)
Cohen, S. 1971 *Images of deviance* (Penguin)
Erikson, E. 1977 *Childhood and society* (Triad Granada)
Gillis, J.R. 1974 *Youth and history* (Academic Press)
Goodman, P. 1971 *Compulsory miseducation* (Penguin)
Hall, S. and A. Jefferson 1976 *Resistance through rituals* (Hutchinson)
Holt, J. 1974 *Escape from childhood* (E.P. Dutton, NY)
Hoyle, M. (ed.) 1979 *Changing childhood* (Writers and Readers Publishing Co-operation)
Hyatt-Williams, A. 1975, 'The early years' and 'Puberty and phases of adolescence' in Meyerson

McRobbie, A. and J. Garber 1976 'Girls and subcultures: an exploration' in Hall and Jefferson

Meyerson, S. (ed.) 1975 *Adolescence and the crisis of adjustment* (George Allen and Unwin)

Murdock, G. and R. McCron 1976 'Consciousness of class and consciousness of generation' in Hall and Jefferson

Musgrove, F. 1964 *Youth and the social order* (Routledge and Kegan Paul)

National Youth Bureau 1981 *Enfranchisement: young people and the law* (NYB Youth Work Unit)

Pearson, G. 1983 *Hooligan: a history of respectable fears* (Macmillan)

Reeder, D. 1979 'A recurring debate: education and industry' in *Schooling in decline*, ed. G. Bernbaum (Macmillan)

Robins, D. and P. Cohen 1978 *Knuckle sandwich – growing up in the working-class city* (Penguin)

Upson, P. 1975 'Adolescents and groups, subcultures, countercultures' in Meyerson

Walvin, J. 1982 *A child's world* (Penguin)

Classroom materials

Basic Skills Unit 1982 *Consumer facts* (COIC, Moorfoot, Sheffield S1 4PQ)
Practical guide for students, on consumer legislation and rights. Includes sections on buying on credit, complaints, gas and electricity, and others.

Evans, M., W. Rice and G. Gray 1983 *Free to choose* (TACADE, 2 Mount Street, Manchester M2 5NG).
Drug education pack in ten sections, Tutor's notes and student material (for ages from 11 to 16). Sections include: medicines, alcohol, tobacco, solvents, cannabis, amphetamines.

Hanson, W.J. 1982 *Enquiries* (Longman)
'Family life', 'Aggression', and 'Courtship' are titles included in this wide-ranging series, which offers readable, well-illustrated material for discussion and case studies.

Jones, A., J. Marsh and A.G. Watts 1982 *Male and female* (CRAC)
A student's workbook on sex roles. Tutor's notes are provided separately. There are sections on: 'Sex and the single teenager', 'Men and women at work', 'Top jobs', 'The kitchen sink', 'Who earns the bread?' and other topics.

National Youth Bureau 1981 *Enfranchisement: young people and the law* (NYB Youth Work Unit: 17–23 Albion Street, Leicester LE1 6GD)
A loose-leaf ring-binder with resource sheets on a wide range of topics. It includes sections on: alcohol, contraception, the courts, education, finance, employment, unemployment and many others. Each section gives factual information about relevant legislation and identifies issues for discussion.

Simnett, I., M. Evans and L. Wright 1983 *Drinking choices* (TACADE: Health Education Council)
Ring-binder training manual designed for a five-day course on alcohol. It includes a teaching plan, students' material and tutors' material. It uses games-type strategies, and covers alcohol use from all possible angles.
Spindler-Brown, A. *Women's studies* (National Extension College)
A resource pack with sections on: 'Women and society', 'Women and politics', 'Minds and bodies', 'Child-bearing and child-rearing', 'Women's creativity', 'Women and work', and 'Women and education'. It includes resources list and outline syllabuses.

11   Widening social relationships

11.1   Classroom discussion of relationships

You may find that the discussion of relationships is the most difficult aim to acknowledge as a legitimate part of your work with students. The value of such discussion may be clear but you may question your right to interfere in such a sensitive area and your right to make judgements about what is or is not a 'satisfactory' relationship. If you are a tutor (or supervisor) who spends a great deal of time and energy patching up difficulties for students on work-experience placements, then you may feel such relationships between students (or trainees), fellow workers and supervisors sometimes cause more difficulty than the students' actual performance on the job. Yet you may still feel that without specialized training not much beyond emergency first aid is possible when it comes to relationships. Or you may object to the aim because it seems to perpetuate the view that students on these courses are seen as deficient in this personal area of their lives, as well as academically.

'Satisfactory' should not be read in a normative sense. Part of your role here will be to work with students to discover what 'satisfactory' means to *them* in connection with their relationships. Principally your aim is to make students more effective social actors:

- better at assessing the constraints of the particular context they are in
- more able to understand the social rules and norms that operate
- more able to judge what is appropriate or possible
- sharper as observers of social interaction
- better able to control encounters and to analyse linguistic and para-linguistic aspects of communication
- better able to understand the politics of their everyday life in the various groups to which they belong (e.g. family, school, work, friends)

In each of these areas your work is to develop with students a systematic way of thinking about their relations with other people. This does not necessarily mean replacing their everyday way of observing and talking about these relationships with a specialist language. Your first aim is to help them develop some objectivity about what happens in their dealings with other people. In achieving this aim you will be increasing their ability to manage situations for themselves. In what ways might their previous experience have limited their ability to do this?

Selecting the range of social relationships

Chapter 10 looked at the limits that social institutions and processes have set on young people's lives. What general conclusions can be drawn from the arguments put forward there? American writers tend to emphasize the difference between age groups, while British studies highlight social-class differences. There is, however, agreement over what the general pattern of growing up is like.

The family is the most important source of support when children are young, and can act as an effective bridge between them and other people. As children get older the family becomes less important. Schooling does not take over the bridging role at all effectively. Schools go on treating students like children: controlling their time and making choices for them. This continues well into the period when in previous times students would have had a more adult role.

Those who can accept and use what the school has to offer remain 'unresponsible' (rather than *ir*responsible) for longest, but accept that the price is worth paying as long as their final opportunity to exercise responsibility will be correspondingly greater. (This assumption is worth testing out with students.) Most schoolchildren leave at the earliest opportunity.

Getting a job (or being trained in one) used to be the way to find an immediate place in the adult world. Now half of those leaving school cannot do this.

Being cut off from most adult activities (apart from those controlled by parents and teachers) and segregated by age into groups has made the social world that young people have created for themselves the most real and important part of their adolescent experience. Adults then feel excluded from it and often resent this. The problem for the 16-year-olds who suddenly find themselves at work or on work experience is that there adults expect them to grow up overnight.

This is why the whole area of personal relationships is so important an element of schemes and courses for the 16–19s: the problem has been created for them by their exclusion from, and then sudden admission to, a complex world of adult activities of which they may have little experience.

Seeing difficulties with relationships as part of this general picture makes your task as a tutor clearer. You can help your students to see that not all problems are 'one-off' difficulties caused by personality clashes; many are produced by a general lack of knowledge on both sides. (This is not to say that students will not sometimes meet problems that need to be dealt with by someone acting in a counselling or tutoring role with individuals or small groups.)

11.2   Forming a relationship

What are the ingredients of the process of developing a personal relationship? To begin with, each of the participants needs to have a clear and reasonably confidently held idea of what kind of person he or she is, to be able to present this picture to the other, and to be able to make a fairly accurate assessment of the same aspects of the other person. It is also necessary to know what the rules of their meeting are: these will determine the expectations each attaches to his or her position.

It is this combination of the social and the individual that makes the area so interesting. As section 11.1 showed, young people are limited as far as gaining useful experience in assessing a variety of social constraints is concerned. The question of their own sense of individuality is also affected in particular ways. We want to avoid the two-dimensional stereotype of the adolescent as a rebellious soul-in-torment coping with skin complaints and an identity crisis. In fact, adolescents are simply people who are expected to cope with a lot all at once, and without much useful preparation. Adults have the same problems all through their lives, but they are usually in a better position to make sure they acquire useful experience, and can often choose the time to make important changes in their lives.

Young people and change
Adolescents are experiencing changes in every area of their lives.

- They have to win recognition for themselves as mature individuals inside their own families.
- They must decide whether to leave school and go on to somewhere new (college, a course, a job or the dole) or whether to delay the decision and calculate the benefits.
- They must establish themselves independently with others of their own age, find compatible groups and friends, and make their first serious sexual relationships.

These changes involve a widening of social relationships. The place to begin a consideration of what these *changes* will entail is by helping students to assess where they stand at the moment.

Knowing yourself
- Turn the previous brief analysis into a series of questions:
  - ★ What kind of person am I?
  - ★ Who else has opinions about this? (How much notice do I take of them?)
  - ★ What impression of myself am I giving?
  - ★ What kind of person have I met here?
  - ★ What kind of group/organization are both of us in?
  - ★ What rules/limitations are there?
  - ★ How free am I to control or change these?
  - ★ Students can use these questions to produce sketches of themselves in various roles. These do not have to be taken too seriously, and

plenty of discussion should come out of the differences that emerge. This idea is the basis for the sample lesson plan for this chapter (section 11.7)

Assisting in students' personal development

Tutors familiar with the aims and strategies of careers education will recognize that the first question on the list overlaps with those which form the basis for self-assessment activities. In the field of vocational choice the aim is primarily to identify aspects of one's personality and ability relevant to work. (This is pursued in more detail in Chapter 12.)

Developmental theories of vocational choice made personal development a legitimate part of careers work. Many of the new lifeskills materials (e.g. Hopson and Scally, 1981) continue this concern with personal ideas, choices and ambitions, but also combine this with an examination of the issues covered by the rest of our list of questions. This expanded interest in self-assessment has its roots in theories of social interaction.

These deal with the process by which one's sense of identity is confirmed and adapted in interaction with others (see Argyle, 1967 & 1973). Classroom activities derived from an understanding of this process are aimed at making students express and clarify self-perceptions, matching them with the perceptions which others hold of them (see Priestley, McGuire *et al.*, 1978).

The uniqueness of the individual

It is not enough, however, to see your students as social beings and to choose a range of topics and experiences that deal only with this aspect of their lives. You need to see each student as an individual, and provide opportunities for him or her to respond to material in a unique way. Unfortunately many tutors tend to see themselves as specialists in one approach or the other: English and communication tutors can feel they have the monopoly over students' creative and subjective responses to experience; and those with a social-science background may consider themselves the experts in helping students to understand the social context in which they operate.

Our argument about social education is that the tutor in this field has to be able to handle *both* views of the students, and to acknowledge the importance of both aspects. You should also be familiar with strategies and materials appropriate to each approach. Two views of the tutor's role that may be particularly helpful are those of Richard Jones (*Fantasy and feeling in education*, 1972) and Carl Rogers (1961), who write about education from the viewpoint of psychotherapy. (Chapter 14 of Carl Rogers' book is particularly relevant.)

Stimulating imagination and creativity

Richard Jones explains how the sorts of learning aimed at in certain kinds of therapy can be used as a model for this kind of individual learning. (His phrase is 'creative learning'.) He criticizes educational learning theories for emphasizing the cognitive aspects of learning at the expense of the emotional ones. Such redefinitions of the tutor's role can provide you with a justification of the need to stimulate imaginative responses, and some ideas about methods of working. The argument about the importance of imagination may have most application to areas such as music, dance and art which are outside the scope of this book (and almost totally absent from the curriculum for this age group, where too often a diet of social realism prevails). The use of literature is relevant here, however, since we expect that many tutors have a professional background that has equipped them to use literature in the classroom.

There is almost certainly no place for the type of literary criticism practised in English examination classes, but carefully chosen extracts from novels, poetry and plays can provide the stimulus for discussion and written assignments in a wide range of contexts and topics. Students can also be encouraged to write creatively themselves and this work can be the focus of classroom activities involving their fellow students. This use of creative writing can help students to reflect upon and to understand better their own ideas and beliefs by providing an additional source of experience.

Helping students to understand and use their experiences
It is important to recognize that the centre of any consideration of personal relationships is the student's *own* view of the world, and that this involves more than just the successful application of human-relations techniques or the effective 'management' of interpersonal relations.

Work on this area with your students should be complemented by discussion of the issues pointed up in the second half of the list on page 169. This should help students to evaluate how useful their experience up to date has been as part of the preparation for assessing the demands that future new roles are likely to make of them. This assessment can be made in relation to each of the social worlds to which they currently belong. A discussion of each of these follows.

11.3 The family

'I think in our family I'm always expected to do chores . . . I'm always expected to be in the kitchen cooking or something like that, with my mother . . . Like my brother's always doing painting round the house, and doing the rubbish, taking the rubbish out . . . We're all given our own jobs.'

– 16-year-old girl.

The quotation (from a study by Kitwood) highlights two issues that can be used as starting points for discussion: the distribution of chores as an indicator of the status of the children's contribution to the home, and sexual differences in this. The same point can be made about the division of labour inside the home as was made in Chapter 10 in relation to family finances – that young people do not often make an important contribution (or practise making one) to the serious business of running a family.

Sharing out the chores

Allocating part of the domestic chores is general, but the chores are usually menial ones. In affluent homes, where children can see parents are not so domestically burdened, these low-status chores can generate a fair amount of resentment. In single-parent families and in those in which both parents work, the message about the necessity of sharing the load can be accepted more willingly.

Variations between the share given to girls and that given to boys follow the same pattern across the social classes – girls always do more than boys. And they do this for longer: boys can often drop their chores when they start work, whereas most girls are expected to carry on with their share.

Since these household jobs are on the whole the low-status 'unskilled' ones (cutting grass, washing up, going to the launderette) it seems likely that many parents see them as good preparation for the disciplines of work rather than as a way of underlining how important a contribution children make to their family life.

Household chores
- Discussion points:
    - ★   What chores do students do?
    - ★   How important to the home are these jobs?
    - ★   How are they allocated?

One exception to the unskilled nature of most children's chores is child care. Taking responsibility for looking after someone else should be the ultimate aim of the 'training' of family life, and many girls (and some boys) look after younger ones or babysit for relatives for years before they leave school. This is one reason why so many girls see a job in child care as attractive – employment in any of their other chores (being a washer-up in a restaurant, or a car-wash or launderette attendant, for example) hardly holds the same attraction.

Restrictions and rules

Chores felt to be unfair or unequally distributed are one source of arguments. The other continuing area of renegotiation centres on restrictions and limits set on an independent social life and use of the home. Again there are variations between the genders and between social classes. Evidence (provided by the studies that are suggested as sources) suggests that middle-class families, in which parents have a greater desire to control all spheres of their children's lives, may experience more conflict about this. There is a general view, however, that overall the modern nuclear family promotes more intense involvement between parents and children, making it harder for all parents to 'let go'. Their opinions about the maturity of their children are often at odds with what the legal age limits allow them to do.

The family as a source of information about work

These negative points about family life suggest that many aspects are unhelpful as a bridge to adulthood. John Holt (1974), in a polemical attack on the modern American family, saw the child as a combination of slave and 'super-pet'. How useful is the family as a source of information about working life and as a support for the choice of job?

Here again the picture shows an unhelpful gap. Since work is carried out away from the home, most young people have no realistic picture of what their parents do. Instead they rely on television and other media as the source of their information. (No wonder many of them still think of nursing as a glamorous occupation.) The message they do get from hearing their parents talk about work is that there are few satisfactions to be gained apart from money. The distribution of chores underlines the division between 'men's' and 'women's' jobs.

As a source of *values* about work, parents can be very influential. As a source of *information*, they are less reliable. Their knowledge is much more likely to be out of date or partial. Again these generalizations mask differences between working- and middle-class families. In the latter a wider selection of occupational roles is often presented, offering attractive status and rewards (both intrinsic and financial). This variety can itself cause problems of choice – middle-class children may want to reject strongly presented parental values about the importance of making an early serious commitment to a career.

Teaching suggestions

The topics picked out in this brief treatment of family life are used as the basis for lesson ideas in these areas:

- chores
- parental restrictions
- preparation for work

Organizing chores
- Conduct a class survey to establish a who-does-what picture of the division of chores in students' families. Follow-up discussion can focus on obvious gender discrepancies, the reasons for different allocations, and the relative fairness of these. Depending on the issues sparked off by the initial survey/discussion, subsequent topics for development could be:
    ★ differences in the allocation of chores when students leave school/college

★   how the students would organize the tasks of running a shared flat
      (this could be done at a group problem-solving exercise)

Caring for a family
● Ask students to imagine themselves in ten years' time, with a family.
   (Give them time to sketch in some of the details – it adds to the
   enjoyment.) Ask them to list the tasks that running a family involves.
   Now present them again (board, handout, or OHP) with the first list,
   of their chores. How many items do the two lists have in common?
   What important tasks in running a family are they not involved in at
   all? How useful a preparation for running their own families do they
   think current experience is? What reasons do they think parents have
   for giving children chores to do if the reason is *not* training them to
   run their own families?

Household skills
● Examine whether students think chores have any value in helping them
   acquire useful job skills. Use the initial list of chores, or a new one that
   combines these with the tasks that their parents keep for themselves.
   Then ask students to brainstorm a list of as many jobs as they can that
   use the same skills. How many of these jobs would they consider
   doing? How does society rate these jobs in terms of money and status?
● Depending on the interests and composition of the group and the time
   available, these topics could extend into a wider consideration of how
   gender roles link with job choices. Students could also compare their
   ideas about desirable patterns of sharing domestic work when they are
   married and when both partners work.

Disagreements between parents and families
● Ask the group to make a spider diagram showing the most frequent
   sources of disagreement between themselves and their parents. Group
   these into broad categories such as 'restrictions on social life', 'use of
   home', 'choice of friends', etc. (But beware of neglecting interesting
   exceptions.) Students can then devise brief improvised role plays
   illustrating typical points about these. Follow-up discussion can lead
   on to consider how differently they think they will behave as parents.

11.4   School

'At work you grow up to be a manager – at school you just grow up to be a kid.'

   – young worker interviewed in a Coventry engineering factory (quoted in Bazalgette, 1978).

Schooling has attracted so much criticism in recent years that it seems unkind in a book written for tutors to present you with yet another negative view of your work. Currently changes in the youth labour market are undermining the whole basis on which teachers have at least managed to motivate most students. Difficult as the job is, it is certainly not going to get easier.

The limiting effects of schooling

Our attention is directed at one aspect of school life in particular – what schools are like as places to grow up in. There is something seriously wrong with this aspect of their role. This is not entirely surprising since the way in which they run as organizations has not been altered fundamentally since mass education began a century ago.

The basic pattern then, as now, was of pupils separated into groups by age, moving round the building at regular intervals to be attended to by small numbers of specialists who saw them in large groups. Since this routine was set, schooling has simply been extended for longer and longer without any serious reconsideration of whether this is the best kind of institution in which to do most of one's growing up, nor any questioning of the increasing discrepancy between the values and practices of schools as organizations and those of other institutions that students move on to.

Looked at from this point of view – the view of schools as organizations preparing students for adult life and the main preliminary to work – what comparisons can be made between schools and other kinds of organizations? What influences do organizatonal patterns have on relationships?

Limitations for teachers

In many respects teachers form a peculiar occupational group. Few of them have ever made the kind of transition into work for which they are preparing students, and their only working roles have been pupil, student and teacher. This must limit the range of roles that they see as possible for students.

Since they themselves are the academically successful products of schooling, they are in some ways in the worst position to appreciate the point of view of all those pupils who cannot or will not accept what school has to offer. They communicate not only knowledge and skills but the values that they attach to the possession of these. This again limits the variety of perspectives schools can offer. Many teachers have values strongly antipathetic to the values and practices of pupils' families and friends and to the working life most of their pupils aim at. It is unlikely that this conflict fails to be communicated to students.

Working patterns

The nature of school work is peculiarly different from that either of the free-time activities or of the jobs that most students aim to do. Its chief characteristics are these:

- There is an emphasis on cognitive tasks which outweighs practical or aesthetic activities.
- There are tasks that in themselves seem unrelated to any other area of students' lives, and that are essentially scholarly, prizing formal literacy over other forms of expression. (Students often try to make these links for themselves; for example, a student, good at English, may say 'I want to be a journalist'. Trying to link these essentially scholarly activities to tasks carried out in the work context is, however, unsound as a basis for vocational choice. Any disillusion that results only seems to emphasize the immaturity of their own judgement.)
- There is training in working patterns that are predominantly individualistic and competitive. This limits students' experience of working with others and of being given the confidence that results from others valuing what they can do. Both these aspects are important ingredients in developing independence.

Passivity of the student role
The student role is an almost totally passive one in an authoritarian structure. The only choice the student has is whether to work hard or not. Another aspect of this passivity is that despite college and university efforts to have student representation on disciplinary and governing bodies (and the Taylor report of 1977 that recommended extending this to schools), only 'alternative' schools seems to have tried to involve students in these aspects of the organization's work. Students continue to feel its results without any opportunity to see how the decisions have been made. (This does not altogether apply to Scottish schools.)

Being assessed
Students are aware that teachers' assessments of them are one of the main reasons for their producing work, yet they have no part in the preparation of teachers' final reports on them. In addition, confidential records exist that remain secret throughout their school career. Again the links that students try to make for themselves show how they can make false assumptions of correspondences between school and work. They expect testimonials and references for jobs to be like school reports: mostly critical. They are often surprised to hear that the main aim of most references is to emphasize positive qualities. This is further evidence of the way in which the opinions of adults such as parents and teachers are experienced as being very similar, and often very damaging. Their judgements are invariably taken personally, even if not intended as such.

Profiling is a form of assessment that attempts to deal with these difficulties, and is discussed in more detail in Appendix 4.

Activities that develop independence

All the aspects listed under 'working patterns' emphasize the authoritarian, solitary and unrelated nature of much schoolwork. Activities that could help to develop maturity would have to provide experiences that schools neglect. Such experiences should include:

- being one of a group that is working on a collective task
- belonging to a group whose members are of very different ages
- being asked to take decisions that have practical consequences
- being expected to take responsibility for others

Interestingly enough many of these activities happen on residential courses, which is why residentials are usually able to accomplish so much in such a short space of time. After a residential, individuals can feel their relationships and their views of themselves have changed a great deal, even in the space of a few days.

It is not possible for all teachers to take students on residentials, but some elements from the list of maturing *experiences* can be incorporated into classroom activities by choosing participative strategies rather than those which keep students in a dependent and passive role.

Schooling as it is has advantages for adults, of course: it frees them for work, it keeps the young off the streets, and its length protects their share of the job market. Since it has such weaknesses from the point of view of encouraging independence, however, there have been suggestions that school attendance should be part-time from 14 onwards. This could happen, it is asserted, without any significant drop in the amount of work covered in school.

Teaching suggestions

The main criticism of schooling made here is that it limits young people's range of relationships and their abilities to exercise decision-making skills. The ideas below concentrate on these areas.

Disadvantages of schooling

- Introduce students to the argument that school is a poor environment in which to grow up. Compile a list of the advantages to adults of extended schooling, e.g. it
  - ★ keeps children off the streets
  - ★ frees adults for work
  - ★ prevents young people from competing for jobs too soon
  - ★ enables parents to know where their children are

Students can add to the list, and then compile a list of their own of the *disadvantages* from their own point of view. Ask them to prepare and present a case for or against schooling after 14. (See 'Assigned opinion' in section 2.3.)

Part-time schooling
● Present students with the proposition that schooling could be made part-time after the age of 14. (Truancy and part-time jobs are already examples of this principle in operation.) Patterns of attendance could be 2 or 3 days per week, or mornings only: students can choose the form they would prefer. Ask them to plan their activities for the rest of the time. Have a list of local community/leisure/training resources available for reference while groups draw up their ideas.

Setting up a class committee
● Ask students to list the decisions that have to be made:
   ★ before their course could start – this should include everything from hiring staff and timetabling to buying furniture and choosing rooms
   ★ while the term runs – this would cover choosing lesson topics and work methods, discipline, exams or tests, grading and writing reports You could provide a checklist to make sure important things are not omitted. Ask students to identify who makes these decisions. This can be developed into a consideration of questions such as:
   ★ which decisions should/could students have a part in taking?
   ★ what sort of group would have to be formed for this?
   ★ what organizing or communication skills would they need to have to be part of such a group?
● This could lead on to the setting up of some kind of formal class 'committee' to look at what decisions they could make about the organization and running of the rest of their course.
● Take the list of 'maturing experiences' on page 177 and combine it with a selection of activities that would give students experience in some or all of these areas. (Typical small-scale examples involve organizing surveys or trips, inviting in people from outside, etc.) Present this to
the student committee to revise and make decisions on.

11.5 Work

'Now I've left school – well, my parents are all right . . . They said from the beginning, "As soon as you've left school and you're in a good job and you're settled, you're all right". Then they sort of let me go.'

(*17-year-old boy, quoted in Kitwood, 1980*)

All investigations into the attitudes of school-leavers to their first job discover the same thing: young people have very high expectations of what being a worker will be like. They invest a very high proportion of their sense of identity in the work they do. For those in unskilled jobs this halo effect can last up to two years before disillusion with their true lack of prospects sets in. Early dissatisfactions used to be dealt with by frequent changes of job: if they didn't like one place they could walk out and get another job. Now this is no longer possible.

Work has assumed this exaggerated importance in their lives because so many of their psychological needs have to be satisfied by their jobs. As their opportunities for taking part in adult activities have become more limited, work has increased its importance.

When they move into their first job (or into work experience) most young people are at least as anxious about how they will get on with the other people as they are about whether they will be able to do the work.

Getting on with people at work

Several things have to happen before one is accepted at work. These include:

- being seen as competent (but not too competent in comparison with others)
- being trusted by workmates
- being competent to carry responsibility
- understanding the limits of this responsibility (not treading on anyone else's toes)
- not letting others down
- being accepted into a group as a friend

School leavers' worries about these things are increased because of the way school life has taught them to see authority figures. They expect adults to be critical; and their experience tends to be that any opinions adults have of them are felt as personal criticisms rather than as objective comments on their actions, even if they were not intended as such. Consequently, all authority figures tend to be seen negatively, and school-leavers' first assumption may be that work supervisors are going to be like parents and teachers. Different strategies may have to be used to cope with all three.

Developing assertiveness

Coping with restrictions
- Increase students' appreciation of the difficulties and possibilities of negotiation, by giving them contrasting problems to consider:
    - ★ ways of dealing with parental restrictions
    - ★ strategies for coping with school rules or teacher's restrictions
    - ★ ways of responding to work rules such as not wearing jeans at work, and not smoking in forbidden places.
  What courses of action are possible? Solutions can be discussed or acted out under three headings: obey or reject or appeal. The level of

necessary personal tact and understanding and the need for a variety of communication skills obviously vary with each alternative.

The example above could be used to give students the opportunity to practise some of the skills of assertiveness, and to help them work out what are appropriate and possible responses in a variety of situations. This will also contribute to helping students build more adequate models for understanding formal and informal organizations.

Alternatively this could be a starting point for developing students' powers of assertiveness in dealing with difficult situations in which being new or lacking confidence can leave one feeling 'taken advantage of'.

Self-assertiveness
- Non-work examples can be used:
  - ★ complaining about badly-cooked food in a canteen or cafe
  - ★ taking back faulty goods to a shop
  - ★ resisting a door-step slaesman
  - ★ telling a boyfriend or girlfriend that you don't want to see him or her any more
  - ★ asking someone out for a date, over the telephone
  - ★ receiving a present you hate from someone you like
  - ★ telling your best friend that his or her new outfit looks awful
  - ★ being irritated at work by personal teasing from an older person
  (Role-play is really the only strategy that is appropriate for this.)

Being in an organization
One of the questions concerning judging a relationship (page 169) involved understanding the rules attached to the meeting. Students often go into workplaces with the wrong perceptions about this, and get into difficulties by applying the social rules of home or school to encounters at work.

This is precisely the area that many employers' criticisms are concerned with. Comments recorded in the studies that school-leavers these days are 'too cheeky' (from a supervisor in the Coventry study by Bazalgette) and that 16–18-year-olds have an 'inadequate general education' show the terms they used to interpret the same kind of events. The positive comments that can occasionally be elicited (in the *A-Z study*, for example) show that it is this area of 'personal effectiveness', as it is called in some schemes, that is more often the key to success or failure in a job.

The following idea aims to help students develop some objectivity about these rules.

Variations in language
- Language is an important marker of relationship differences. Begin

with students' everyday experiences. Ask them to list all the styles of greeting they use in one day, and ask for the reasons for these. Elicit and record the important categories: age, status, social background, familiarity. Then ask them to devise simple improvised conversations based on instances of people misjudging situations. (*Language in use* has relevant lesson suggestions in the 'Starting work' unit.)

11.6 Friends

Previous sections explain that work has assumed too great a significance as a marker on the route to adult status because of a lack of adult roles in other areas of adolescent life. However, work does have one thing in common with the family and school: it is run by adults. What light do surveys and research studies throw on the world that young people organize for themselves?

Exclusivity of friendship

The most obvious point to be made is that it is a very exclusive world – self-contained and offering no admission to anyone outside the age-group. Debarred from activities that have any real economic or political significance, young people respond by creating a social world that is inward-looking. Most energy is directed towards establishing and evaluating social relationships and the chief preoccupation is with forming a personality for oneself.

This particular environment, organized as it is around interpersonal relations, has been compared to a prolonged 'sensitivity training'.

Gender differences

There are again gender and class differences in the particular patterns of this social world. Boys tend to gather in small groups or gangs whose reasons for coming together are organized around activities. Girls on the other hand form more intense friendship-pairs, and treat the whole business of developing a personality at a much more serious level. They acquire in the process a wider range of social skills than boys of the same age, skills which match their more developed sensitivity to the working of relationships.

Gender differences
- Give single-sex groups a variety of case-study problems to consider (this can be done in the form of a quiz). Compare the answers they come up with. For example:
  - ★ A friend arrives on your doorstep and says he/she has just been thrown out after a violent row at home. What do you do?
  - An effective solution would:
  - ★ stop the unpleasant effect

★   identify the cause
★   prevent a recurrence
Judge the solutions according to these criteria. Do girls' and boys'
solutions treat problems better/worse/differently?
● This can lead on to a consideration of whether girls are better at
dealing with sensitive issues where feelings are involved, or whether
boys are underestimated in this respect. Do parents differ along the
same lines?

Class differences
Surveys show that class differences become apparent in the timing of the move
'out': middle-class adolescents move later into an independent social life.
Though for middle-class boys at least, a wide range of possible characters
exists to be tried out, working-class boys have a much stronger consensus view
of what is acceptable masculine behaviour.

Identifying with the group
Pressure towards conformity is the strongest characteristic of the friendships
of adolescence, however. A nice balance has to be struck between carving out
a personality that is at the same time individual without being too different
from that of one's friends. This may be helped (or hindered) by the fact that
though conformity is the price demanded for admission to the group, young
people often belong to several groups that have different, often conflicting
values and expectations.

   The point has already been made in Chapter 10 that the picture of teenagers
that televison and newspapers reflect is selective and unrepresentative.
Subcultures whose members have picturesque or extreme dress and behaviour
may make better subjects for journalists or sociological studies, but only
a minority of young people belong to such groups. The voyeuristic interest
of adults in extreme groups may be the result of their exclusion from
adolescent social life. They resent being left out, and this allows them to
endow this social life with an atmosphere of tribal foreignness that lets them
suspect the worst.

Conflict and continuity with parents
This is not the picture represented in large-scale studies. Arguments with
parents and value clashes do occur, but these tend to be centred on domestic
issues such as restrictions on the use of the house, chores, and children's rights
to make their own decisions. (This issue is taken up again in connection with
political literacy – see Chapter 17.) When it comes to the values that young
people hold about more general issues then there is a strong consistency with
traditional values. Attitudes to work are dealt with above; those connected
with personal relationships (including partnership and marriage) also seem to
conform to the picture most adults would prefer young people to have, rather

than to challenge it. Indeed, young people often express opinions that take a much harsher moral line than that of their parents.

The phrase 'sensitivity-training' was quoted earlier as an example of how one study construes the adolescent preoccupation with interpersonal relations. The derogatory overtone is intentional in the context of the argument that the author (Kitwood) presents – that society is leaving them little else of importance to do.

We have chosen four areas of students' current experience (family, school, work, friends) to examine the overall question: 'What sort of basis for future relationships do current ones provide?' Previous sections illuminated ways in which each of the social worlds to which your students belong may help or hinder the transfer to the wider network of roles offered by adult life.

Friendships

- Ask students to make personal timetables of how they spend their week. These need not be shared. Then ask them to see how wide an age-range of people they come into contact with, and try to establish whether meetings with adults are primarily in formal or informal contexts.
- Ask students to list the friendship groups to which they belong. (The timetables produced above could be used again here.) Discuss (or ask them to discuss in buzz groups of which you are not a part) how differently they behave or are seen in these various groups.
- This can develop into a more general consideration of 'Who knows you best?' This is such a diffuse and personal question that the discussion needs to be focused, at least initially, by a piece of stimulus material. Try giving students a list of personal adjectives and asking them which ones would be likely to be used about themselves by various people – mother, father, teacher, boyfriend or girlfriend, etc. This can link with a discussion of the expectations various people will have of them in different roles.
- Compare and discuss the values they hold about various issues that will be important in their future, such as work and marriage. This could begin by examining their current ideas about friendship. Again such personal topics need to be dealt with by strategies that protect students' confidentiality while giving them plenty of opportunity to share and compare ideas. Lists of value statements can be used as questionnaires; extracts from interviews can be used as discussion starters.

Analysing press reports

- Examine a selection of press extracts about young people to identify the underlying attitudes and assumptions that adult writers and readers seem to share.

11.7   Sample lesson plan

Length of session: 1 hour.
Group size: 20.

Resources
- Blackboard/OHP; students need paper.

Aim
- To examine how social context affects behaviour.

Objectives
- To elicit students' present ideas about effects of surroundings on behaviour.
- To help them analyse the behaviour, language and dress that distinguishes their different roles.
- To get students to describe themselves in different contexts.

Method
Phase 1: Checklisting (10–15 minutes)
a   Ask the whole group this general question: 'Do you always act the same wherever you are, whoever you're with? What affects your behaviour?'
b   List responses on a board or OHP.
c   Turn this list into a series of questions (use those on page 169 as a checklist).
d   Confirm that students accept this list and ask them to copy it down.

Phase 2: Writing self-portraits (20–30 minutes)
a   Ask the whole group to suggest their various social identities; list these on the board or OHP. Examples include: son/daughter; boyfriend/girlfriend; student/employee; grandchild; best friend/enemy; footballer/dancer.
b   Ask students to choose two from the list and write contrasting portraits of themselves, using the checklist of questions as a prompt.

Phase 3: Comparing descriptions (15–20 minutes)
a   Ask volunteers to read out their sketches.
b   Discuss the differences and the reasons for them.
c   End by arriving at the question: 'So what is the real you?'

Follow-up
- Creative work. Ask students to produce a portrait of their 'real' selves. This should be in *anything but* continuous writing: e.g. paste-ups of favourite photos, poems, drawings, song lyrics; short audio tapes of favourite music or book extracts. Make a group display.
- Developing empathy. Ask them each to choose to be someone else in the

group and study all the material about that person until they feel they know him or her well. They can then describe an event from the other person's point of view.

11.8 Resources list

Tutors' background reading

The social-education tutor's task is a complex one: it involves you in many roles – tutor, teacher, trainer, counsellor – not all of which are naturally complementary. What we are recommending in this chapter on social relationships is that you should be able to work with your students in a way that compensates for the limitations in their experience. These limitations result to a large extent from the way society (through the institutions of family, school and work) has now organized the business of growing up. Sources recommended here are chosen because they provide one or both of these things:

- a broad view based on factual research for tutors who are interested in pursuing the issues in more depth
- plenty of illustrative evidence that can be turned into teaching material

There are many 'transition' studies that give a broader picture of those areas of young people's lives dealt with briefly in this chapter. The 1972 report on *Youth: transition to adulthood* was in many ways one of the most comprehensive and clear analyses of the way in which society currently restricts the opportunities and rights of its young. The Coventry study (Bazalgette, 1978) of young people in their first jobs contrasts their experience at work with their experience in school and reinforces the same point made by the American study mentioned above about the limitations of schooling. Interviews provide illustrations of the criticisms. Another research project on the transition to work (Hill and Scharff, 1976) has some valuable points to make about the way in which group work and experiential learning are key strategies that should be used by tutors to support and develop students' understanding. *The serious business of growing up* (Medrich *et al.*, 1981) is an extended American survey with a detailed chapter about chores and the connection between these and attitudes to work. Their sample (nearly 800 children) also provides a useful reminder of the realities of family structure – half the children had working mothers and nearly half lived with single parents.

The study by Kitwood (1980) has theoretical chapters on methodology and explanation that might be obstacles for the non-specialist. The extracts from interviews however are extremely valuable. They offer extended first-hand opinions on all the subjects touched on here: family, school, part-time work, work and unemployment, free-time activities and friendship.

Interview studies seem to be forming a genre. They have the great advantage of being very readable, always succinct and are often very funny. At the same time they can be a useful source of teaching material: the opinions can be turned into questionnaires, lists of contrasting opinion, statements for comparison, etc. Quotations can be used as discussion starters and experiences and anecdotes are source material for case studies and role-plays, having the advantage of immediacy and topicality that is often difficult to find in literary sources. Studies should avoid the pitfall of concentrating on the picturesque minorities, so we have recommended ones that are based on large samples and are representative of opinions from young people from different regions, social classes and cultural groups.

Too much too young (Fisher and Holder, 1981) is instantly accessible, and covers an enormous range of topics. Here the interview quotations are shorter, and are intercut with authors' comments. Since the authors were market researchers rather than academic sociologists, however, these inter-pretations would make sense to all readers. (It is a major irony of much field research on young people that in its final published form it is beyond the comprehension of those who have provided the evidence.) The two previous books we have recommended, and the next, are books that contain much that your students might want to look at too.

Tales out of school (White and Brockington, 1983), as the title suggests, concentrates on various aspects of school, teachers, work, and unemployment. It also includes plenty of personal opinions on YOP experiences. The extracts have the advantage of being long enough to be used as case studies in their own right.

Argyle, M. 1967 *The psychology of interpersonal behaviour* (Penguin)

Argyle, M. 1978 *Social interaction* (Tavistock)

Bazalgette, J. 1978 *School life and work life* (Hutchinson)

Fisher, S. and S. Holder 1981 *Too much too young* (Pan Books)

Hill, J.M.M. and D.E. Scharff 1976 *Between two worlds* (Careers Consultants Ltd.)

Holt, J. 1974 *Escape from childhood* (E.P. Dutton & Co. New York)

Industrial Training Research Unit 1979 *The A-Z Study* (ITRU)

Jones, R. 1972 *Fantasy and feeling in education* (Penguin)

Kitwood, T. 1980 *Disclosures to a stranger* (Routledge and Kegan Paul)

Medrich, E.A. *et al.* 1981 *The serious business of growing up* (University of California Press)

President's Science Advisory Committee 1972 *Youth: transition to adulthood*: a Report of the Panel on Youth of the Committee (University of Chicago Press 1972)

Rogers, C. 1961 *On becoming a person* (Constable)

Watts, A.G. 1983 *Work experience and schools* (Heinemann)

White, R. and D. Brockington 1983 *Tales out of school* (Routledge and Kegan Paul)

Classroom materials

Adams, C. and R. Laurikietis 1980 *The gender trap*, revised edn. (Virago)
Book 1: 'Education and work'; Book 2: 'Sex and marriage'; Book 3: 'Messages and images'. Tutor's (and older students') discussion books on sex typing. Background information and questions to stimulate discussion on a wide range of relevant issues.

Brandes, D. and H. Phillips 1978 *Gamesters' Handbook* (Hutchinson)
140 games for use with groups. Two sections: social games, to develop trust and integration; and personal-development games, to promote self-awareness.

Brandes, D. 1984 *Gamesters' Handbook Two* (Hutchinson)

Careers Consultants Ltd. *Personality*
A card game to develop group relationships. It has a simple card format, and multiple uses.

Haggerty, C. 1984 *In place* (Careers Consultants Ltd, 12–14 Hill Rise, Richmond Hill, Richmond, Surrey TW10 6HA)
An index of materials for personal development, life-skills and careers education. Over 200 entries.

Hopson, B. and M. Scally 1981 *Lifeskills Teaching Programmes No 1.* (Lifeskills Associates)
Loose-leaf binder of exercises for self-assessment, communicating, assertiveness, and managing relationships.

Jones, A., J. Marsh and A.G. Watts 1982 *Male and female*, revised edn. (CRAC)
In the CRAC 'Life-style' series, students' workbook (and tutor's notes) on gender differences at home and work, stereotypes, sexual relationships, and life-styles.

Porter, S. 1979 *Problem page* (Edward Arnold)
Student's workbook with 30 brief exercises (case study followed by discussion questions) on problems arising out of relationships with friends, parents, and the opposite sex.

Priestley P., J. McGuire, D. Flegg, V. Hemsley, and D. Welham 1978 *Social skills and personal problem solving* (Tavistock Publications)
Tutor's handbook of methods and exercises for self-assessment, personal and social-skills development.

Walker, D. 1982 *Kith and kin* (Edward Arnold)
Student's book in play-script form of various problem situations facing a fictional family. Follow-up questions are intended to open-up discussion (or stimulate role-play) on relationships, marriage, etc.

12　On from the course

12.1　Helping students decide what to do next

Considering with students questions such as 'What am I getting from this course?', 'How will it help me with what I want to do next?', 'What choices are open to me?' is an intrinsic part of vocational-preparation courses. Curriculum elements like induction, negotiation, guidance and counselling create an 'official' space in which this can happen.

The ABC core objectives include ones directly concerned with helping students decide what to do when the course finishes. This brings social education into the area also covered by careers education. These questions about personal choices are also likely to arise in connection with various other topics, particularly where the social-education session is used to provide a back-up to work experience.

The whole question of what to do next will be inextricably linked with the way in which unemployment is affecting your students. This is so important that we have devoted the whole of the next chapter to unemployment – for this reason it is not part of the discussion here. You may prefer to read Chapter 13 first.

12.2　The overlap with careers education

You may not be the tutor with specific responsibility for giving students detailed information about opportunities after the course, or with helping them choose between options, but as a social-education tutor you have more in common with the area covered by careers work than have other tutors, and you probably have more time with students in which to look at certain topics than a specialist careers tutor might have.

We are not going to describe careers education here. Some topics distinctive to it – interviewing students individually, record-keeping, and aptitude or interest-testing, for example – are not relevant here. If you want to find out more about what a complete careers-education curriculum includes, consult some of the texts given in the resources list (section 12.8).

In order to make 'informed and realistic' decisions about the future, students need:

● information about current job opportunities in general

- knowledge of the local labour market
- an informed idea of likely future developments in these
- details of education and training courses available to them
- a rational procedure for choosing between options

Special concerns of social education
In a sense the social and personal aspects of careers education have been colonized by social education, though careers-education programmes were able to claim them as their own only because the rest of the curriculum neglected them.

Your areas of concern are likely to be:

- relating the issue of choosing a job or kind of training to the self-descriptions produced in other lessons and in profiles
- giving students a general picture of the context in which they will be looking for work or choosing a course
- helping them to develop their own strategies for making informed choices and decisions

Before you can draw up detailed activities for students and plan sessions with them, you have to decide what your particular stance on the issues is going to be. Virtually all the topics involved – work, unemployment, YTS, etc. – are controversial. There are no ready-made solutions. All tutors have to come to terms in their own ways with the need to find working roles they can live with. You just need to be clear about how you balance the considerations.

Choosing your position
The FEU survey of social education (Lee, 1980) describes the variety of approaches that are currently being used. *Developing social and life skills* (FEU, 1980) describes ways in which these different approaches can be put into practice.

The most important tasks for you as tutor in this area are to be clear about your own working principles and to keep a check on internal consistencies in your curriculum. Two types of social-education aims have been distinguished. These can be broadly summarized as 'activist' and 'adaptive'. Within each approach aims can be concerned with change or adaptation at an individual or societal level.

Activist aims
Activist aims emphasize:

- developing political and economic understanding
- developing in students a commitment to change as one of their values
- helping students to acquire the relevant collective-action skills to initiate change

- using these to try and improve their present circumstances on the course, at work, or in the neighbourhood
- increasing the individual students' ability to change his or her own circumstances – for example, you can teach assertiveness techniques, or you can help students to analyse the skills of social interaction they need in order better to control social encounters

Activist social-education programmes seek to challenge or change the status quo, so are likely to be seen as disruptive by anyone who is unsympathetic to this aim.

Adaptive aims
Adaptive aims emphasize:

- developing students' understanding of societal norms – the aim itself may be normative, e.g. 'fitting in at work'
- developing students' self-awareness about their own values, but not seeking to change these
- allowing the students the autonomy to make informed choices entirely on the basis of their own values and perceptions

At an individual level, these last aims are typical of the non-directive counselling approach. Tutors are careful not to disclose their own values and not to allow their own values and personal beliefs to influence the decision-making process.

For a detailed discussion of these alternatives and more examples of how the aims are interpreted, see *Beyond coping* (Lee, 1980: pages 51–3). Watts (1978) first drew up the model to trace the connections between tutors' values and their approaches to teaching about unemployment.

Your programme will probably not have aims that are restricted exclusively to one point of view. The aims you select will depend on your own combination of social and political beliefs. Look at your course to see if there are:

- inconsistencies in the programme that are produced by tutors when views conflict
- aims that are rejected because the tutors disagree with the belief underlying it
- aims that are simply neglected by omission rather than rejected

Are your students clear about what the tutors' views are? Are they allowed to disagree? Are students being denied any useful experiences or insights because of gaps in the programme?

Earlier in this chapter we pointed out the likeliest areas of involvement for social-education tutors. Each of these will be explored in turn. The links between your aims and your values will affect the detailed objectives you select for various activities.

12.3 Self-assessment

Self-assessment is one of the major areas with which social education concerns itself. In the case of future choices the main questions that you will want students to consider will be:

- what activities or subjects do I like?
- which ones am I good at?
- what kind of jobs would I like, and which are available to me?
- what kind of training courses or schemes would I consider?
- what effect will my values have on my choice?
- what kind of person am I, and how does this affect the kind of job or course I want?

The regular discussions which you or another tutor may have with individual students to complete their profiles are one place in which these questions can be considered. This serves the same purpose as the one-to-one careers interview, and is what might be called the rational approach. There are a number of reasons why it is of limited value for a tutor simply to ask the questions of individual students.

- Students may be intimidated by the one-to-one interview. They are less likely to offer answers they feel unsure of, or to admit they don't know, or to give an answer they feel the tutor will disapprove of.
- It is essential to know what your students' attitudes to these issues really are. When it comes to questions to do with work and jobs there are great gaps between the experiences of tutors and students which are largely the result of age and class differences.
- The opportunity to compare self-perceptions with their friends' opinions of them can produce feedback that is more useful than a tutor's opinion.

Your basic approach will be to explore the questions through classroom activities in which students work in groups or pairs. Individual tasks also have a place, but here the students will be working on the questions without you; and in most cases it will be more appropriate for them to share the results with each other.

Self-assessment
- Ask students to produce self-profiles under different headings: skills; qualifications; leisure interests; part-time jobs held; personal qualities.
- Pair interviews could obtain the same information. Students could then read out what they have found out about each other.
- As an individual task, students could write notes under the five headings, or answer 'prompt' questions – e.g. 'List the three things at school/college that you are best at'.

- A third alternative is to devise a card-sorting activity that deals with the same area – e.g. under the 'skills' area students select from a pile cards that name their skills. Other piles could name personal qualities, preferred working conditions, etc.
- In follow-up interviews students can use the information to complete a 'personal record' (a less formal curriculum vitae).
- Ask students to try filtering the information to produce descriptions suited to different audiences – potential employer, pen-friend, computer-picked date, etc.
- 'Personal qualities' can remain a private area, i.e. students need not be asked to disclose what they've written. A common technique is to provide lists of adjectives ('shy', 'amusing', 'aggressive', etc.) and to ask students to select those that describe themselves.
- Close friends can compare lists so that each student can match their self-perception with that of someone who knows him or her well.
- Again the selection can be made through the eyes of someone else ('Which ones would your tutor/mother/father tick?')
- Students can select different sets according to different social roles they may have now or in the future, such as friends, employees, or parents. These lists can be of skills or personal qualities or both.
- Ask students to write testimonials for themselves, but from your point of view.
- Students can write their own testimonials anonymously, then exchange them to be read out so that others can guess the subject. (You need a fairly high degree of trust in a group for this exercise.)
- Ask students to describe the sort of skills and personal qualifications they think a good tutor/student/supervisor/employer/employee ought to have. (These can be brainstormed by different groups.) When you and they have argeed on the criteria, these can be used to rate various examples. Again confidentiality needs to be observed, especially if it's you they are judging.

Many of the items in the resources list (section 12.8) have ideas and materials for this area. Since the topic is potentially so important because it is directly personal, most teaching ideas recognize that making the activity enjoyable (by using a quiz or game format, for example) removes the intimidating aspect. All such strategies can produce clear and beneficial effects on motivation and group cohesion.

12.4   The job market

The second area with which many tutors are involved is a continuation of the self-assessment activities. It is complementary to the compiling of a self-description in that it involves identifying the sort of jobs that are available and that would be suitable. It is one of the elements necessary for decision making.

There is no point in talking in a vacuum about jobs. As a background to this kind of matching activity you need to have a broad picture of what jobs there are, and a realistic knowledge of what local and regional job opportunities are like. Your own sources of information about this are those agencies that have to collect such information themselves. Local-authority planning departments frequently have employment market reports and surveys. Local employment offices collect monthly statistics on vacancies, unemployment numbers, travel and work patterns to send to the Department of Employment. This information can be adapted into a form suitable for use with students.

These are the kinds of questions you will need to look at with students:

- who are the main local employers?
- what is the range of small/medium/large firms?
- what jobs do people I know have?
- how did they get them?
- what jobs are open to me if I travel/work locally?
- what is the future of work locally?
- what kind of things do I want from work?
- what training/courses are available?
- what kinds of work are available apart from being employed full-time?

Local employment information
- Students can consider employment information by reproducing it in various forms:
    - ★   factual reports
    - ★   graphical forms, e.g. maps, charts and diagrams
    - ★   3-dimensional models of the locality
- This last suggestion could expand into an environmental project, looking at possible future developments and at desirable local-authority policy directions.

Having established what sort of job market they are in, your students then have to identify a possible niche for themselves.

Job matching

Matching up a picture of the students' skills, abilities and relevant personal characteristics to the demands of different jobs has become a standard part of many careers education programmes. It is also the basis for the official way in which careers officers and careers teachers match up students and opportunities. It has been criticized for being a bureaucratic answer to a problem that is too complex to be solved in this way. (See Watts, 1981.) The limitations of the method are these:

- your students may be well aware that they lack the practical experience that would have tested the abilities they claim to have
- they may have pressing short-term reasons for wanting a job that are not recognized in this kind of activity (e.g. wanting to get out of school and earn money)
- their reasons for wanting work may seem too nebulous to be pinned down in a list: perhaps in a general way they would just rather be in an adult environment than at school or college
- the experiences of their friends and families may also convince them that this is not the way people they know got *their* jobs: they may have a clear intention of working in the kind of job that is not part of the formal economy and therefore never gets into the career officer's files
- they may feel so sure that getting a job will be hard or nearly impossible that they see no point in assuming that such a thing will happen, even for the purposes of a classroom activity

Of course it would be a mistake for you to present job-matching activities as a simple process with parts which will click into place like those of a well-oiled machine, producing a job opportunity like a slot-machine obligingly dispensing gum. There are still important reasons, however, why work needs to be discussed from the point of view of the choices to be made.

- Even if students do face unemployment directly after the course, at some point in the future they are likely to find work.
- Even students who become unemployed will have to make choices between different ways of spending their time (Chapter 13 discusses these in detail).
- Working-class students are not so locked in by their opportunity structure that they have no chance to use some discrimination of their own: unskilled jobs may have little intrinsic interest or status, but they can vary a great deal as far as job tasks, health risks or physical surroundings are concerned.
- Not having qualifications at the end of the fifth year does not mean that there is no possibility of finding some kind of training or continuing-education course.
- Something useful has to be made of each student's work-experience placement. The success or failure of this period as one in which useful learning can happen should not be allowed to rest on the likelihood of the student getting a job immediately after the end of it.
- Students need some kind of criteria by which to choose a YTS or training course. Even if their main motivation for being drawn into a scheme is to get the training allowance they should be clear about which alternative might suit them best.
- There is plenty of evidence that girls' ideas of possible jobs are more limited in scope than boys'. Your aim should be to extend their list of options.

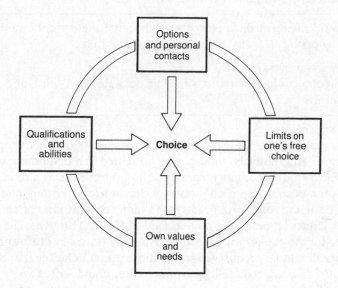

Figure 12.1   Decision-making about jobs

Making choices
The elements of decision-making about jobs are shown in Figure 12.1. The diagram is not arranged as a linear sequence because different people will start in different places, and will give different weightings to these elements.

Picking a job
● How do students see the process of picking an ideal job?
  ★ Ask groups to make a simple flowchart diagram of how they made other choices – boyfriend/girlfriend, their most expensive purchase, sport, etc.
  ★ Pool ideas and discuss them.
  ★ Extract common elements and write them on a board or OHP. Do your students accept this model? Agree on a form that can be used to find out more about how decisions are made. (Groups can come up with different designs, from which the best can be chosen.)
  ★ Test this design by asking students to interview people they know to see how they got their jobs, chose where they live, chose who they live with, etc. (Pairs can follow up one important choice each.)
The results of these interviews may produce different explanations. As long as each student ends up with some picture of the process that they feel

accurately reflects what they have found out, and that they feel they could use, these differences will not really matter.

We have been looking at short-term choices because these are the students' most pressing problem. Other points are worth making:

- no choice is necessarily final
- different choices have variations in their possible short- and long-term implications

The results of choices
- Students can explore these by compiling biographies of older people they know. Alternatively, these can be presented in a diagrammatic form. Each student (or pair) represents the subject's life as a road drawn on a poster. Important events or decisions are written in at points along the road, with roadsigns to indicate what kind of choice it was. (A ladder is sometimes used instead of a road.) Students can 'tell' the life-story to the rest of the group, using the poster as illustration.
- Students should be encouraged to put those present choices that they make into an imagined life-long context. They could write two autobiographies for themselves, showing how different choices might lead to different futures.
    ★   In pairs, they could interview each other briefly about what they intend to do after the course; have a short period to flesh out the details, then read out a scenario for their partner's future.

A close look at the options has become more important as the choices become more complex since the introduction of unemployment measures.

Youth Training Scheme
Discussion points range from the pragmatic . . .

- Is it better (or possible) to take a course that may offer a qualification, or to have the MSC allowance during, and a reference after, a period of work experience?
- How can students assess the possible value of a work-experience placement before they start?
- Courses and schemes have a bewildering (and often remarkably uninformative) range of titles: what do these mean?
- Does taking a YTS course jeopardize one's chances of getting on to a training course later?

. . . to the more controversial.

- YTS trainees are at work but not in employment. Without contracts of employment their rights as workers are severely curtailed. (Find out what these limits are.)

● What are students' views about the political purposes and justifications behind YTS?

● What are the students' opinions and values about being a YTS trainee? (This could be done by sentence completion: '3 good/bad things I've heard about YTS are . . .'; or 'If I said I wanted to go on a YTS scheme my parents/friends would think . . .'.) Students can design a questionnaire of their own to survey opinions in their group or college. Those interviewed should include trainees.

Job families

One new element in the design of YTS and the vocational-preparation area is the concept of job families, and the idea that there are certain common skills that distinguish the jobs in each family. How far-reaching or long-lasting the influence of this training concept will be remains to be seen.

Official rhetoric about YTS and the entry into work makes much of the fact that the ideas of job families and 'transferable skills' could revolutionize the content of training courses. This is seen as the answer to the problem of preparing a workforce to cope with rapid and unpredictable technological and labour-market changes. At present it seems that employers still need to be convinced that these more general skills are more useful than specific skills, which is hardly surprising.

The question of the transfer of knowledge or abilities from the context in which they were learnt to a different context is extremely complicated. It seems unlikely that training will have so quickly solved such a long-standing problem. Certainly in principle it provides an answer to the key question of what it is useful to train students to do when you cannot predict what jobs they will eventually have. It is also the foundation of the vocational-preparation concept, which is based on the principle that a broad-based general training is the best foundation for future occupational choice.

Connected with the idea that some job skills are generalizable is the new way that the MSC uses to classify jobs. All careers-education programmes have had to operate with some kind of occupational classification system. This varies from the simple ('practical, paper, people') to the complex ('practical, investigative, artistic, social, enterprising, clerical'). The new system groups jobs into eleven 'families'. A family comprises those jobs demanding the same generalized skills. These categories cannot be made to include all the jobs that there are, nor are they discrete – some jobs straddle different categories. If the vocational-preparation field develops as intended then this classification system should correspond to the content of courses and schemes, and with the selection of vocational sampling options or work-experience placements.

Certainly students need some way of classifying jobs, either to make a connection from their present abilities to possible jobs:

- what can I do at the moment?
- what jobs use these abilities?
- where are these jobs available?

or to interpret a picture of the employment market they are in:

- what jobs are there locally?
- what skills do they need?
- have I got these skills?
- can I acquire them?

For classroom purposes some kind of logical way of grouping jobs and training is necessary. You may want to use, select from or adapt the eleven families into a form students can use. The families are listed in Table 12.1. If you have to use the list as a way of describing your course content and organization for submission to a course-approval body, then it seems advisable to be consistent in the way you present your range of vocational sampling options or placements to students. However it would be misleading students to pretend that controversy over these does not exist.

Table 12.1   Occupational training families

Group number	Broad description of occupational band	(Tutor can enter local job opportunities/work-experience placements/in-college vocational options)
1	Administrative, clerical and office services	
2	Agriculture, horticulture, forestry and fisheries	
3	Craft and design	
4	Installation, maintenance and repair	
5	Technical and scientific	
6	Manufacturing and assembly	
7	Processing	
8	Food preparation and services	
9	Personal services and sales	
10	Community and health services	
11	Transport services	

It is important that students are not expected to use terms like 'transferable skills' without a chance to test out some of these arguments in discussion, particularly about the vocational skills they are being taught.

Describing work skills
- What are the problems when some some skills go out of date?
- Do different jobs share the same skills? (Students could work from the job-families list for this exercise)
- Think of three examples of jobs that you know something about, which are done by people you know, and which are jobs you might consider for yourself. What skills and abilities are needed to do them? (This needs to be as realistic as possible.)
- What is the connection between what you learn and do at school (keep the two distinct) and being prepared for work?
- What makes people good at their jobs? (See the *A–Z study*.) Pick someone you have seen at work. Is it a matter of personal qualities or job skills?

'Owning' one's skills
The phrase 'skill ownership' come from Hayes *et al*. It recognizes that many students coming off courses and YTS schemes are likely not to get jobs, or may find themselves redundant within a short time. The key problem this gives course designers, trainers and tutors is to find credibility for the vocational skills taught.

It may be that the idea of 'skill ownership' and the associated concept of transferability have caught on not so much for the effectiveness of the surface argument but because it meets the underlying need for courses to win credibility with students and trainees. One way of achieving this is to claim that what they are taught will be useful whether they get a job or not.

Certainly, deciding how much emphasis to place on preparing students to look for work is one of your first problems when planning activities. For many students this may be their main motive for taking the course.

This is the key controversial issue we mentioned earlier in this chapter. It is important that tutors do not over-use or misuse the vocational motivation of students when planning work-related activities.

Choosing your teaching objectives
Whatever your particular views, these will determine the selection of detailed objectives for achieving the overall aim of helping students decide what to do at the end of the course. Your views also influence important decisions about the designing and pacing of particular activities during the course.

For example, you may have planned all the activities directly connected with looking for work and applying for courses (interview practice, letter writing, form filling, etc.) for a late stage of the course, to coincide with the time when students do most of their job searching. This 'rehearsal' aspect of the classroom activities might succeed in motivating students, but you might become unhappy with other results:

- the timing is likely to create extra anxiety around the activities
- there is likely to be heightened competitiveness in the group
- there will be depression in those who have not got a job when others succeed
- the 'failures' fail to learn anything useful from the activities because they feel the only validation of the usefulness of these lies in their producing a successful application

If these things happen, it does not mean that the activity (practising formal interviews) is in itself worthless, but that the objective (to increase students' chances of getting a job) is not well-chosen; it cannot succeed because of factors outside your control.

The same activity could be chosen as a way of reaching other objectives:

- helping students to analyse job interviews as one example of formal interaction
- understanding different types of questioning
- appreciating the effects of non-verbal communication
- increasing their command of an unfamiliar linguistic register
- understanding the politics of such encounters to see who holds what kind of power, and how this can be dealt with

The ubiquitous job interview is a common – perhaps too common – part of vocational-preparation course, but this one activity can lead to very different kinds of learning. The selection of learning objectives is inextricably linked to your own viewpoint, or can be the result of the *absence* of any clearly defined set of beliefs.

Our view is that, given the predictions about structural youth unemployment, any tutor who over-emphasizes the importance of getting a job as the objective of a class activity is doing his or her students no favour. Such work-related activities as there are should always be linked with other non-work areas and topics.

Local employment survey
- Ask students to conduct interviews and a survey to discover:
  - ★   what jobs their friends or their families have got
  - ★   their own part-time experience
  - ★   how people they know got their jobs

  Summarize results to describe local employment patterns. Compile a list of all the different ways that they have discovered of getting a job.
- Give students a research project – to discover the local range of unemployment schemes and YTS options. Sources for this information

include careers offices, job centres, local press and radio, and direct contact with employers. They can produce information, short-listing the options.
- Review the information students have collected and fill gaps (i.e. add jobs or courses they've missed out).

Analysing jobs
- Group a range of jobs they have discovered into 'families' (Table 12.1 can be used). A small-group activity will produce most discussion as lists are likely to vary.
- Identify the demands of these jobs. Categories could include: common skills; general social skills; job-specific skills; training.
- Interview a variety of people (covering professional, skilled, semi-skilled, or unskilled) to discover how they judge their jobs.
- From these discuss findings and discover what criteria people use to evaluate jobs. (Ideas can be pooled on a blackboard or OHP, and then sorted into a list.)
- Such a list should cover those items listed below. Ask students to rank these in order of personal importance.
  - ★ any training provided
  - ★ qualifications or relevant experience needed
  - ★ wage levels
  - ★ physical conditions
  - ★ desirability or status
  - ★ fringe benefits
  - ★ alternative working patterns (e.g. can the job be done part-time or seasonally?)
  - ★ how are men and women distributed in these jobs – does there seem to be equal opportunity?
  - ★ ingredients of job-satisfaction – how do the jobs compare in this respect?
  - ★ effects of the job on social life, free time, and family life
  - ★ health risks

Working from these lists, ask the class to draw conclusions about the sort of needs that are met by work.

Satisfying these needs without work
- Students, working in groups, can suggest ways in which unemployed or leisure time can be used to satisfy some of these needs.
- Organize a discussion in which one speaker puts the case for paid work and another supports the idea of living without employment. (Assigned opinion is a suitable strategy here.)
  - ★ Invite outside speakers who will be willing to put these arguments, and to discuss their views with students. (Get the students to

organize this.) You may need to advertise in the local press/radio to find someone subsisting happily in the 'alternative' economy.
● In small groups, compare the list; and explain and justify choices.

Projects
● Build a map of local free and commercial leisure, sports and educational resources. Small groups in teams interview users of these to find out how satisfied they are with them, how often they use them.
● Collate the information students have found about the local area and its jobs, unemployment, YTS, leisure and training resources. This can be produced in various forms
  ★ a newspaper or broadsheet for the group's own students to read, or for distribution to other students
  ★ a display or programme mounted by the group (audio-tape plus photos) on the local area and what it has to offer
  ★ a full-scale programme (e.g. video-film) for showing to other groups
● Compile a list of sources of information about jobs:
  ★ official – from job centre or careers office
  ★ local – from press or radio
  ★ unofficial – from friends, relations or by direct contact with employers
  Brainstorm the advantages and disadvantages of each source.
● Divide into small groups, each taking one of the sources of information identified above. Analyse the method by which application would have to be made. The range should include phoning, letters, forms, personal contact, scanning job cards, and press advertisements.
● Carry out a group survey or pair interviews to produce a list of the group's spare-time activities. Pool the group's findings to produce a list of skills possessed by group members. Could these be useful in jobs? Or in alternatives to full-time jobs?
● Each student can apply the results of the previous activities and come up with a personal choice of:
  ★ 3 possible jobs
  ★ 2 YTS options
  ★ 2 activities he or she could take up if unemployed

Analysing interviews
● Identify elements of interviews (as an example of a formal encounter). This can be done by watching a video or a simulated interview. Students should have a checklist of the things they are to note:
  ★ dress
  ★ furniture arrangement

★ body language (eye contact, posture, facial expression)
★ formal spoken register
★ open and closed questions
● Compare the interview with similar and contrasting examples of formal social encounters:
★ being disciplined
★ asking someone for a date
★ addressing a meeting
★ selling a second-hand car
Role-play with small groups, taking one example each. In the debriefing discussion concentrate on: the varying degrees of formality; how these are marked; appropriate dress; language and responses. Ask students to choose the kind of encounter they find *least* easy and role-play it.

Follow-up work on language
● Students could pick up and explore any of these:
★ decoding reference sources of information (including small ads)
★ written styles
★ aspects of formal and informal written and spoken registers
(See Chapters 14 and 15.)

12.5 Part-time work

Recent evidence about part-time jobs can be found in *Child labour in London* (from the Low-Pay Unit). This reports the findings of a 1982 survey of 1000 London schoolchildren aged 11–16. It has plenty of information about the kind of jobs that were being done and there is clear evidence of exploitation in the form of long hours, low wages, and widespread illegal unemployment. While nearly a third of those surveyed did part-time work, four out of five of these were working illegally; and there was ample evidence that employers were using these children as a cheap substitute for adult labour. These sharp criticisms usefully balance the rather rosy view that any kind of experience at work is worth having. The study also gives a clear account of the legal position *vis-à-vis* part-time work for schoolchildren, including the ILEA bye-laws.

Despite the report's criticisms of the kind of work that school-students were doing, there is no denying the potential usefulness of such jobs. Most students take a part-time job as a source of money and would probably rate this as the most important thing they get out of it. Less tangible but equally useful gains worth discussing are the value of the practical experience as a contrast (and useful antidote) to the irrelevance of schoolwork, and the chance that such jobs offer of being accepted by older people.

Finding part-time work
● Carry out a brief class survey to establish the range of experience of

part-time work. (Since some of it may well be officially illegal, confidentiality must be promised.) This should include activities that do not earn a wage but that offer useful job skills, such as baby-sitting and bike repairs. Students, in groups, can compile lists of the advantages and disadvantages of working while at school or college. Compare these lists for discussion.

- Develop this into the compilation of a register of ideas for getting part-time work; listing contacts, describing how to set about it, noting the pitfalls to be avoided. This should also include a description of the legal restrictions. You will also have to give students (or help them to find out) the local education authority bye-laws restricting part-time work while at school. Students could produce some or all of this information as a broadsheet for class (or more general) distribution.

12.6   Work experience

If you are the tutor responsible for organizing sessions in which students talk about what happens on their placements, you may find it useful to structure these with some of the group activities suggested in section 2.2.

Students could compile the results of these reviewing activities into a diary, log-book, or folder. Many of the activities suggested here could form the basis for assignments for students taking City and Guilds Certificates in communications or numeracy.

It is obviously important that work experience should be carefully organized and monitored, since it can offer many ways of achieving some of the core objectives. In general terms your aim is likely to be to help students move up from the level of the particular and personal anecdotes that they bring, to develop a systematic view of what is going on in their workplace.

Teaching suggestions
School is a poor basis from which to make comparisons with work organizations. Students rarely perceive schools as workplaces or teaching as simply a job. The following suggestions aim to develop their perceptions of organizations and working conditions as a preparation for work experience.

Making use of work experience
- Provide students with a simple family-tree structure of an imaginary firm. Explain how this represents a hierarchical structure and levels of responsibility, wages, training, etc. Ask them to list all the jobs done in school. (They can do this in pairs or as a group activity.) This should include work done by all teaching and non-teaching staff. Now ask them to draw up a family tree of their school or college structure. You could provide them with a skeleton handout as a guide on which to enter the job names.

● Develop this idea by applying this framework to the workplace. Ask students to use the family tree they produced earlier as a model for making a plan of the organization of their work-experience placement. Keep this to department or section level to avoid making it too complicated. (If the family-tree style of diagram causes problems, a triangle with names plotted on it is acceptable and simpler.) Ask them to compare these and explain how the work tasks and decisions are organized. This could be done as a more formalized presentation exercise, to develop confidence.

● Introduce the idea of the formal and informal structure by giving some examples of how problems occur when a newcomer falls foul of one or the other, e.g.

★ a young newcomer tries to copy older workers' familiarity with superior and is ticked off for being 'cheeky'

★ a new worker gets into trouble with workmates for unwittingly exposing their 'shortcuts' to a superior who is forced to take action

★ a newcomer who wants to be liked by workmates agrees to do a favour such as covering up for an absence that then results in a serious mistake in the work process

★ a newcomer faces a dilemma about imitating behaviour she or he does not personally approve of, in order to be accepted

★ a newcomer is ticked off by a superior for a mistake and responds personally (having a row or walking out) rather than using the grievance procedure

All these ideas can be treated as case studies, role-plays or problem-solving exercises. Students on work experience will have examples of their own.

● To deal with the possibility of conflict between students' perceptions of work experience (as one way to a job offer) and your own view (that it gives a general introduction to working life), ask students to list the things they think they are gaining from work under three headings: vocational (i.e. using skills and contacts); social (making friends); personal (increasing confidence). How important are these different benefits to them?

12.7 Sample lesson plan

Length of session: $1\frac{1}{2}$ hours
Group size: 15.

Resources
● 15 copies of a skeleton worksheet for interviews and sentence completion.
● 15 copies of a checklist of competences based on the table on page 47 of *Common core – teaching and learning* (FEU, January 1984): you will need

to adapt the items and the language to a form that makes sense to your students.
- A prepared handout, listing jobs and job families in the local employment market.

Aim
- To identify transferable skills learnt on work experience.

Objectives
- To analyse work skills of placement.
- To distinguish between those that are particular to that job and those that could be useful after the placement has finished.
- To produce a self-profile that can be used in follow-up interviews.
- To identify the choice of jobs or unemployment activities.

Method

Phase 1: Pair interviews (20 minutes)
a   Students interview each other in pairs for 10 minutes each. Each has to find out exactly what the other *does* on work experience (i.e. not what they expected to do, or what the firm's brochure says they might do, or what they hope to do in the future.) The interview should cover all aspects of their day under four headings: solitary tasks; group tasks; equipment used; social times. (These could be used as column headings on the first skeleton worksheet.)

Phase 2: Self-description (10 minutes)
a   On the reverse of the worksheet is a list of sentence starters: 'I can now . . .' Students should now complete these sentences using the information provided in the interview.

Phase 3: Identifying skills currently practised (20 minutes)
a   Explain the difference between a general competence and a job-specific skill.
b   Give each student a copy of the handout that lists core competences. Ask each student to identify those of which they have experience, using information from their placements. (Circulate while this is going on, to help with any problems.)

Selecting new ones to learn (10 minutes)
c   Students also add these sentences to the phase-2 worksheets: 'I also want to learn how to . . .'; 'I would like to be better at . . .'

Phase 4: What next? (30 minutes)
a   Give out copies of the handout showing jobs and job families in the local

employment market. Ask each student to find three jobs they could apply for from the list – jobs for which they now have some relevant experience. *Either*

b Give out a list of training courses or YTS placements, or some college prospectuses. Ask each student to find a course or scheme they could do. *Or*

c Link these findings with ideas for unemployment activities.

Follow-up activities

● Individual interviews can explore these choices, give information about how to apply or find out more.

● Reproduce the information students have found out about their experience in another form, such as in part of an application letter. Students could use the phase-2 handout to write references for each other.

12.8   Resources list

Tutors' background reading

Sources recommended here are only a small selection from a field that is by now overcrowded with research reports and surveys. If you need a general picture of the spread of work that has been done, you might find it helpful to look at the comprehensive annotated bibliography published by the MSC: this has summaries of publications on the transition to work, vocational guidance and careers education, youth unemployment and special schemes. The summaries are not evaluative so their usefulness is limited, particularly since some titles are up to twenty years old with information and arguments that have been superseded by more recent work.

Given the current circumstances in which school-leavers are entering the labour market it is important for tutors to be knowledgeable about alternative patterns of work and the advantages and disadvantages of going it alone. Watts' paper on informal economies has an extensive discussion of the informal household, communal and black economies. This could provide you with plenty of useful ideas to follow up with your students.

If you are interested in looking at careers education in more detail and devising a comprehensive programme that combines interviewing and teaching activities, you could look at two influential books for teachers: *Careers guidance* (Hayes and Hopson) and *Exercises in personal and career development* (Hopson and Hough). Watts' earlier paper on the implications of unemployment for careers education puts forward an outline curriculum.

Further Education Unit 1980 *Developing social and life skills* (FEU)

Gleeson, D. (ed.) 1984 *Youth training and the search for work* (Routledge and Kegan Paul)

Hayes, C. *et. al.* 1983 *Training for skill ownership* (Institute of Manpower Studies, University of Sussex)

Hayes, J. and B. Hopson 1972 *Careers guidance* (Heinemann)

Hayes, J. and B. Hopson 1972 *The role of the school in vocational development* (Heinemann)

Hopson, B. and P. Hough 1973 *Exercises in personal and career development* (CRAC)

Lee, R. 1980 *Beyond coping: some approaches to social education* (FEU)

MacLennan, E. 1983 *Child labour in London* (Low Pay Unit)

Manpower Services Commission 1983 *Youth unemployment and special measures: annotated bibliography*. Research and Development Series No. 1, Jan. 1983 (MSC)

Watts, A.G. 1978 'The implications of school-leaver unemployment for careers education in schools' in *Journal of Curriculum Studies*, **10** No. 3, Sept. 1978

Watts, A.G. 1981 'Careers education and the informal economies' in *British Journal of Guidance and Counselling* **9**, No.1, Jan. 1981

Classroom materials

British Youth Council *Young Worker* (BYC: 57 Chalton Street, London NW1) A pack of discussion notes and posters on issues including unions, health and safety, the organization. Includes a 'tea-break' simulation of a work dispute.

Broadcasting Support Services *Numeracy resource guide* (BSS: 252 Western Avenue, London W3 6XJ) This contains reviews of materials: books, packs, games, and puzzles. Sections on social mathematics and adult materials include some relevant to tax and insurance.

Burgess, B. 1984 *Problem solving at work* (Framework Press, St. Leonard's House, St Leonardgate, Lancaster, LA1 1NN) Task sheets and tutor's notes. Six sections, on group decision-making, making sense of disorganized information, role-play, simulation and case studies for various vocational areas (horticulture, textiles, building and construction, electrical engineering, retail and community care).

CRAC *Work-experience projects* (CRAC) Classroom-based simulation material. Packs for jobs as transport clerk, receptionist, proof-reader, sales promoter, policeman, policewoman, bank cashier.

Hutson, H. 1984 *Learning from work experience* (Longman Resource Unit) Eleven student booklets with tutor's notes. Includes: 'Learning at work', 'Analysing your own job', 'Why choose that job?', 'People you meet at work', 'Problems at work'.

Inner London Education Authority *Making a living* (ILEA Learning Materials Service, Publishing Centre, Highbury Station Road, London N1 1SB) A pack of student workbooks, on finding vacancies, applications and interviews, unemployment and retraining, starting and keeping a job.

Jordan, J. 1982 *Workfacts for young workers* (Basic Skills Unit)

A practical information booklet for students on all aspects of starting work, also relevant for those undertaking work experience. Topics include contracts, part-time workers, pay, tax, health and safety, time-keeping, time off, equal chances, complaining.

Law, W. 1977 *Decide for yourself* (CRAC)

A student's workbook, plus worksheets and tutor's notes. Decision-making programme exploring values and choices in depth.

McGuire, J. and P. Priestley 1981 *Life after school* (Pergamon)

Lots of teaching suggestions for social education, student self-assessment and communications work. Contexts include: social interaction, job search, leisure, money, rights, and meeting the opposite sex.

Ridgway, B. 1982 *What are you going to do now?* (Edward Arnold)

This deals with the transition from school to work/college. Advice and activities for students, on: finding a job, the shop floor, unions, pay, conditions, unemployment, work, and social attitudes. Course advice is included (some now outdated).

Walker, D. 1984 *Just the Job* (Edward Arnold)

Three sections about the experience of work, including self-assessment, job assessment and applications. Useful for practical, written, discussion and research tasks. Could also serve as stimuli for imaginative drama or documentary work.

Williamson, H. 1981 *Chance would be a fine thing* (National Youth Bureau/MSC)

A series of brief case-studies of young people entering the labour market, and their experience on YOP.

13   Unemployment

13.1   Problems of discussing unemployment

Within the ABC list of core objectives, unemployment has a fairly minor place, subsumed under Aim 2. Into this objective is packed enough detail to fill a course on its own, were it to be properly dealt with. Indeed a detailed curriculum outline has existed for some time – see Watts (1978). It is almost as if the whole subject of unemployment is so embarrassing that all its aspects have been parcelled up and bundled into a corner in the hope that their implications can be minimized. The implications of treating the topic in depth with your students are, of course, potentially very threatening. There seems to be no way that a tutor can face the prospect of talking about unemployment comfortably.

Inform your students about the scale of the problem and you will disturb them and increase their sense of helplessness. Go on to outline possible future developments and they may feel justifiably apprehensive about their own futures (and so will you, of course). If you are working with students who have already been unemployed, then you are opening up a topic where their experience probably extends beyond yours. Inevitably you will hear about their pessimism, their discouragement, their unhappiness and their fears about going back on the dole. Given current figures about the chances of finding a job after YTS, what faces them at the end of the course is something that it will not be comfortable to talk about openly.

One thing is absolutely certain. Even if the word is never mentioned (and there are probably many classrooms where this is so) it will be at the back of everyone's mind, students' and tutor's alike. It is one of the keys to each student's motivation, and fundamental (in their eyes) to their whole reason for being in the classroom at all.

Both the relevant information and people's attitudes to the issue can play a major part in determining whether they are successful in learning any of the things that their tutors and supervisors are trying to teach them. These factors affect not only whether students learn while they are on the course, but whether any of that learning is valuable enough to be retained and used in other contexts after they have left the course.

Transfer of learning
One thing of definite value has already emerged from research into good practice on courses and YTS schemes. Courses seem to be considered useful

by students if they teach things that the students can make use of after they have left, and this applies whether they get a job or not. This is where the whole idea of transfer of learning becomes most relevant for supervisors and tutors of vocational skills. While this book is not intended primarily for them, the issue is worth expanding on a little here; it has relevance for social-education tutors, particularly those doing a social-and-life-skills input for a primarily vocational course. These are the people most likely to have to deal head on with the subject of unemployment.

Some sort of trainers' mystique seems to be collecting like an obscuring vapour around the term 'transferable skills'. It remains to be seen whether these will become the key to the design of industrial training courses in the next decades. That debate is not our concern here, though relevant references are included in the resources list (section 13.8).

We use the word 'transfer' to refer to the result that validates any educational activity: that what is learnt can be taken from its original context and related by the learner to new contexts, in such a way that it increases each individual's ability to understand and control something in the world for themselves.

Broadly speaking, a course that has been planned to take account of the fact that students might get a job or be unemployed uses the principle of transfer as follows. Vocational skills may be taught as part of the preparation for paid employment or work experience. Related communications and numeracy work (reading labels, writing orders, compiling stocklists, measuring, costing jobs, etc.) is used as back-up to ensure success in the vocational field and to boost students' levels of achievement generally.

But a scheme that does not look beyond this is not doing enough for its students. Some courses identify non-vocational uses for the same skills, often allowing students to use domestic versions of equipment alongside industrial ones. They may be allowed to take tools home, or bring do-it-yourself jobs in to be done in workshops. Self-employment possibilities may be explored, or ideas about using the skills in other forms of organization, such as co-operatives, for cash or barter to supplement the dole or supplementary benefit. These latter topics bring us back into the area that can involve the social-education tutor, for it is a fact that it most often falls to these tutors to make these connections for students, and to discuss unemployment as an issue in itself.

Unemployment within social education
In raising the issue of unemployment at the start of this chapter, we spelt out all the negative aspects of teaching of the topic. These have to be acknowledged by you as the tutor before you can begin to find positive answers to the questions: How can I deal adequately with these issues? What strategies are appropriate? What content is necessary?

Being aware of these negative aspects does not mean you need to emphasize them in your teaching. What this chapter is intended to do is to present positive ways of acknowledging the problem, and then helping students to find their own way of dealing with it. It is important to remember that although unemployment now faces two out of three school-leavers, the period out of work though it may be long is unlikely to last for the rest of their lives.

It is vital to find some positive approach to teaching about unemployment: all writers on the subject make clear that it is no temporary phenomenon. Patterns of working life, attitudes to work and expectations about it will have to change in order to adjust to the structural changes that are forecast for the labour market. These permanent changes include:

- greater demand for highly skilled people, hence greater emphasis on qualifications
- increased periods of unemployment for the unskilled, inexperienced, and unqualified, many of whom will find getting a job difficult in the first place

It is also important not to present these positive strategies as a glib or superficial answer to what is both an economic and a human problem far beyond the capacities of any tutor or any group of students to solve. However well planned, YTS schemes or courses do not create jobs (except for part-time staff!). A suggestion to students that they get 'on their bikes' and go and clean windows offers no substitute for what a fully-waged job might have given them.

But (to raise another political echo) there is no alternative. The limitations of the activities suggested here will be clear to both you and your students.

First we deal with the general context of unemployment as a social phenomenon: scale, geographical and ethnic variations, and discernible trends in the impact of technological changes on the labour market.

13.2   Trends in unemployment

The overall picture of unemployment is of course profoundly depressing. Between 1980 and 1985 there will be over 8 million school-leavers in EEC countries, of whom only 1 in 3 will find a job. One writer (Merritt, 1982) gives estimates which put unemployment in the mid-1980s at nearly 5 million in Britain; at 12–15 million in the EEC; and at 35 million in the industrialized countries of the OECD.

The birth-rate bulge of the 1960s exacerbated the figures in the early stages of this phenomenal increase, but it is no longer the major reason for the high figures. There will be 9 million more on the job market in the mid-1980s, though recession, technological changes and the decline of the manufacturing industry are destroying jobs faster than they can be created. Forecasts estimate Britain will suffer a job loss of some 16 per cent (i.e. 4 million jobs) by the end of the 1980s.

Britain is particularly badly hit when compared with other Western

European countries. There are greater numbers of long-term unemployed (defined as those with continuous registration of over 12 months) than in the 1930s, a larger proportion of our workforce is unemployed (the mid-1983 rate was 13.3 per cent, a total of 3.1 million), and the 'hidden unemployed' number over a million. This last figure contains one of the largest proportions in Europe of married women who do not register themselves as unemployed.

The problem of how to communicate this picture to students needs careful thought. The figures and statistics are intimidatingly large. If you deliver them strictly as information, on a handout or as exposition, the effect can be overwhelming.

Without any comparative measures, e.g. the size of the working population, they are meaningless. (In fact, the number of men in the labour force has remained at around 16 million throughout the last 20 years.) It is easy enough to abstract them from sources yourself, and present the same information in a less intimidating form, such as a quiz. Let us stress that this is not to belittle the importance of the figures; but as students are likely to try and interpret the phenomenon at a personal level, you want to avoid a reaction such as 'What chance have I got then?' before you can go on to consider the implications in detail.

The future of work
Writers on the subject (see the sources recommended in the resources list, section 13.8) seem to agree what the ingredients of these high levels of unemployment are, but there is no agreement about how much weight is to be attached to each of them, or what solutions are best attempted in order to help employment pick up again.

Different models of the economy produce different solutions, and though competing theories may rest on different arguments, in one respect there is agreement. Something like 5 million unemployed in the mid-1980s seems inevitable, and job losses in many industries and occupations are an irreversible trend. Many people are going to have to get used to the idea of living without paid employment for periods in their lives. These people include some of your students. In order to adapt to this fact the structure of working life would have to change radically. By 2000 everyone would need, for example, to be working a three-day week. Some writers are pessimistic about the likelihood of this, partly because of employers' reluctance to employ more labour (UK overtime levels are the highest in Europe), and partly because of the difficulty of undermining the values of a consumer society in which most people measure their satisfactions (and confirm their sense of identity) by the goods and services on which they spend their wages.

The three-day week alone would not solve the problem. Other forms of leave have been mooted: sabbaticals, built-in leave for training and education, earlier retirement for both sexes. More jobs would be created by new occupations in an expanded public sector, more social, care and health workers with increased facilities, and enlarged service and leisure industries.

Just as there is disagreement over what causes the problem, so there is disagreement over how to pay for these new working patterns and jobs. Such public expenditure has to be balanced against that which is already taken up in supporting an unemployed workforce: an MSC estimate for 1981 allowed £4380 each year for each unemployed worker (cost of dole, estimated by adding the benefits and lost tax revenue) multiplied to a national total of £12.45 billion.

Students can be asked to suggest changes in working patterns that *they* regard as desirable, and to evaluate the pros and cons of the alternatives. (See the 'Teaching suggestions' on page 232.)

The effect on jobs of technological change
Recession and birth-rate bulges apart, changing technology seems likely to be the major cause of job loss. Something like 62 per cent of all occupations will be at risk. This may be because new products (such as digital watches and word processors) supersede old ones, or because work processes are changed. A single micro can replace hundreds of circuitry components in a manufacturing process, and can control robots that replace human labour. Entirely new information systems (like electronic mail) can produce the phenomenon of the paperless office.

In a discussion of the impact of technology in *The collapse of work*, the writers (Jenkins and Sherman, 1979) envisage the people-less supermarket. Shelf-stacking and carrying would be performed by robots, stores and ordering facilities would be centralized and computerized, costing and payment handled by computerized checkouts. Not even the customers would have to be there – they would choose their goods from a stocklist picked up on their television screen, and pay by telephone with a credit card.

Changing work patterns
● There are plenty of aspects that can be considered by students in discussion or problem-solving tasks.
   ★ How many new products can they think of that did not exist 5 or 10 years ago?
   ★ What new products and services might be developed?
   ★ What new shops or services exist in their area that were not there 5 or 10 years ago?
   ★ As a result of these changes, what new jobs are there?
   ★ What jobs would disappear? (The supermarket example could be used as a way into this issue – see the sample lesson plan, section 13.7).
   ★ What kinds of skills or training will be needed?
   ★ What might it be like to live in the same area in 20 years' time? (This could be the stimulus for imaginative writing or drama.)

- Consider the social effects of these developments. What would it be like:
  - ★ to work in a paperless office,
  - ★ to shop by phone,
  - ★ to be diagnosed by a computer instead of by a human doctor?

The workers who disappear

Jobs that require a great deal of personal judgement will be least affected. Jobs in offices, banks and the finance sector are already changing. The paperless office does not need filing clerks or copy typists but will still need a personal assistant. The new information systems are eliminating jobs dealing with routine tasks at the semi-skilled level. In manufacturing all kinds of unskilled manual jobs are at risk where micros can replace components or human labour and simplify production processes. That much is bad news for unskilled workers (and job-seekers). On the other hand, projections also show that new technology will de-skill a great many jobs and reduce demand for semi-skilled labour.

The car with a built-in computer to diagnose faults will not need routine servicing by mechanics. Looking after that microcomputer requires a lower level of skill than a motor mechanic has, though designing the system and producing the software requires greater skill.

This aspect of the new technology seems to indicate that new occupations at the unskilled level will still be there. It is the semi-skilled level that disappears, leaving at the top a few highly skilled people to design the systems and programme them.

The sources recommended in the resources list (section 13.8) contain plenty of detailed examples that can be used as case studies to help students assess job losses in greater detail. Jenkins and Sherman use digital-watch production as one instance. The issue can then be localized by students working from a description of their local job market, trying to predict job changes in their area.

Who is hardest hit by unemployment?

The most important thing to stress alongside the national statistics and generalized statements about changes in working patterns is the highly localized nature of unemployment. Regions such as Northern Ireland and the North of England (one-and-a-third times the national average level) were hit first and hardest, the West Midlands suffering slightly later, the South-East feeling the effects latest of all – predictions estimate that London will not feel the worst effects until the end of the 1980s.

Regional unemployment
- Consider the figures given in Table 13.1.
  - ★ Why do students think there are such differences?

★ Ask students to turn the list of figures into a map showing the distribution of unemployment nationally.
★ What is the picture like in their local region?
★ Ask students to produce a local map.

Within the regions towns are differently affected. In the West Midlands, notably Birmingham, one manufacturing job in three has disappeared since 1979. In inner-city areas such as Liverpool, unemployment among the under-18s is nearly 100 per cent. In the new high-tech towns like Cambridge and Newbury, the picture is reversed: in 1982 Newbury had only 60 school-leavers out of 600 who were still without jobs.

Young people and unemployment
Young people are the worst-hit section of the population, being inexperienced and less skilled than the more productive older workers, and so more likely to be made redundant in many cases. In April 1981 an unskilled worker was six times as likely to be unemployed as a professional worker. Unskilled men are worse hit by unemployment than unskilled women.

Between 1982 and 1983 there was an increase of over 20 000 in the number of unemployed school-leavers, bringing the total to 126 000. The government publication *Social Trends* (1984) includes a special chapter on the unemployed, (Chapter 13). Many of the statistics provided can be used as the basis for numeracy or communications work, particularly where you want students to appreciate the differences in impact that information can have if presented

Table 13.1   Average regional rates of unemployment (1982)

Region	%
UK as a whole	12.2
Northern Ireland	19.4
Scotland	14.2
Wales	15.6
England	11.6
South-East	8.7
North-West	14.7
West Midlands	14.9
South-West	10.8
East Anglia	9.9
East Midlands	11.0
Yorkshire and Humberside	13.4
North	16.5

(Figures taken from Social Trends 1984, HMSO)

graphically. Figures about the unemployed, grouped by age group, can be presented in a table (see Table 13.2) which students can use as the basis for the following activities:

Unemployment among young people
- Consider the totals displayed in Table 13.2.
    - ★ Why do younger age groups form a higher proportion of the unemployed than of the employed?
    - ★ Why do young women form such a large proportion of unemployed women?
    - ★ Why do you think there were more boys than girls in YOP when the girls seem worse affected by unemployment?

Table 13.2 (Reproduced from *Social Trends* 14, 1984, Chapter 13)

Unemployed claimants: by sex, age, and duration, April 1983

United Kingdom   Percentages

	Duration of unemployment (weeks)						Total
	Up to 2	Over 2, up to 8	Over 8, up to 26	Over 26, up to 52	Over 52, up to 104	Over 104	
Males aged:							
16–19	*11.1*	*14.3*	*27.8*	*27.7*	*15.7*	*3.4*	*100.0*
20–24	*4.6*	*11.8*	*24.2*	*23.1*	*20.1*	*16.2*	*100.0*
25–34	*4.4*	*10.9*	*22.9*	*20.4*	*21.0*	*20.3*	*100.0*
35–49	*4.3*	*10.2*	*21.6*	*19.1*	*20.9*	*23.9*	*100.0*
50–59	*4.0*	*8.0*	*18.9*	*19.3*	*22.2*	*27.6*	*100.0*
60 or over	*3.1*	*6.6*	*16.9*	*20.6*	*26.9*	*25.8*	*100.0*
All males aged 16 or over	*5.2*	*10.5*	*22.4*	*21.5*	*20.8*	*19.5*	*100.0*
Females aged:							
16–19	*11.9*	*14.8*	*29.9*	*28.0*	*13.0*	*2.6*	*100.0*
20–24	*6.0*	*14.3*	*29.6*	*25.9*	*14.4*	*9.8*	*100.0*
25–34	*6.8*	*15.3*	*31.3*	*27.0*	*13.0*	*6.6*	*100.0*
35–49	*5.8*	*14.2*	*26.9*	*23.8*	*17.3*	*11.9*	*100.0*
50 or over	*3.5*	*8.1*	*18.6*	*21.1*	*22.7*	*25.9*	*100.0*
All females aged 16 or over	*7.4*	*13.9*	*28.3*	*25.8*	*15.2*	*9.5*	*100.0*

Source: Employment Gazette, Department of Employment

Compiling charts and diagrams
● Use this content to practise interpreting graphical and statistical information.
   ★ Using OHP or worksheets, demonstrate the construction of barcharts or histograms using the same information.
   ★ Ask students to express the same information in writing.
   ★ Compare the different presentations and decide which is the most effective and accessible method.

Currently most 16-year-old school-leavers join the dole or YTS; and many 'graduate' into unemployment from YTS, or into unskilled work and then into unemployment. Long-term unemployment is growing faster for the under 25s than any other group.

Ethnic variations in unemployment
A 1982 survey by the Commission for Racial Equality confirmed that black school-leavers of Afro-Caribbean origin were worse hit than whites in the same areas, and that Asian school-leavers also experience discrimination in their search for work. In absolute statistical terms there is not a significant difference between female unemployment in ethnic-minority groups and that in the indigenous white population, but as far as discriminatory practices are concerned, school-leavers obviously experience the effects of prejudice. Overall, considered as a proportion of economically active men aged between 16 and 64, men in the two major ethnic minority groups (West Indian; Indian, Pakistani or Bangladeshi) are nearly twice as likely to be unemployed as men of white ethnic origin.

Ethnic unemployment
● Female differences in unemployment between ethnic groups are not so marked. What are the reasons behind this?
● What do students believe are the reasons for the differences in the unemployment rates?
● Ask students to find out what their rights are if they believe they have been discriminated against.

Women and unemployment
Of the several groups who suffer disproportionately, women form the largest, as already stated. Britain has the highest percentage in Europe of female 'discouraged' unemployed who do not bother to register. Primarily this is because they do not have a record of paying sufficient contributions to earn them benefit. There is also evidence – see the Youthaid background paper by Hirsch, 1983 – that some benefit offices categorize married women with

children as 'not available' for work (and therefore not entitled to benefit) in any case. This high proportion is particularly worrying when considered alongside another estimate – that by the mid-1980s nearly half the working women in the EEC will be breadwinners, either because their partners are unemployed or because they are bringing up children on their own. It seems that the realities of family life in the coming years will mean that more women will need to hold onto jobs – current public opinion, as reflected in the media, seems to be against this. The welfare state system of benefits is itself based on an outdated concept of the family, which assumes that the wife is supported by a working husband.

The implications of this for girls leaving school are alarming. As the participation rate for women in the labour force has been growing in recent years, girls' expectations at sixteen of getting a job and spending at least some years at work are positive. Those interviewed for the MSC studies of unemployment in Cornwall and Tyneside (1980) were more optimistic than boys of the same age. However, the girls find it harder than boys to get work and consequently become more pessimistic and therefore more likely to drop out of the labour market altogether and give up the search for work. Many see marriage as a solution to the question of what to do with their lives. The facts about the future for female breadwinners show how dangerous such lowering of expectations and making of short-term choices with long-term implications can be.

13.3   Predictions of social change

Putting all the special 'at risk' groups together and looking at the resulting picture, many writers make gloomy predictions about the social implications of these trends. Girls and women may be subject to social pressures that direct them back into the home, losing all the advantages gained by the changes in attitudes to women in recent years.

Changes in the skill demands of jobs may produce a 'knowledge class' and a 'serf class' that greatly exacerbates class and social divisions. Some writers envisage an underclass of under-28-year-olds who have never worked or who have only had brief periods of unskilled work. Some scenarios have them passively adjusting to this situation, dropping out of the search for work for large parts of their lives but retaining the values of a consumer society and therefore suffering the financial and psychological deprivations felt by 'failures'. Alternatively, and more positively, they are pictured subsisting successfully in the informal or black economy and losing their commitment and allegiance to traditional social and economic work values.

Either way, potential for social change or social unrest seems a possibility – another interesting survey finding is that among the young the unemployed show more interest in politics than those in work, either because they see official political channels as a possible route for change or because they see party politics as ineffective and so voice support for the idea of more direct, even violent action to promote social change.

The classic catch question for many 16-year-old job seekers seems now to be 'Do you want a job?' rather in the way that 'Have you stopped beating your wife?' used to be asked of men. Say 'Yes' and great numbers are doomed to disappointment. Answer 'No, I shan't bother' and be condemned to being one of the 'sub-employed'. Not surprisingly one writer (Merritt, 1982) calls these the 'impotent generation'. No wonder that writers anxious to find some kind of positive response to these implications say that the 'collapse of work' has to be redefined as the 'ascent to leisure'.

It is important to remember that these kinds of predictions are fictional. Extrapolating from survey findings to produce a social trend is a risky business. However, such ideas are useful starting points from which to encourage your students to consider their own reactions to the figures about youth unemployment and the opinions of some of their contemporaries.

Future prospects
- Imagine your life in 10 or 20 years' time. What kind of life-style do you want?
  - ★ Ask students to write descriptions, or to video- or audio-tape role-plays.
- How would not having a proper job affect these ambitions, financially and personally?
  - ★ Review the previous descriptions. What would you not be able to do?
- What ideas about the future do you think young people of your age should have?
  - ★ Design a questionnaire to help students to find out their fellow students' views.
- What should they do about these prospects? Start protesting? Drop out? Live for the present?
  - ★ Organize a discussion in which students have to present arguments for these alternatives.
- What would be effective ways to act to change things?
- Compare your life chances with those of your parents at the same age. Do your parents have a realistic understanding of what your lives will be like?

This section concludes our description of those aspects that comprise the general picture of unemployment. Your main aim in introducing students to this picture is to give them up-to-date information and a chance to discover how they stand in relation to this overall view.

Your responsibility does not end there, however. Your students also need answers to the question, 'What do I do about it?' The sections that follow narrow down the focus to the personal and practical level.

13.4   The personal effect of unemployment

Being without work still carries a social stimga. One researcher in a region of high unemployment found it difficult to make contact with the network of unemployed men in the area in order to interview them, even though they existed in hundreds. It was as though they lived on the other side of a curtain, isolated from 'normal' society.

The word 'schizophrenia' is used by different writers to describe both the gap and the conflict that exist between those whose lives and opinions are safely defined by a job and those who are excluded from this kind of ready-made solution.

Poverty

The first and most obvious result of joblessness is lack of money. The income gap between wage-earners and the unemployed is wider now than it was in the 1930s, so in relative terms the unemployed are worse off. In November 1982 there were 7 million on the officially defined poverty line or supplementary-benefit level, including 1.7 million unemployed and their dependents.

Ill health

There are obvious links between lack of income and poor physical and mental health. There may not be the absolute malnutrition of the 1930s, but this has been succeeded by high levels of stress and physical illness. This affects both the unemployed and their families. One depressing finding (reported by Hirsch, 1983) is that YTS trainees who showed an improvement in their general mental state while on the course (measured by a questionnaire assessing self-confidence, ability to concentrate, etc.) lost this advantage after they had left the course and rejoined the dole. In other words the experience had not changed their fundamental attitude to work. Even young people in routine jobs said that the best thing about the jobs was 'just having a job at all'. So even a job with low wages and little intrinsic interest is felt to have some kind of value.

A 1979 survey asked people to imagine they had a private income sufficient to live on. Would they still want to work? Three-quarters of these interviewed said they would, and the proportion was higher amongst teenagers.

The persistence of the work ethic

Obviously it is difficult to alter basic attitudes to paid employment. Young people are surrounded by influences that act to prevent them doing this easily, even though this may seem the most rational response to the difficulties of their situation. Work has increased in its significance as a marker on the route to adulthood during the same period that it has become less available. A disturbing finding in the *Into work* study (MSC, 1980) was that many parents of the young unemployed held unsupportive attitudes towards their children's lack of jobs, despite living in the North-East where mass unemployment had been a fact of life for a long time. Evidently parents too find it difficult to move from a position in which getting a job is seen as the most important thing about growing up. This cannot be unconnected with their own dismay at finding their children financially dependent on them for longer, and the accompanying personal tension when the children have to remain dependent at home for longer than either party would like.

As a means of opening up discussion on these issues with students, direct questioning may seem far too intrusive – indirect approaches such as role-play (see the teaching suggestions on page 233) may stimulate discussion about the same issues.

Phases of unemployment

The stages of unemployment have been identified (Figure 13.1). Failure to find a positive solution at Stage 2 means that a person may go straight from

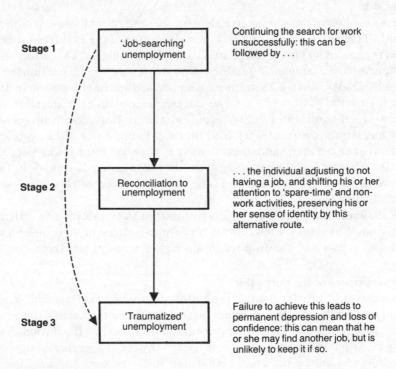

Figure 13.1   Stages of unemployment

Stage 1 to Stage 3. Such a diagrammatic representation is very impersonal: for an illustration of the process that would have more impact on students you will probably want to select from first-hand accounts. Marsden's *Workless* (1982) and Youthaid's *A dossier of despair* (1981) have descriptions of adults' experiences; White and Brockington's *Tales out of school* (1983) contains school-leavers' accounts.

Checklist – the problems of being unemployed

- lack of money
- boredom resulting from
  - ★ unstructured time
  - ★ limited social life
- loneliness
- likelihood of family conflict
- encountering the disapproval of others
- having to find alternatives to paid employment as one's primary goal

These extra problems are created by long-term unemployment:

- skills one has acquired become rusty or go out of date
- one may lose contact with sources of information about local job opportunities and developments
- personal values change or confidence is so eroded that fitting into the work routine becomes more difficult: this reduces the chances of keeping any job that might be found
- the social network of contacts may change permanently so that one becomes part of a sub-society: this may make it difficult to rejoin the more familiar social network of the employed
- long-term goals may become difficult or impossible to achieve

When discussing with students the problems caused by unemployment the above checklist can be used as a prompt. You may prefer to ask students to identify the problems for themselves. You will then have a more accurate idea of how they perceive the difficulties. A closer focus on the issues can be reached by adding the question 'What are the worst things about being 16 (or 17, or 18) and out of work?'

It is also very important to give those who may already have been unemployed a space in which to talk about their experiences. Small task-group exercises allow them to do this but in a more structured and protected situation than if they were asked to admit to the problems in front of the whole group.

13.5   Selecting the right teaching approach

Obviously the level of detail appropriate for your students will vary according to their age and the course they are following. In all cases it is essential that you are familiar with local unemployment figures and trends. The main divisions are discussed below.

Pre-16 year olds
This includes those on a pre-vocational course who have not yet left school. A great deal of the topics in this chapter are general background information for such students. They will need to know why they may be in one or more of the high-risk groups. It will be useful to raise the ideas in the problems checklist (page 223) and the positive strategies section (13.6) to establish the point that individual answers can be found; but you will probably not want to go further at this stage. Information about local developments may be vital for choices that they have to make in the fifth year.

16+ students on a vocational FE course or YTS
These students need more detail about some of the individual strategies. You will probably want to give equal weight to these and to the job-search and further training topics in Chapter 12 (unless local conditions invalidate these proportions). You will want them to compile a folder in which they can keep addresses, suggestions and so on, to refer to later. Perhaps more important, though more difficult to achieve, is an actual named person to contact after they have left. Local support groups for the unemployed may already exist in your area.

Students who have already been unemployed
With these students the most important place to begin will be with their own recent history. Here the counselling aspect becomes most important (see Appendix 2). How they feel about their own experiences on the dole will colour their reception of anything you may have to say. It will be essential to *begin* with the problems checklist to create such a space, and then go on to individual strategies as soon as you feel the air has been cleared sufficiently. All the topics that follow then constitute an agenda for a student's plan of action. Information needs to be detailed, practical and stored in a permanent form (such as a plastic folder).

13.6   Coping with the effects of unemployment

The best place to start looking for solutions to some of the difficulties is to begin by asking students to pool their own ideas.

Problems of unemployment
- Give small groups or pairs one of the problems from the checklist and ask them to brainstorm solutions.
- Pool these and discuss generally.
- Collect the group's preferred ideas and compile an agenda of tasks

to be done, information to find out, etc.
- Allot tasks to individuals or pairs to follow up in subsequent sessions.
- Later sessions can be led by the working group or pair who can tell the others what they've found out or give them tasks to do.

Where sessions are to be run by students it is advisable to meet them briefly before the class to check if special materials or resources will be needed, and to see if what they want fellow students to do will fit into the time available.

Job-searching strategies

The previous chapter dealt with job-searching ideas and techniques in detail. If you are dealing with students who have already been unemployed, it is worth looking again at their job-search techniques partly to check that they have identified all the sources of information adequately, and partly to spend time rebuilding confidence that their interview techniques are good enough. Nothing erodes the ability to present a confident self-image more quickly than repeated rejection. Note that we are not talking only (or even principally) about job interviews here. The opportunity should be created to work on self-presentation skills for many of the purposes mentioned below – e.g. selling your own product or service, or running a management committee for a co-operative.

Money

Two areas are worth looking at here. Firstly, how would your students manage on the limited income provided by the dole (or by supplementary benefit if they are not eligible for unemployment benefit)? This links with the ideas for budgeting exercises in section 10.5.

Money and the unemployed
- Ask students to compare existing spending patterns with those they might have on the dole.
- What would be the effects on their home life?
- On their social life?
- Ask them to pool ideas about ways of earning the limited amount (currently £4) permissible while still claiming benefit.
- Ask them to think of barter arrangements that would help their budgets (e.g. doing repairs for someone in return for meals).

Claiming benefits is in itself a complex, time-consuming and often emotionally fraught business. There are materials that offer help with this (see the resources list, section 13.8).
   Your role here is basically:
- To make sure your students have the right information about
   ★ which offices to go to

    ★   which forms to ask for
    ★   where to go to get independent help and advice about problems
        (i.e. the address of the local Citizens' Advice Bureau, Law Centre
        or Claimants' Organization).
● to give students help and practice with relevant communication
   aspects, such as filling in the forms accurately and – a much more
   complex matter – coping with encounters with officials.

Training and courses

The previous chapter looked at ways of helping students choose training courses in more detail. It is worth looking at some particular aspects in relation to unemployment. Lack of opportunity to practise some skills can mean that these disappear. If your students are currently acquiring vocational skills then it will be helpful to get them to think of ways in which they could use them if they do not get a full-time job, either by advertising locally to work at home, or by offering their services to voluntary or community organizations for some hours each week, or by taking evening or day-time courses to keep up existing skills and possibly learn new ones. It will be important to link students' ideas about choices they may make with the likely pattern of local employment developments.

The need to structure one's time

'Structured' time is that which is filled with regular activity of significance both to the doer and to others whose opinions are important to him or her. The activity may be satisfying in itself or paid for in wages that can be exchanged for satisfying goods or leisure activities. Paid work has come to provide the most convenient answer to the problem of filling time. Financial hardship apart, it is the lack of structure and of recognition that goes with joblessness that causes the most physchological damage. This is compounded by the additional problem of social isolation.

    Solutions must present worthwhile or useful activity plus company (with cash or material benefits as a useful spin-off).

Making a personal timetable

The most important determinant of how much practical work you do with students on the question of how to occupy 'unemployed' time, and how much detail you need to go into, is of course the students' current situation and immediate expectations. You could approach the problems directly by compiling a personal timetable of options for each student. For tutors working with those who are already unemployed or who expect shortly to become unemployed this is obviously necessary. If you are raising the topic for the first time or introducing it as a possibility at some time in the future (for example with pre-16-year-olds, or with those on full-time courses) then a more general approach is possible. It would still probably be useful to plan activities that result in personal lists of activities which students can keep for future reference.

Possible activities for students
● Questions to use as starting-points include:
★ What spare-time activities do you have now that you want to continue?
★ Are there new ones you would like to take up?
★ What new skills would you need to learn?
★ What skills do you have that you could use to earn some money?
★ What part-time work do you do now or know of?
★ What opportunities for voluntary work are there in your area?

The point of these questions is to generate a list of activities that they can then choose from. If you know your students and the locality well enough, you could produce a handout that lists all the activities you think they might possibly consider. The specialized unemployment materials in the resources list (section 13.8) also provide ideas. These can then be evaluated by students working individually or in pairs through a checklist judging each item in the way shown in Table 13.3.

The table could be completed as an individual task, though there may be more benefit in asking students to fill it in in pairs, as discussion about the answers may uncover useful points to bring up later.

Evaluating alternatives to work
● When students have completed the table, they can address general issues:
★ Can they still clearly distinguish between 'work' and 'leisure' activities?
★ List all their leisure activities on a board or OHP or chart. Can these be done as jobs?
★ Would this spoil the students' enjoyment of them?
★ What training opportunities does the group as a whole want to find out about?
★ Pool all the money-making suggestions to compile a group register of ideas.
★ What information do they need to have about self-employment, organizing a co-operative, etc.?

There is obviously a long way to go from discussing ideas at this level to turning them into practical possibilities. The resources list (section 13.8) gives materials that go into the practicalities of self-employment in more detail. Follow-up interviews with people who've tried it would also be worthwhile.
A notional weekly timetable could be produced by students as a follow-up

Table 13.3   Activity evaluation checklist

Activity	Could it earn you money?	Does it save you money?	Does it provide any money-saving benefits?	Does it cost money to do it?	Does it provide you with company?	Does it need special skills or training?	Would your closest friend think it worth doing?	Would you still think it worth doing in a year's time?	Score for enjoyment on a 1–5 scale

exercise to the completion of the table. They would need to consider certain compulsory items that might have to be included in an unemployed week, such as time spent going to claim benefit, visit the job centre or careers office, doing housework, etc.

Personal values
The 'Decisions' workbook (see resources list) has a questionnaire exercise that is intended to discover students' values by looking at their preferred activities. This aspect of how one makes a choice cannot be ignored.

In order to allow students the freedom to make their values explicit you may have to allow them to enter into the 'Activity' column of the questionnaire here some activities of dubious legality – they may be criminal (e.g. stealing) or part of the black economy. Students will feel free to do this if the completed sheet is to remain anonymous and is not to be collected by the tutor. Unless the exercise does reflect their values it will have no directly practical use. If you do not want to let these 'illegal' activities go unchallenged, however, you may want to devise a subsequent activity that picks up the issue for discussion. See Chapter 16 for appropriate strategies for dealing with moral issues.

The final columns of our questionnaire all concentrate on the 'values' aspect of each activity. Whether students think the activities worth persisting with, whether their commitment is shared by people who are important to them, and whether it affords much enjoyment are all indications of its place in their personal value systems. This provides a useful way in to a reconsideration of their values about work so that alternatives to paid employment become possible choices.

Reaching this stage in your discussions with students means that their values about work will necessarily play a major part in deciding how far they can be influenced by any of these practical suggestions.

Dealing with social isolation
It is easy enough to say that being unemployed may cause social isolation, but very difficult to affect or make compensation for this. The preceding comments on helping students learn how to structure time should go part of the way to meeting the problem that one's sense of identity is confirmed partly by work and work companions. Tutors actually working with students who have been or who are currently unemployed will know that group counselling strategies are the only appropriate ones to create the necessary kind of supportive atmosphere in which this difficult subject can be explored. Tutors working with students who have not yet had that experience will be raising the subject to alert them to possible difficulties they may encounter, and to deepen their understanding of how unemployment alters lives. We have mentioned the curtain that researchers felt separated the unemployed from the rest of society. Public disapproval of those who are out of work goes very deep and produces a feeling of private shame, even in communities where unemployment has become endemic.

The importance of companionship
There are practical reasons for this isolation. Lack of money limits a person's social life and separates him or her from friends. The survey of leisure facilities suggested elsewhere (see page 202) could usefully include special mention of free activities or arrangements for the unemployed. Marsden's book (1982) and the Youthaid publication *A dossier of despair* (1981) are full of personal evidence that could provide case studies for discussion.

Understanding family conflict
Children who have to live at home for longer, and couples and families thrown into each other's company for a greater amount of time, can generate a deal of resentment and friction. Asking students to imagine the problems of living at home into their late teens without a job will open the subject up for exploration. Role-play is obviously a suitable strategy for exploring some of the manifestations of family conflict.

Being disapproved of can produce a feeling of rejection that contributes to isolation. The point has already been made that parents' attitudes and values can be unsupportive. Any lack of sympathy that may exist can be exacerbated by tension inside the family, but is more likely to have its roots in the simple fact that parents may have values that are out of date as far as the job scene of the 1980s is concerned. Whether this is true or not for your students can be confirmed by asking them to conduct a survey that includes interviews with all age groups.

Ways of changing work values
Social values change much more slowly than economic conditions. Many surveys (e.g. *Into work*: MSC, 1980) show that, however elusive it may be, most young people retain the idea of a paid job as their main goal. It is much easier to talk about the need to change the work-based ethic than to accomplish it at a personal level. Trying to convince a group of students on a vocational course that the collapse of work should be redefined as the ascent to leisure is no task for the faint hearted.

Most of your activities with students will focus on their short- and medium-term aims such as what to do when the course ends, rather than tackle such deeply rooted issues. However if you accept the overall argument that a life of uninterrupted paid work has become an out-of-date expectation for large numbers of people, then it does not seem enough to concentrate only on the bread-and-butter topics such as claiming benefit, job-searching, alternative ways of earning money, etc. Equipping students with these positive strategies is essential, but you may well feel that you want to tackle the long-term view.

In any case it will be difficult to avoid engaging with students' opinions about some of the alternatives suggested here; it is after all one of the fundamental facts about teaching that, however accurate or useful your information may be, its acceptance by the student will depend on their perception of its value. It is of little use giving the advice that a YTS scheme may have useful experience if your students see being on YTS as something they would be ashamed of. However practical your suggestions about alternative ways of earning money may be, it will be essential to discuss what attitudes the students themselves hold to these suggestions. Marsden's study of the unemployed in an area of high unemployment makes it clear that when an unemployed person worked for money in the black economy this earned considerable social disapproval, whereas an *employed* person doing the same was simply thought to be using his or her initiative and energy to supplement earnings. We are not advocating that you must try and change students' attitudes head-on. That would be insensitive, and probably doomed to failure in any case. What *is* your proper area of concern, however, is to discover where students' values may be in conflict with a course of action that they have chosen for themselves or that awaits them. You can justifiably present them with any inconsistencies between their opinions and their actions. The obvious example is where students disapprove of being unemployed, seeing it as the individual's fault, even where it is likely that they will be on the dole themselves.

Changing traditional attitudes
The main stumbling blocks to changing traditional attitudes to work can be summed up as follows:

- *Adults who reinforce the work ethic:* Other tutors, trainers or work experience supervisors may see your efforts to change students' work-based values as disruptive. Trying to make being unemployed respectable can be subversive. Work experience, as the *Learning at work* study (Hilgendorf and Welchmann, 1982) showed, reinforces the work ethic – even if the trainee is heading for the dole.
- *Parents and friends:* Influential figures in students' lives may still see getting a job as the most important thing to achieve. Your students might think that asking them to change their own views is unfair: it places the responsibility on them to change a social pattern while older and more powerful models are not providing an example – and they would have a point.
- *Informal work*: Your students might see attempts to make voluntary or leisure activities respectable as naive or uninformed. Their knowledge of the local workings of the informal or black economy is likely to be greater than yours. This may make them sceptical about the validity of the basic argument that work values need to be changed because jobs are scarce.
- *Ambitions*: The matters at issue cannot be restricted to the question of work alone. For some time your students will have held medium- and long-term goals that are based on the assumption that they will have regular paid employment. Challenge this and you may force them to question their ambitions in many areas. Their resistance may be correspondingly greater.

We do not pretend to have solutions to these difficulties, but here are some suggestions:

● *Adults who reinforce the work ethic:* Try to make their attitude explicit and available for discussion rather than allow it to remain an implicit influence. Suggest that students organize a discussion forum in which supervisors or other tutors can be invited to join. Questions can be discussed beforehand, or even circulated if the participants are reluctant.

● *Parents and friends:* First discover exactly what their attitudes are (students can compile a questionnaire or tape interviews), then try to assess how justifiable they seem. Can the attitudes realistically be transferred to the students' own situation? Do students accept these influential figures' attitudes about other issues such as marriage, sexual relationships, money, and so on?

● *Informal work:* Try to examine all aspects of working in the informal or black economy with students. Make sure the disadvantages as well as the advantages are clear. Such work may provide a living, but effectively puts one beyond the support of the welfare state (pensions, sick pay, etc.). What are the long-term implications of such work for the individual and for society? (See Watts, 1978.)

● *Ambitions:* Explore these in detail. What kind of money will students need to support them? Are they consistent with what is known about current social trends? Are students willing to contemplate acceptable alternatives?

● *Living without work:* This has a lot in common with what it would be like for a school-age child who was learning to live without school. The sense in which school and work are dissimilar *ought* to be that whereas schooling should encourage the learning of things in which one is interested, with conditions arranged to allow this to happen, at work one has to perform tasks for someone else's benefit. Needless to say, by the end of their fifth year this contrast is not real for many students. Some elements of schooling and work are more alike than dissimilar. This is precisely the argument referred to in Chapter 10 – that mass schooling was initially organized partly to inculcate the values and behaviour appropriate to an industrialized workforce.

In order to begin to learn to live without work it may be necessary to unlearn many of the habits that schooling teaches through what has come to be known as the hidden curriculum.

Changes in working patterns

● Introduce students to the view that a 'life at work' is becoming an unrealistic expectation for many. Consider ways of controlling and distributing periodic unemployment more fairly. Ask students for suggested changes in working patterns (brainstorm; small-group exercise). Alternatively present your own list of options, e.g.
  ★ 3-day week for all

★ overtime ban
★ no jobs for under-18s
★ compulsory retirement at 60
★ prevent mothers with pre-school children from working
★ prevent wives with working husbands from working
★ prevent husbands with working wives from working
★ raise taxes to finance public works

● Students form small groups, each one with the task of deciding government policy for the next five years. Pool options and discuss. A time limit may be necessary for the small-group task.

Political simulation

● For a more detailed look at why change is difficult and why no one wants to make the first move, try a simulation. One group is the government; others represent interested pressure groups (union, employers, school-leavers, married women, pensioners, etc.).
★ Stage 1: The government decides its policy, while each pressure group puts its case together.
★ Stage 2: During a forum, time policy is announced. Pressure groups then present support or objections. (Government deliberations can be 'leaked' to groups before their formal announcement.)
★ Stage 3: The government reconvenes to finalize policy while sub-groups agree on a plan of action if the policy is actually adopted.
★ Final whole-group evaluation: If you want to use this as part of a series of political-education sessions on how pressure groups work, try in the final session to make students be as explicit as possible about the power base that their particular pressure group may have (or lack), and the precise forms of action that are open to them (e.g. individual or collective, constitutional or direct, etc.). This would
   probably entail at least one preparation session.

Family conflict

● Try a variety of brief scenarios for students to act out which focus on family tensions. If they are reluctant to role-play these, write the ideas up as case studies, fleshing them out with more biographical detail.
★ Family One: The father is unemployed; there are two children of school age. The wife, previously at home full-time, has just been offered a part-time job. Would it hurt the husband's pride if she took it? Could the couple change their domestic roles? Do the children object?
★ Family Two: A 17-year-old has been unemployed for six months. He has the chance of going on holiday with a friend, so asks for a

sub in the form of an advance on his birthday money. This provokes a row about how much he is contributing (in cash and chores) at home.

★ Family Three: A couple (aged 18 and 20) decide that they want to leave their separate homes to get married or set up home together. Neither has work at present. Their parents raise objections.

★ Family Four: A working single-parent mother has an unemployed daughter, who is on the point of giving up her search for work, claiming she'll soon be married anyway.

Small groups have some time to discuss their roles and work out how each one views the problem before the action starts. The actual scene can take place over the dinner table. These brief descriptions have been written to highlight the involvement of children and older dependents. You can easily write others to explore different aspects (relations between couples, for example). The core of such a role-play is to begin by identifying a point of conflict for the participants.

Life without school

● Ask students to identify all the similarities between formal education and work. (Syllabus-bound activities, timetabled period, importance of time-keeping, discipline, etc.) You record the ideas as a list. You can have a checklist of your own, but be sure to take down ideas in the students' own words. Ask them to imagine that they are parents who have chosen not to send their children to school. Discuss the similarities between the problems facing students in such a position and those facing an unemployed person.

● Ask students to organize a class discussion of the merits and disadvantages of opting out of school. They should invite speakers who may be local members of the national organization (known as 'Education Otherwise' – 25 Common Lane, Hemingford Abbots, Cambridgeshire PE18 9AN) of parents who choose to educate their children themselves. (Try to get the children along with the parents.)

Writing or taping autobiographies

● Focus on students' personal ambitions. Take as a starting point the list of options that students were asked to produce for themselves earlier (see the teaching suggestions on page 202). Ask your students to construct different autobiographies that might result from different choices. There are various ways of doing this:

★ They can be written as contrasting narrative autobiographies, looking back over 10 or 20 years.

★ Students can interview each other about their past lives, on audio-tape or by taking down notes that can be read out later.

★ You can write a handout of questions that will elicit a picture of their lifestyle, e.g. 'Where do you live?', 'What do you look like?', 'Who are your friends?'

Skills for self-employment

● A great deal of communications and numeracy work can be attached to detailed exploration of some of the alternative-work suggestions – being self-employed, running a co-operative, etc. Materials are suggested in section 13.8 that explain what steps would be necessary. Tutors should analyse these step-by-step accounts for the appropriate learning opportunities and organize suitable activities as part of a simulation. Communications activities could include:
★ writing one's own publicity material
★ persuading a bank manager to make a loan
★ selling one's product or service directly to the public
★ organizing a survey to assess a potential market
★ estimating setting-up production costs
★ setting up and running meetings of a co-operative
★ interviewing people who want to work with you

All these could involve practice in:
★ telephoning
★ writing letters, reports, notes, and memos
★ using charts and statistics
★ talking and negotiating to persuade, influence, inform, and obtain information.

13.7 Sample lesson plan

Length of session: 35 minutes.
Group size: 25

Resources:
● Handout showing floorplan of supermarket.

Aim:
● To identify job losses arising from technological change in one type of employment.

Objectives
● To list present jobs in the workplace (in this case a supermarket).
● To compare this list with the possible job list after automation.
● To identify areas of job loss, particularly those affecting school-leavers.

Method
Phase 1: Job-listing (10 minutes)
a   Ask the group to list all the jobs they can think of which exist in a large supermarket. List these on a board or OHT.
b   Ask students to place these jobs in ascending order of skills or qualifications necessary.

Phase 2: Analysing job losses (5 minutes)
a   Give each student a copy of the handout with the floorplan of an automated supermarket. (This should also include customer, television screen and telephone in corner of the page.)
b   Explain the procedure by which a customer would order and pay for goods from home.
c   Students enter these stages as labels on the diagram.
    (10 minutes)
d   Put two questions to the group:
    ★   Which jobs have disappeared?
    ★   What new jobs will there be?
    Students work in pairs to list these.

Phase 3: Describing new jobs (10 minutes)
a   Ask for answers to the first question, and cross these jobs off the chart on the board or OHT.
b   Now ask:
    ★   Which of these are jobs that school-leavers might do?
    ★   What are the skill levels of the new jobs?
    ★   What sort of workers will be needed for these?

Follow-up
●   Identify further areas of school-leaver employment in the locality, and try to estimate the effects of changes here. This could be by project, survey or interview.
●   Identify possible areas of training and providers of courses.

13.8   Resources list

Tutors' background reading
We have used the current edition of *Social trends* (HMSO) and Hirsch's background paper on youth unemployment as the two main sources of factual and statistical information. The latter also examines explanations of the causes of youth unemployment and alternative theories about solutions. Both are useful resources for tutors and potential sources of information for students.
    The collapse of work (Jenkins and Sherman) and *World out of work* (Merritt)

both give comprehensive overviews of the present and future scale of unemployment, detailed examples of the impact of technological change and outlines of possible future trends in technological change and in new working patterns.

For first-hand accounts that convey clearly the impact of unemployment on individuals and their families we have suggested three sources: Marsden's *Workless*, Youthaid's *A dossier of despair* (both dealing with adult unemployment), and White and Brockington's *Tales out of school*, which has school-leavers' impressions. All would furnish material for case studies.

Hilgendorf, L. and R. Welchman, 1982 *Learning at work*, Research and Development Series No. 9 (MSC)

Hirsch, D. 1983 *Youth unemployment: a background paper* (Youthaid)

HMSO 1984 *Social trends* (HMSO)

Jenkins, C. and B. Sherman 1979 *The collapse of work* (Eyre Methuen)

Marsden, D. 1982 *Workless*, 2nd edn (Croom Helm)

Merritt, G. 1982 *World out of work* (Collins)

Manpower Services Commission 1980 *Looking for an opening: a study of unemployed young people in East Cornwall* (MSC)

Manpower Services Commission 1980 *Jobless: a study of unemployed young people in North Tyneside* (MSC)

Watts, A.G. 1981 'Careers education and the informal economies' in *British Journal of Guidance and Counselling* **9** No. 1, Jan. 1981

Watts, A.G. 1978 'The implications of school-leaver unemployment for careers education in schools' in *Journal of Curriculum Studies* **10** No. 3, Sept. 1978

White, R. and D. Brockington 1983 *Tales out of school* (Routledge and Kegan Paul)

Youthaid 1981 *A dossier of despair* (from: Youthaid, 9 Poland Street, London W1V 2DG)

Classroom materials

City of Sheffield Employment Department *New technology* – whose progress? An information pack, containing sheets on a wide range of topics including: 'Women and new technology', 'Control and deskilling', 'Robots', 'New technology in shopping'. Could be used directly in the classroom, or adapted further to make worksheets, case studies, etc.

Curnow, R. and S. Curran 1980 *The silicon factor* (National Extension College)

Discussion notes in a pack. Seven sections, on 'Technology and the second industrial revolution', 'Microelectronics and the education and training system', 'Use of new information processing technology in the home', 'Microelectronics in the home', 'Impact of the new technology on work and lifestyles', 'Economics and political implications'.

Dauncey, G. 1982 *The unemployment handbook*, 2nd edn. (National Extension College)
Personal handbook of detailed practical information and self-help strategies. (Tutor's resource material.)
Dauncey, G. 1983 *Facing unemployment* (CRAC)
Students' workbook with exercises and practical suggestions on organizing one's time, making local contacts, planning activities.
Dauncey, G. 1983 *Nice work if you can get it* (National Extension College/Yorkshire Television)
Chapters on the background to unemployment; personal strategies for coping, money and benefits, job-sharing, organizing self-help groups, examples of local community projects.
Hall, P. 1983 *Work for yourself* (National Extension College)
A guide for young people who want a positive alternative to just being unemployed or stuck in a job they don't like, and who are willing to try working for themselves. Chapters on self-profiling, part-time and holiday jobs, service jobs, making and selling things, self-employment, and co-operatives. Chapters include first-hand accounts by people who've tried it for themselves.
Hopson, B. and M. Scally 1982 *Work shuffle* (Lifeskills Associates)
Card-game format, with tutor's notes giving suggestions for various activities to help students reassess their work values.
Jamieson, A. and CRAC 1982 *Claims, benefits and rights* (CRAC)
In the 'Survival and Job Skills' series. Students' work book, serving as a guide to forms, leaflets and claims. Includes relevant ones for supplementary benefit, unemployment, maintenance grants and self-employment.
Jones, A., J. Marsh and A.G. Watts 1980 *Time to spare: leisure in modern society* (CRAC)
In the 'Life-style' series. Student's workbook (and tutor's notes) on alternative ways of spending time. Exercises on making choices to do with holidays, organizing time, structuring 'work' and 'spare' time, investigating local opportunities.
Phillips, C. and C. Swanson 1982 *Minding your own business* (COIC/MSC)
Guide to self-employment. Explanations and exercises on market research, costing and operating as self-employed. Includes case-studies (not all of successes!) of young self-employed people.
Ruthven, K. 1983 *Society and the new technology* (Cambridge University Press)
Tutor/student background book. Chapters on the new technology and society, economics and unemployment, education, privacy and democracy, international relations.

14 Getting the message across

Basic aim

14.1 The need to teach communication

Whether you are working with them in a classroom, out on a survey or visit, on a residential, or in their workplace, one of your main aims will be to help your students to communicate.

You don't have to be a communications or English specialist to do this. Course integration and close liaison between members of your teaching team should mean that everybody contributes to the development of the students' fluency and confidence in communicating. The wide variety of contexts involved should help the development of versatility and flexibility in the use of language. Whatever you and your students are doing and whatever the end product, the process will involve the sending and receiving of messages. Communication is commonplace and vital; it needs to be effective.

The medium may be written text, diagrams and pictures, or the spoken or broadcast word. For convenience we have divided the area into two aspects. This chapter looks mostly at speaking and writing; the next at listening and reading. The division is not arbitrary, but it is somewhat artificial. In practice these skills are closely related and they should be developed together. Most of the teaching approaches described in the first part of this book encourage students to practise all aspects of communication. Creative writing, literature and the media (Chapter 7) and communication workshops (Chapter 8) include suggestions for integrated assignments and projects that combine the sending and receiving of messages, both of which are active processes that can only be developed by practice.

14.2 What is communication?

Communication entails putting your own message across and interpreting the messages you receive. It is the basis of human social activity. Sometimes the messages are intentional, but often they are unintentional. It involves the sending and receiving of wishes and feelings as well as instructions.

The 'encoding' and 'decoding' of communication signals depend upon the sharing of symbols, which in turn depend partly upon the social and cultural context. You cannot communicate in a social vacuum. The relationship between participants, the physical location, and the nature of the activity or task all contribute to the meaning of any verbal or visual message. So in seeking to develop communication skills it is essential to work in a real or simulated context that is meaningful and relevant for the students. This is one reason why communication is seen as a core-skill area the teaching of which needs to be practised throughout all parts of the course, not just in an isolated 'communication' slot.

Your students need to develop what is often termed 'communicative competence'. This is the ability to select and use the form of language that is most appropriate for the specific social situation. Sometimes precision is the most important aspect; sometimes expansiveness, imagination, or humour. You shouldn't think of teaching language as an end in itself. You are developing in your students the ability to use language as a means, a medium through which they can acquire new concepts, communicate their own interpretation of them and gradually develop their own personal means of expression. This is very important because language is so much a part of our identity and self-image. Your students' self-confidence and motivation should increase as their communication skills develop.

Language functions

Language is used in many different ways, for different purposes. A number of linguists and educationalists have devised systems and categories to describe this variety of function. One of the best known models remains that of James Britton (1970). He described three main functions which he called the expressive, the transactional and the poetic. These were further divided into sub-categories. He then looked at the relationship between these and the participant role and the spectator role, between what is said and what is done.

Expressive

This is central to Britton's model and describes the type of personal language that can be used in writing and in speech. The writer is probably a spectator, describing personal experience and reflecting on it. The writing is often imaginative. The tone is informal because it expresses the personal voice of the writer. It may resemble speech: certainly it will be direct, possibly intimate. To make full sense of such communication, the listener or reader needs to empathize with and probably share some of the experience of the writer or speaker.

Your students will need to develop their skill in expressive writing before they can communicate effectively in a transactional mode. One of the problems you may face is that your students may not have been given the opportunity to develop this ability to express themselves in a personal, informal manner. Much of the communication work in vocational-preparation courses, particularly that in a vocational or social-education context, involves the transactional use of language – to get things done and to interpret. Unless students have established a foundation of successful communication in the expressive mode they will find it extremely difficult to communicate in a more formal, impersonal manner.

Transactional

Transactional uses of language arise when the writer or speaker is a participant. It is concerned with carrying out operations, with the giving and receiving of instructions, and with persuasive argument. There is usually information to be conveyed and objects and processes to be described in an objective way. It might involve the interpretation of diagrams or statistics. Summarizing or note-taking skills are often needed.

These are the types of communication skills that we think of first when we talk about the communication element in vocational-preparation courses. And this raises problems. To use this type of language accurately and efficiently your students need to be at home with more formal styles of writing – the passive voice, the impersonal tone. A process may be described and represented in words and diagrams by one person as a message to be understood and acted upon by a second person who has different experience and who is working in a different context. Your students will need practice in communicating in a precise, unambiguous way. But they will need first to have become adept at using expressive language.

This is yet another reason why creativity and imaginative personal writing needs to be encouraged. 'Vocational' should be interpreted in its widest sense, to include personal creative pursuits – music, drama and poetry as well as technical skills. But we need to distinguish between personal, imaginative writing and the tightly disciplined world of literary creation.

Poetic

Britton sees the poetic as the most sophisticated use of language. It shares the imaginative and personal dimension of the expressive use but it is experience worked upon and shaped into art. 'Poetic' is the name given to the highly ordered, carefully selected and balanced language of plays, poetry and novels.

It is unlikely that you would wish or expect your students to spend much time developing their expertise regarding this, the most complex, function of language. Encouraging them to write in the expressive mode should give them access to the world of creative and personal expression without burdening them at this stage with the more disciplined rigours of the writer's craft. That can come later for any students who choose the path.

Your teaching

What you as a social-education tutor can do is to foster the desire to communicate and help to develop the language tools to do it well. Begin with the expressive and work towards the transactional.

You should alert your students to the need for a degree of accuracy. A curriculum vitae needs to be carefully composed and correctly spelled and punctuated. But you are not really concerned with what could be termed 'mechanical accuracy' – spelling, punctuation and grammar. Your chief concern is in helping your students to get their message across through effective communication. It is a question of finding the right balance between ensuring sufficient accuracy for the content and purpose of the communication and encouraging your students to be uninhibited and free in their expression.

If you cover their writing with corrections you will probably discourage them from writing at all. On the other hand, if you leave all errors uncorrected you will deny them the opportunity to achieve a more standard form of English which might eventually help them obtain their ambitions – vocational or social. A workshop session should help you deal sensitively with each individual need.

We can list the functions of language as follows:

- expressive
  - ★ personal experience
  - ★ informal tone
  - ★ imaginative, creative
  - ★ exploratory
  - ★ individual voice of writer as spectator

- transactional
  - ★ instrumental, to get things done
  - ★ facts and information
  - ★ objective description
  - ★ persuasive argument and opinion
  - ★ interpretation of diagrams and statistics
  - ★ summary and note-taking
  - ★ writer as participant

- poetic
  - ★ sophisticated
  - ★ highly ordered
  - ★ novels and short stories
  - ★ plays and poetry
  - ★ disciplined, creative language of literature

A similar breakdown is now recommended by the FEU (Figure 14.1).

Example G
Communication Skills and the ABC Core (Aim 6.3)

"English is rooted in the processing of experience through language . . . Once it is understood that talking and writing are means to learning, those more obvious truths that we learn also from other people by listening and reading will take on a fuller meaning and fall into a proper perspective." Bullock Report.

A good deal of work has already been done on the concept of Language across the Curriculum though sadly, despite the exhortation of Bullock, little has been trasferred into classroom practice. The checklist below, the result of a matching process, emerged when the four modes of language were compared with the checklist in *A basis for choice* (Aim 6.3). Clearly, the list is intended as a general guide and embraces most aspects of communication skills teaching with which the specialist may already be familiar. Full details of the objectives are given in Appendix 2 [of this document].

The 4 Modes of Language

TALKING

6.3.2 read and understand written questions and requests;
3.3 distinguish fact from opinion;
3.11 give clear verbal explanations to a variety of audiences;
3.12 contribute to group discussion;
3.13 use the telephone effectively;
3.14 experience and evaluate verbal encounter;
3.15 practice communication in a variety of groups;
3.16 experience various roles in these groups;
3.17 experience the communication requirements of certain jobs;
3.18 match the form of communication to the purpose;
3.19 critically evaluate a mediun of communication.

LISTENING

6.3.3 distinguish fact from opinion;
3.5 understand oral information;
3.12 contribute to group discussion;
3.13 use the telephone effectively;
3.14 experience and evaluate verbal encounter;
3.15 practice communication in a variety of groups;
3.16 experience various roles in these groups;
3.17 experience the communication requirements of certain jobs;
3.18 match the form of communication to the purpose;
3.19 critically evaluate a medium of communication.

READING

6.3.1/2/4 understand a variety of data;
3.3 distinguish fact from opinion;
3.9 express graphic data in written form and vice-versa;
3.17 experience the communication requirements of certain jobs;
3.19 critically evaluate a medium of communication;

WRITING

a. *transactional*
6.3.6 communicate competently in written form;
3.7 explain and describe events in writing;
3.8 make notes for own use;
3.9 express graphic data in written form;
3.10 fill in forms correctly;
3.17 experience the communication requirements of certain jobs;

3.18   match the form of communication to the purpose.

b. *expressive*
6.3.6   communicate competently in written form;
3.7   explain and describe events in writing;
3.18   match the form of communication to the purpose;
3.19   critically evaluate a medium of communication.

However, if the notion of skill embraces a student's 'individual synthesis of knowledge, skills, experience and attitudes' (*Basic skills* FEU, 1982), then it is by no means only the specialist who can engage in teaching communication skills. Indeed, the acquisition of skills is a developmental process and the touchstone of success must necessarily be the flexibility and transferability of acquired skills.

Figure 14.1   Uses of language (FEU Common core-teaching and learning, January 1984)

14.3   Teaching about communication

Your students need to develop their ability to communicate in a wide range of situations. Typically they will role-play interviews, encounters with supervisors on the job and with people they may meet off the job – police, bank and shop staff, social-security officials. They will write formal and informal letters, make real and simulated telephone calls, interview people on the street for surveys, discuss with their peers and express their feelings about social issues in talk and writing. A glance through the strategies (Part I) will reveal how many different learning contexts you and your colleagues involve them in, each calling for a range of communication skills.

Given this variety it is worth introducing them to some of the more significant aspects of communication. An appreciation of the contribution of, say, non-verbal signals, to getting their message across may help them to develop their expertise.

Here is a suggested programme of topics you should cover, fairly briefly, probably during communication or social-education lessons.

- non-verbal (gesture, eye contact, posture)
- paralinguistic (pace, intonation, volume)
- distinguishing facts from opinion (association and connotation, bias and tone)
- prejudice and stereotypes (sexist and racist language)
- register (selecting the appropriate level of formality and vocabulary for the context)
- grammar and non-standard varieties of English

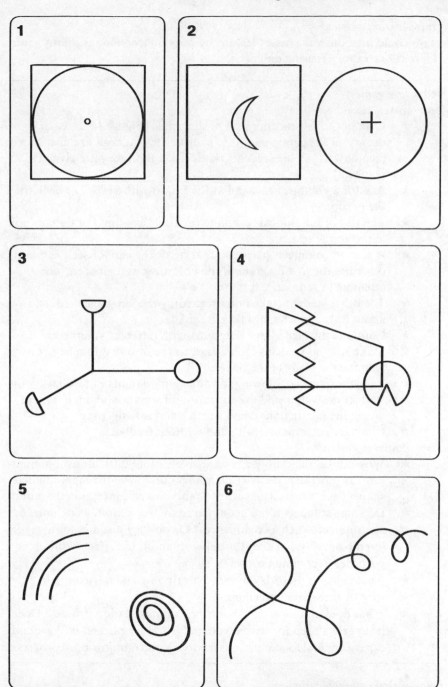

Figure 14.2 Diagrams for the diagram game

Introductory session
You could introduce a series of lessons by playing a communications game.
Here is one example, using diagrams.

Diagram game
- Instructions:
  ★ Give out to all students a set of diagrams (Figure 14.2 – each is
    drawn on a separate page of a pack). The diagrams are distributed
    face-down. Ask the students not to look until they are given the
    go-ahead.
  ★ Ask for a volunteer to stand at the board with his or her back to
    the group.
  ★ The rest of the students examine the first diagram, but do not look
    ahead to the rest.
  ★ A second volunteer, placed so that he or she cannot see the board,
    describes the first diagram to the volunteer at the board, who
    attempts to reproduce it there.
  ★ The other students take notes regarding the language used, and
    about how and why mistakes are made.
  ★ Continue through all the diagrams with different volunteers.
  ★ Make sure no students look ahead to the next diagram before a
    volunteer is ready at the board.
  ★ Vary the game by allowing for different amounts of feedback – the
    student drawing could ask for more information and the student
    giving the instructions could watch what is happening.
  ★ Compare performance with and without feedback.
- Points to discuss:
  ★ Why do the diagrams get progressively more difficult to communi-
    cate? Is it because the later diagrams don't have the more familiar
    shapes (like 'square') that are probably shared concepts in the group?
  ★ Do some students try to get a precise reproduction, using units of
    measurement such as centimetres? Or do they just aim for a vague
    resemblance? What does this tell you about the effect of different
    purposes in communication?
  ★ Are analogies used? Is number 5 a rainbow and a fried egg in a
    pan, or three arcs and ellipses?
  ★ What does all this reveal about the communication process? Does
    it suggest a need for shared vocabulary, concepts and background
    experience and for continuous feedback and monitoring of progress?

Non-verbal communication
Our body language, dress, hairstyle, facial expressions, and gestures all signal
messages about ourselves, our beliefs and attitudes. Such non-verbal

communication is an important aspect of communication for your students to study: they need to be aware of the effect their own body language may have on others. It is not a question of setting out to change the way they present themselves but of alerting them to the possible results of the decisions they make regarding their appearance. They can then choose for themselves depending upon what they value most at the time – their selected identity image or the impression they make on a prospective employer or equivalent. The choice is up to them; your job is to ensure that they make their choice on the basis of knowledge.

These are some of the aspects you might consider with your students.

- *eye contact:* what are the effects of maintaining it or of looking away?
- *gesture*: does this impede communication or accompany speech in a helpful way?
- *posture:* how does this convey confidence, anger, resignation, etc.?
- *facial expression:* should they smile at an interview, etc.?
- *proximity:* how close should they stand or sit; how do they protect their personal space?
- *orientation:* what position do they take with regard to another speaker or listener?

You could point out that cultures differ in the signals used and in the significance and meaning that is given to eye-contact, proximity and gesture. You may well have students who have experience of different languages and countries who could contribute their knowledge to the discussion.

Here are two activities you could use to explore some of these aspects.

Gesture game
- Instructions:
    - ★   Ask one student to sit on her/his hands and to give instructions. Suitable subjects might be: setting the timer on a video recorder; wiring a plug; making coffee; putting paper into a typewriter. Your hope is that the student will be hampered by lack of gesture.
    - ★   Talk about this, and then repeat the exercise using hands.
- Points to discuss:
    - ★   What do we use gesture for?
    - ★   How does it accompany our speech?
    - ★   Is it ever redundant?
    - ★   Does it ever distract and get in the way of communication?

Identity game
- Instructions:
    - ★   Ask for a volunteer, but stress that it must be someone brave because everyone will make comments about him or her. It might be better to use yourself or to bring in a brave colleague.

★ Ask the rest of the group to spend five minutes writing down as many assumptions about the volunteer as possible. Assumptions made might concern whether the volunteer lives with parents, a partner, or alone; is married or single; likes modern or old furniture; drives, or rides a bike; reads a particular newspaper or magazine; votes for a particular party; has some favourite author, TV star, or singer.

★ Next get pairs to compare their notes.

★ Then ask for a report back in the whole group.

★ Give the volunteer a chance to speak in answer if he or she wishes.

● Points to discuss:

★ How do we use non-verbal clues to make judgements about people?

★ Is this how stereotypes are formed?

★ What is the significance of this for your students?

★ Do they believe they should choose their clothes, make-up, hair style, and so on to make a particular impression?

★ When they role-play interview situations do they think of the impression they make through their use of eye contact, posture and
so on?

Paralinguistic communication
Tone, intonation, pace and volume all contribute to the message being communicated. By changing the stress we can alter the meaning.

Changing the message
● Instructions

★ Give out slips of paper with lines of text, or show the text, a line at a time, on the OHP. Suitable lines would be:

'I've just seen her again.'
'Sit there and he'll get the drinks.'
'United have done it again.'

★ Ask a volunteer to read one line out.

★ Ask the group to listen and then give opinions on how many people are present, what their attitudes are, and what's happening.

★ Ask the volunteer to read the line again, ideally in the same way.

★ Then ask someone else to read the line again in a different way, to give a fresh interpretation.

★ Continue with the other lines.

● Points to discuss:

★ How does the intonation, pace and tone determine the meaning?

★ What is the relevance of that for your students?

★   Do they need to practise speaking to ensure that they select the most suitable tone, intonation for their message? (This is particularly important if you have speakers of English as a second language or dialect.)

Distinguishing fact from opinion
Here you may introduce your students to the emotive aspects of language, to the multiple signals we receive from words and their associations. You might also like to look now at the sections on creative writing, literature and the media (Chapter 7) and at section 15.3 on media studies, where these ideas are discussed in the context of receiving messages from the media.

Association
● Instructions
   ★   Write pairs of words on a board or overhead-projector transparency (OHT). Suitable pairs might be: parent/child; us/them; successful/unsuccessful.
   ★   Ask your students to write down the first ideas that come into their heads.
   ★   Brainstorm their ideas and write these all up on a board or OHT.
   ★   Draw out similiarities and categorize their ideas.
● Points to discuss:
   ★   Which associations did they have in common?
   ★   What does that reveal about the nature and function of associations?
   ★   Are these associations socially, culturally, or class based?
   ★   Can we separate denotation from connotation, that is the 'objective' meaning of words from their associations?
   ★   How do we use this powerful aspect of language to convey our own attitudes and emotions?

Emotive language
● Instructions
   ★   Select a short passage from the newspaper or a magazine, or write your own.

   ★   Retype it with alternative words at regular intervals, one giving a generally favourable message, the other unfavourable. An example is: 'The (cunning/clever) investigator found more evidence. Her (strength of purpose/obstinacy) helped her to . . .'
   ★   Ask a volunteer to read the passage aloud, selecting one word or phrase from each bracketed pair to convey a favourable or unfavourable attitude towards the subject. The volunteer should try to remain consistent.
● Points to discuss:

★   Do the alternatives 'mean' the same thing?
★   Is language ever 'objective' – free from an emotive dimension?

Prejudice and stereotypes

Discussing emotive language and word associations and looking at ways to distinguish 'fact' from 'opinion' may lead you on to an exploration of the links between language use, attitude formation and prejudice.

It is probably best to select just one or two areas of concern. Sexism and racism would be good choices because one or other or both may be of direct relevance to your students, either because they have experienced prejudice or because they feel it.

We are not suggesting a direct onslaught by you on your students' attitudes. You probably don't feel prepared or equipped to do that, and the chances are that it wouldn't be effective anyway. But a sensitive, imaginative and gentle introduction to this aspect of language should be a worthwhile and positive experience.

Sexist language
●   Instructions
 ★   Give your students the examples taken from *The Guardian* newspaper's regular feature 'Naked Ape' (Figure 14.3). Ask them whether these illustrate what is meant by sexist language. In discussion, bring your students round to perceive that, although the examples display sexism – that is, discrimination on the grounds of gender – they don't contain sexist language as such.
 ★   Look at the passage about repairs and rented accommodation (Figure 14.4). Help your students, in discussion, to identify the sexist language – the use of 'landlord' and 'he' to include females.
 ★   Look at the list of job and role descriptions (Figure 14.5). Discuss the changes that are taking place. Do your students feel that separate job titles are needed for females and males?
 ★   Follow up with a survey of the boards in the local Job Centre.
●   Points to discuss
 ★   What effect does the use of 'he' to include 'she' have on the attitudes of males and females, both to themselves and to each other? Why do females feel excluded?
 ★   Identify the ways in which language use is currently changing in our society, due partly to the influence of such writers and researchers as Dale Spender (1980). Examples include the use of 'chairperson', 's/he', 'craftsperson'.
 ★   How does this use of language affect social attitudes? Why do we expect girls to train for certain jobs and boys for others?

Bangor Technical College offers everything from angling to wood carving and yoga and one obviously for women called "Making the best of yourself!"

Belfast Telegraph

"I AM sorry to see that the Gazette has succumbed to the current use of 'Ms' to indicate the female of the species in its Student Lists and Examination Results etc. As probably they are almost 100 per cent single, it is quite likely they would prefer to be known as such (and therefore 'available'!)"

Letter from Peter Readings in Guy's Hospital magazine.

WE WELCOMED the 70 incoming male undergraduates and the 42 women, at a freshmen's dinner . . . According to the most experienced observers, this proportion of men to women is likely to persist, being the normal one.

The Warden, writing in the Wadham College Gazette.

"THE undermentioned gentlemen have permission to occupy rooms as stated. Name: Miss J. I. Elliot Miss K. R. Batty, Miss K. A. Hagan, Miss J. E. Bendor-Samuel . . ."

Notice posted in Christ Church College, Oxford.

THE FIRST batch of highly qualified entrants into the course consisted of 24 pretty women and one very happy-looking man.

Principal's report, University of Glasgow.

"IN SPITE of the fact that most candidates were girls, the maths and science results were excellent."

Report by J. Almond of the Academic Board meeting at Hardenhuish School, Chippenham, Wilts.

"THE WIFE of a student will normally be admitted for the period of her husband's authorised stay without restriction on taking employment . . .

"The husband of a student will need to qualify for entry in his own right and will not normally be granted leave to remain solely because his wife is studying in the UK. If full-time employment is required a work permit must be obtained.

Leaflet from the United Kingdom Council for Overseas Student Affairs.

Now there's a profound thought; is the OU feminine or masculine? I think it's a woman. It likes to dress up for degree ceremonies and is bitchy about those who don't wear the correct dress. It also sulks when you criticise it.

Sean Ward in Sesame, the Open University newspaper.

Figure 14.3 Examples of sexism (Naked ape: an anthology of male chauvinism from the Guardian (1981) Edited by Andrew Veitch (Duckworth))

When you rent a place to live the landlord is responsible for keeping it in good repair. If he refuses to do this you should first get advice from an Advice Centre, Citizens' Advice Bureau or from the Council's Housing Department. The Council could take your landlord to court if he doesn't get the necessary repairs done. Or you can get a builder to carry out the work. When you've paid him you can take the cost off the rent but you should not stop paying the rent altogether.

Figure 14.4   An example of sexist language

foreman	supervisor
chairman	chairperson
cameraman	camera operator
fisherman	fisher
laundress	laundry worker
airline steward	flight attendant

Figure 14.5   Alternative job and role descriptions

If you wish to take this further, look at the illustrations in books and at cartoons to see how they reinforce stereotypes – the woman at the sink, the boy engaged in active play, the girl looking at a book or nursing a doll. If you compare recent children's story books with those of ten years ago you may find striking differences in the way children are presented according to gender roles. Writers and publishers have become aware of the need to avoid restrictive labelling. Your students, however, may need a long time to digest and ideally to accept these changing social attitudes.

You could also look at racist language and images. Children's books will again provide examples. Consider the effect of illustrations that show only white people. Are black people ever portrayed as achievers? Or are they always in a disadvantaged or menial role? Look for 'tokenism', the coloured-in drawing of a white person, or the use of racial stereotypes – e.g. all Indians, Africans and Italians looking the same.

Register
Your students need practice in identifying situations that require formal written or spoken language. You could help them by introducing them to the concept of 'register'. The social context and the subject matter will influence the type of language used in any situation. In addressing a friend we use a more

casual, informal style of speech or writing than when dealing with someone in authority over us. Our style of talking in a pub or at a party is almost certainly different from that adopted in a job interview or a conference. Most of us have learned to switch from one register to another as the occasion demands. But it is a complex process. Not only are some items of vocabulary specific to certain situations, the syntax – that is, the grammar – differs too.

Formal, standard English usually involves the use of the impersonal and the passive. There are long sentences with subsidiary ideas embedded in them, often separating the subject from the main verb. Your students may find it difficult to read this language with understanding; producing it in speech or writing is even more difficult. This is one of the main concerns of Douglas Barnes (1971). Although he described the school sector his research and ideas are relevant for further education and youth training generally.

You can help your students learn gradually by showing them a variety of examples of writing and by encouraging them to use different styles themselves.

Register
- Instructions:
  - ★ Give out passages of text that illustrate different styles and levels of formality. Useful sources would be: passages from textbooks in vocational and technical areas, in sociology, law and economics; letters concerned with job applications and to friends; extracts from specialist magazines and journals like computing, dress-making, music.
  - ★ Explore and analyse the language together in discussion. Look at sentence length, and at the number of main and subsidiary ideas in the sentences. Check whether the passive voice is used. Is the tone personal or impersonal? Are there words that are only meaningful within the subject area? Is this jargon?
  - ★ Ask the students each to bring in one piece of writing from an interest, hobby, or vocational area of their choice and to explain its meaning to the group.
  - ★ You could then role-play dialogues with deliberate mismatches of formality. One student selects a formal tone, the partner a casual, informal one.
- Points to discuss:
  - ★ Why is it important to select a suitable level of formality and tone in writing and in speech?
  - ★ What is the effect of a wrong choice?
  - ★ Do subject areas and hobbies need their own specialist terms or do they use unnecessary jargon?

  Try to bring your students round to recognize the advantage of being able to operate in a range of registers, both written and spoken. Recognizing the need is, of course, only the first step. The ability to operate effectively in a range of registers will come slowly and will require a lot of effort from you and from your students.

Grammar and non-standard varieties of English

You will probably work with some students whose language use is non-standard. This might be because they are second-language or dialect speakers, or because of the influence of their social class.

It is important to avoid negative labels. Varieties of English that differ from the standard are generally different, not deficient. Part of your effort will be to foster respect for dialects and other non-standard forms. Your students may not recognize the positive aspects of their own language use. Students whose speech and written work is influenced by West Indian dialect, for example, may not be aware of its grammatical consistency and expressive power. They may have picked up messages of disapproval and feelings of inferiority with regard to it, from their parents or peers or from the prevailing social attitudes in the West Indies and in Britain.

There is, however, a thriving and vigorous form of language, much influenced by Jamaican dialect but also by British urban dialects. This is used by young black, and occasionally young white, students. Published poets like Lynton Kwesi Johnson have helped give status to this form of language but it is still generally regarded as less suitable than standard British English for most situations.

By encouraging the creative use of such dialects you can help your students develop respect for and an interest in a form of language they may feel at home with. This is particularly important when you are dealing with spoken language because insensitive attempts to change the way people speak can be devastating to their self-images and confidence.

This is not to say that there is no place for helping your students to develop expertise in the use of standard British English. There are occasions when it will be very much to their advantage that they can reproduce as polished and sophisticated a form of standard English as possible. What you need to develop is versatility, the ability to select the appropriate type of language for the situation.

In writing this usually mean grammatically correct standard English. This is not the place to look at ways of teaching grammar or spelling, but all teachers are also teachers of English and you need to negotiate agreed standards of accuracy with your students and to help them meet them.

Varieties of English
- Give out a poem or passage of text written in a fluent, powerful, but non-standard form. One poem by Lynton Kwesi Johnson is reproduced here (Figure 14.6) as an example.

- In pairs or small groups unravel the meaning and then write a short paragraph trying to convey this meaning in standard English. This will probably have to be in prose unless you have accomplished, fast-working, poets in your group.
- Compare the two forms. Which is the more expressive? Why? When would the standard English prose be the more appropriate and hence expressive?

If you have students who are willing and able to use a dialect form creatively themselves then encourage them to do so. But remember that although writers like Lynton Kwesi Johnson have written in dialect, they have worked to develop their written skill. And they can probably operate equally fluently and

DOUBLE SCANK

I woz jus about fe move forwud,
tek a walk thru de markit,
an suss de satdey scene —
yu know whey a mean —
when I site bredda Buzza
bappin in style
comin doun FRONT LINE.

him site a likkle sista
him move fe pull a scank
but she soon suss him out
sae him dont in the rank;

soh when shame reach him,
him pap a smile,
scratch him chin,
but de sista couldda si thru him grin:
bredda Buzza couldn do a single ting.

"Hail, Buzza!" I greet him.
"Love!" him greet I back.
"I a look a money, Buzza:
come forward wid some dunny."

de bredda sae him bruk
him sae him naw wuk
him sae him woman a breed
him sae him dont even hav a stick a weed;

but I site diffrant:
de bookie man jus done tek him fe a ride!

Linton Kwesi Johnson (1975) *Dread Beat and Blood* (Bogle-l'Ouverture Publications Ltd.)

Figure 14.6   An example of non-standard English

effectively in a standard form. This is true of many English dialect writers too. Generally the dialect is a spoken form and so you shouldn't require, or even encourage, students to write in it unless the impetus comes from them and they are anxious to try. It might be more realistic to role-play using dialect as a spoken form.

Varieties of English
- Can your students identify situations in which they might choose to use a non-standard form of English and others in which standard English would be more appropriate?
- Why do we have an accepted standard? Do they know how it came about?
- How do social groups use 'in-language' to reinforce their identity and keep others out?

A programme such as this, which explores a number of aspects of language use, will not by itself develop your students' ability to communicate effectively, but it should acquaint them with the issues and foster a desire to become a versatile and skilled communicator.

Fluency in written and spoken communication
Ideas and approaches for helping students speak and write clearly and effectively can be found in the strategies section (Part I). For oral skills look particularly at:

- discussion and small-group teaching (sections 2.1–2.3)
- asking questions (sections 3.1–3.4)
- role-play, simulation, gaming-simulation, games (sections 4.2–4.5)
- visits, survey methods, residentials (sections 5.2 and 5.4–5.6)
- the media (section 7.4 and 7.5)
- communication workshops (sections 8.2 and 8.3)

For written skills look particularly at:

- case studies, projects, survey methods (sections 5.1, 5.3, 5.4 and 5.6)
- creative writing, literature, the media (sections 7.2–7.5)
- communication workshops (sections 8.2 and 8.3)

Multi-skill and integrated assignments (section 8.2) are particularly useful because students tackle both spoken and written tasks in an overall, relevant context. This is more realistic than practising speaking and writing separately.
    Below are a few additional pointers.

Developing spoken skills
- Aim for clarity and appropriateness.

- Help your students to become confident and autonomous, assertive but not too pushy.
- Always place them in realistic situations. Don't ask them to speak if normal practice would be to write.
- Encourage the development of a standard form while fostering respect for dialects.
- Never criticize accents or spoken deviations from standard unless they are likely to cause a breakdown in communication or unless the student has specifically asked for help in developing another way of speaking. In any case go easy and correct on an individual basis, never in the middle of a discussion with the whole group present.
- Feed in ideas, content and structure *before* you ask students to talk. Before a discussion or dialogue can happen there needs to be a shared body of knowledge or experience. Use newspaper articles, prompts on the overhead projector or board, or written questions.
- Allow students to remain silent on occasion. If they are always silent, encourage gently, by eye-contact, gesture and only as a last resort by calling on them by name.

Developing written skills
- Aim for clarity and appropriateness.
- Encourage a suitable degree of accuracy.
- Try to develop imagination and creativity alongside functional effectiveness.
- Help your students to categorize their tasks, to distinguish between reports, memos, notes, letters, poems.
- Practise presenting reasoned, logical arguments and persuasive writing.
- Use different stimuli to inspire students; never give an essay title or assignment without some kind of introduction or initial guidance.
- Brainstorm ideas on a topic with the whole group and use the board or overhead projector to demonstrate how these first ideas can be organized and placed in a structure with introduction, paragraphs, and a conclusion.
- Encourage the use of varieties of English and non-standard forms but ensure that your students understand the social consequences of selecting an inappropriate register or dialect. It's their decision but they need to be able to make an informed choice from a basis of skill and knowledge.

14.4 Sample lesson plan

Length of session: 2 hours (be flexible about phase timing)
Group size: 12.

Resources
● Possibly a 'guest'.
● OHP, board, flip chart (two of these).

Aims
● To heighten students' awareness of the effect their own body language may have on others.
● To alert them to the possible consequences of the decisions they make regarding their dress and the general image they choose to present.
● To give them practice in group negotiation.

Objectives
● Students will identify aspects of non-verbal communication.
● Students will explore and demonstrate their awareness of its significance in attitude formation through practical work and discussion.

Method

Phase 1: Activity (15 minutes)
a   If possible, before the students arrive, arrange the seating in a circle.
b   Without formally introducing the topic, ask for a volunteer to sit on her or his hands.
c   Ask the volunteer to give instructions to the whole group on one of these: making coffee, wiring a plug, rewinding and playing a cassette. (Choose appropriate activities for the experience of the group; it is not a knowledge test.)
d   Ask the rest of the group to observe carefully. With luck, the task will prove difficult and there will be pauses, laughter, and a failure to communicate.
e   Now ask the same volunteer to give the same instructions with hands available for gesture. This task is likely to prove easier.

Phase 2: Whole-group discussion (15 minutes)
a   Lead a discussion arising from the activity. Points to bring out include:
    ★   Was communication hampered by lack of gesture?
    ★   How did this affect the volunteer's facial expressions?
    ★   What do we use gesture for?
    ★   How does it accompany speech?
    ★   Is it ever redundant and does it ever distract?
b   Draw towards a first consideration of what non-verbal communication is – i.e. part of it is gesture, part facial expression.

Phase 3: Activity (pairs) (15 minutes)
a   Invite a visitor into the room or ask for a brave volunteer or use yourself as subject.

b   Divide the group into pairs.
c   Ask them to spend five minutes writing down as many assumptions about the subject as possible.
d   Reveal a list of example questions on an OHT, chart or board and lead a brief question-and-answer phase to ensure everybody understands the task.

Phase 4: Buzz groups (20 minutes)
a   When the five minutes is up, combine the pairs into fours.
b   Ask them to appoint spokespersons who will take notes and report the group's discussion to the whole group.
c   The group task is to compare their assumptions and to agree a consensus view of the subject.

Phase 5: Report back (15 minutes)
a   Ask the three spokespersons to report back.
b   Write a summary of each report on the board/chart/OHT.
c   Allow the subject to comment if he or she wishes.

Phase 6: Whole-group discussion (20 minutes)
a   Lead a discussion on the exercise. Points to bring out include:
    ★   How did students use non-verbal clues to make assumptions about the subject?
    ★   Is this how we judge people?
    ★   Is this how stereotypes are formed?
b   Widen the discussion to a consideration of non-verbal communication generally. Points to bring out include:
    ★   What is the significance of these two exercises for your students?
    ★   Do they believe they should choose their clothing, make-up, hair-style, etc. to make a particular impression?
    ★   Do they adapt their image to suit particular occasions – interviews, encounters with authority, social gatherings?

Phase 7: Summary and conclusions (10 minutes)
●   From the discussion, draw up on the board a summary of aspects on non-verbal communication introduced (there is a list on page 247).

14.5   Resources list

Tutor's background reading

Language use
Britton, J. 1970 *Language and learning* (Pelican)
Halliday, M.A.K. 1973 *Explorations in the functions of language* (Edward Arnold)
    Difficult, but worth the effort.

Open University (1972) *Language in education* (Routledge and Kegan Paul/Open University Press)
   A useful range of essays covering wide field.

Non-verbal communication
Argyle, M. 1972 *The psychology of interpersonal behaviour* (Penguin)
Argyle, M. 1975 *Bodily communication* (Methuen)
Goffman, E. 1971 *The presentation of self in everyday life* (Penguin)

Sexist language
Adams, C. and R. Laurikietis 1980 *The gender trap: 3. Messages and images*, revised edn. (Anchor Press)
   Useful teaching suggestions.
Miller, C. and K. Swift 1982 *The handbook of non-sexist writing for writers, editors and speakers* (Women's Press)
Piercy, M. 1976 *Woman on the edge of time* (Women's Press)
   A novel introducing changed language use to avoid use of 'he' and 'she', etc.
Spender, D. 1980 *Man-made language* (Routledge and Kegan Paul)
   Recommended background reading.
Veitch, A. (ed.) 1980 *Naked ape: an anthology from The Guardian* (Duckworth)
   Useful source and teaching material

Register
Barnes, D. 1971 *Language, the learner and the school*, revised edn. (Penguin)
   Recommended.

West Indian dialect/Black English
Bloom, V. 1983 *Touch me, tell me* (Bogle-l'ouverture Publications Ltd)
Herbert, C. *In the melting pot* (Enterprise Publishing Project: 136/138 Kingsland High Street, London E8 2N3)
Johnson, L.K. 1975 *Dread beat and blood* (Bogle-l'Ouverture Publications Ltd)
Shore, L. *Pure running (a life story)* (Enterprise Publishing Project)
Simon, D. 1983 *Railton blues* (Bogle-l'Ouverture Publications Ltd)

Classroom materials
Adult Literacy and Basic Skills Unit *Chalo kaam kare* (ALBSU)
Intended for ESL students, but the materials are useful for native speakers too. Originated as support worksheets to accompany Radio Leicester programmes. There are 20 themes, each with well designed worksheets and information, on such topics as travel (timetables, maps, 24-hour clock), employment (payslips, trades unions, discrimination at work), unemployment (benefit, signing on), and taxation and money (bank accounts, tax forms).

Armitage, A. 1981 *Do it yourself* (Edward Arnold)
Practical guidance and exercises in social and life skills. Resource material dealing with the transition from full-time education to employment. 10 units: 'Self and others', 'Time off', 'Getting about', 'Post and telecommunications', 'Around the house', 'Buying and selling', 'Money management', 'Health and safety', 'On the road', 'The law', 'Work'. For literacy, communicatons and numeracy work, oral and written, with some simulations.

Armitage, A. 1984 *What do you Say?* (Edward Arnold)
Guidance and exercises in oral communication. Looks at non-verbal and technical aspects of speech, logical argument and defence of opinions. Contexts chosen include informal (social) and formal (job interviews).
There are some assignments, which could be used as teaching materials involving written and oral work.

Baber, M. 1982 *16+ English* (Stanley Thornes)
Materials and tasks that encourage students to think about the ways they use language. Also includes sections on study and research skills.

Cooper, A., P. Legott and P. Sprenger 1984 *Matters of fact* and *More matters of fact* (Edward Arnold)
Each publication contains 30 comprehension exercises dealing with communications at a level suitable for City & Guilds 772 Communication Skills.

Doughty, P., J. Pearce and G. Thornton 1971 *Language in use* (Edward Arnold)
Ring binder of teaching units on language use. Sections include 'Language in individual and social relationships', 'Language and culture', 'Language in social organizations'.

Inner London Education Authority *Living in a city* and *Working in a city* (ILEA Learning Materials Service, Publishing Centre, Highbury Station Road, London N1 1SB)
Students worksheets on communications, social and life skills, and numeracy, for use in workshop settings. Packs with teacher's notes.

Jenkins, J.P. 1981 *Put it across* (Edward Arnold)
40 self-contained assignments in reading, comprehension and writing.

Leach, R. 1981 *Communicating with the system* (National Extension College)
Series of workbooks on: 'Children and education', 'Jobs and money', 'Housing', 'Health services', 'Consumer rights', 'Law and politics', plus teacher's notes. ESL communications materials, for use with adults.

Leach, R. 1983 *Coping with the system* (National Extension College)
An 'Inter-Action Guide'. Workbook addressed to adult ESL students. Chapters include: 'Jobs and money', 'Housing', 'Health', 'Consumers', 'Law', 'Politics'. Brief guide to each area, plus resources.

Mace, J. 1980 *Learning from experiences* (Adult Literacy Support Services Fund. Obtainable from the BBC's Broadcasting Support Services, 252 Western Avenue, London W3 6XJ).

Ring binder plus audio cassette tape. Tutor's notes plus student material for use with adult groups on literacy and communication. Sections on using literature, group work and teaching writing. Includes a Resource Guide.

Parsons, C.J. 1982 *Assignments in Communication* (Edward Arnold)
Social and life skills. Contextualized tasks to develop communication, social and life skills, numeracy skills and problem-solving abilities. 40 assignments in 4 contexts – college/school, work, the home, and social life.

Ridgway, W. 1984 *Words at leisure, Words about work* and *Words about town* (Edward Arnold)
Lesson materials – mainly for comprehension.

15   Receiving the message

15.1   Communication as a two-way process

Communication is concerned with receiving messages as well as with sending them. Indeed it is not just artificial but misleading to separate the two. The way a message is transmitted affects the way in which it can be received. Your students will have spent their lives before you meet them reacting and responding to or deliberately ignoring or missing a host of signals. These will have been beamed their way by people older than themselves, often in authority over them, by their peers – friends and less trusted contacts – and by younger people. They will also have been receivers of other messages, in a less direct way, through such media as television, magazines, and fashion advertisements.

We have chosen to look at two areas where you can help your students to recognize some of these messages and to make informed decisions before they react. These areas are study skills and the media.

15.2   Receiving the message through study

Whatever the content of your course and whichever strategies you use, your students will not benefit fully unless they have learned how to study. They will need practice in listening with understanding, in note-taking, in information-retrieval skills, in reading for reference and for thorough comprehension. And they will need these skills for their life outside the classroom. Political literacy and functional literacy are both partly dependent upon reading comprehension to make sense of forms and leaflets, for example. Ideally these skills will be developed in other parts of the course, as well as in communication and social-education classes. You can play a part, however, in alerting your students to techniques and in providing the opportunity for practice, by setting assignments that use specific study skills.

Apart from such explicit goals as improving their ability to read, note-take, and use libraries, you should be aiming for an increase in your students' confidence and self-awareness and in their ability to assess their own needs and to experiment with different ways of learning.

Learning to learn
The FEU has produced a free publication called *How do I learn?* This contains

tutors' notes and worksheets for an introductory course. Rather than tackle the usual study-skill topics, it seeks to stimulate the students into identifying the basic strategies by which they can learn, through reflecting on their previous experience. Introducing the classification – learning by memorizing, by understanding and by doing – it begins by asking course participants to list things they have learned in the past and to classify them. The next step is to sort given activities and achievements into the three categories. There then follow a series of lessons concentrating on different types of learning. You would probably be able to use some of the lesson plans and worksheets with your students as an introduction to study skills. Certainly there are lots of ideas that could be used even if you needed to adapt the materials.

An alternative first session might be to hold a brainstorming session (section 2.3) with your students to identify the situations (on the course, at work, at home) in which they need to note-take, to summarize, to take messages, to listen, and to read. You could then negotiate a series of lessons with them to cover the main study-skill areas, using their ideas as the contexts for practising.

You might come up with the following details.

- *reading tasks* – leaflets, newspapers, textbooks, forms, letters, exam papers, library catalogues, memos, record and cassette sleeves
- *listening tasks* – messages, note-taking, following instructions, television and radio
- *writing tasks* – notes from books, lessons, discussions, reports, scripts, letters, forms
- *speaking tasks* – asking and answering questions, giving messages, instructions, participating in discussions

The most important aspect of this approach is that your students become aware that there are many different strategies involved in learning. The method appropriate for learning the highway code, for example, is different from that which is appropriate for learning how to ride a motor bike. One can be learned in an armchair; the other is definitely practical.

Organizing resources

Time

You could begin with a quiz to draw out your students' attitudes to study (Table 15.1). This could be worked at individually or in pairs during simulated interviews with one student asking the questions and the other noting the answers. Either way the resources could be compared and discussed in pairs and then in groups of four before you lead a general discussion.

The statements in Table 15.1 are only ideas to get you started. You will be able to write your own set of statements, appropriate for your particular students and the kind of tasks they do. Try to have a mix of positive and

Table 15.1   Quiz: attitudes to study

Attitude	Yes	No
• I always study as hard as I can		
• I usually find it easy to get going		
• I plan a study schedule week by week		
• I keep a record of the number of hours I put in each week		
• Sometimes I find it difficult to get started on a task		
• I usually manage to get everything done in time		
• I get distracted if I try to study for too long a period		
• Sometimes I get started on one task and move on to another because I get bored		
• I work best when I'm alone and it's quiet		
• I sometimes worry that other students are working harder than me		
• I don't know whether I'm doing enough study each week		
• I work better at some times of the day than others		
• I find it difficult to decide which task to do first when I have several		
• Some weeks I do a lot of work and others none at all		

negative statements and tell them you won't be taking their papers in. They don't have to reveal their responses if they don't want to.

During the general discussion, try to reduce anxiety by pointing out that everyone finds it difficult to get going sometimes and that we all take on too much or do too little at times. They need to review their own situation and work out a weekly plan which will give them time for leisure and sufficient sleep as well as time for study. If your students have nowhere to work at home, try to arrange a place in your centre where they can work, or encourage them to investigate the possibility of using their local library for private study.

Another activity would be to get each student to draw up a time plan for one week and to insert all the things they do. They could then pinpoint the times when they could study. The next stage would be to draw up a weekly schedule.

Encourage them to attempt the more creative and taxing assignments at times when they are most alert, the routine work when they are more likely to be tired. They should then make daily 'to do' lists and learn to give these priorities. They could work in pairs and practise on each other's list.

Your students are unlikely to be on academic courses with an emphasis on exams. You are not concerned with high-pressure cramming and exam-study techniques, but with establishing a pattern for quiet reading and study which they can use through their lives. So treat the subject very gently and ease them gradually into a routine that suits their individual circumstances.

Study materials
Your students may not be aware of the materials available for recording and storing their notes and assignments.

It is probably worthwhile taking a selection into class and demonstrating their use. If you work in a centre that has a bookshop for students, so much the better; you can show them the stock. If you do not have that possibility you will have to take in your own and colleagues' materials. Here are some suggestions.

- folders
    - ★ cardboard envelope folders (limited use – they disintegrate)
    - ★ hardback folders with visible envelopes for materials (useful for project reports, photos and so on)
    - ★ transparent folders with different coloured tops and zips (useful: see-at-a-glance contents and different colours for coding)
- files
    - ★ transparent files with the top or side open (ideal for individual reports or sets of worksheets)
    - ★ flat files with metal prongs (fiddly to use)
    - ★ box and lever-arch files (bulky to carry around); useful home storage but expensive)
- binders
    - ★ ring binder (popular for large amounts of material because this can be resequenced and added to easily)
    - ★ side binder (can make a paper or assignment appear more permanent and professional)
- clipboards and pads
    - ★ there is a variety of clipboards
    - ★ plain, ruled, and graph refill pads are available
    - ★ paper can be punched or unpunched
    - ★ paper can be with or without a margin
- extras
    - ★ paper clips, bulldog clips

★ yellow highlighting pens
★ correcting fluid

Your students will probably not have much money to spend, so help them to make sensible choices for a system which won't cost too much and which will give them flexibility. It's important that they develop a system quickly at the beginning of the course.

Using books

The distinction between 'using books' and 'reading books' is a crucial one. Students at all levels tend to plod laboriously through a book, however unsuitable, believing that their aim should be to read every word from cover to cover. It isn't surprising that they get distracted and bored at an early stage and abandon the exercise. Alternatively, they may flick through in a haphazard fashion, gleaning little of value and remembering nothing as they have no organizational framework into which to slot the snippets they do read.

Your students will probably need to use books if they attempt a project (section 5.3) or take part in a syndicate (section 2.3). This means that they would be better advised to develop the skill of quick reference and zip through several texts on their topic rather than to read one book for thorough comprehension. We are assuming a basic level of literacy for this exercise although we also recognize that you may well have students in your groups who have not received this level and who will need extra help if they are to be included in this study-skills programme.

Preview
- Take in a pile of library books that have something to do with a chosen project topic.
- Give them out – one book between two students – and ask students to look quickly at the following (five minutes should be enough).
  ★ title
  ★ date of publication (to see if the information is recent)
  ★ preface (to check the author's purpose)
  ★ contents page (to look up project topics)
  ★ index
- The first time you do this your students will probably still be stuck on the preface after five minutes. If so, reallocate the books and try again. They should improve gradually.
- Next get them to flip through the book looking at the headings, layout, and visual information.
- After another five minutes ask them to say whether the book is worth looking at in more detail for their project. Try to get them used to the idea of rejecting several books before they select one or two that will be worth spending more time on.

- Next give out books on different topics.
- Give pairs of students another five minutes to work out what their books are about.
- Swap books and go through the procedure again.
- Finally, write up on a board or OHP the title of each book and a few words for each pair summarizing the content.
- Discuss any differences of opinion, and where the pairs found their information – in the contents list? in the index? in the headings?

Skimming and scanning
Skimming is the process whereby you skip through a passage or book. Instead of attempting to read every word you go quickly and selectively through the text, seeking out headings and main points. Your student will have needed to do this for the preview exercises.

Scanning also involves skipping much of the text, but your purpose is different. Instead of trying to get a general impression of the content you will be looking for specific information, usually to find answers to specific questions.

So-called rapid-reading courses usually concentrate on increasing scanning speed. The eye moves in jerks across lines of text. These are referred to as 'fixations'. You can increase your reading speed by reducing the number of fixations and by increasing the speed of the return sweep. When we read we also tend to make backward eye movements instead of always going on to the next forward 'fixation'. More experienced readers do this less often, so another aim is to reduce this tendency. The fixations of both fast and slow readers tend to last for a quarter of a second. It is a bit like taking a photograph. The eye doesn't do the reading: the brain does that through interpretation, linking past knowledge and experience to the new information. Each span of words is therefore cleared (in the sense of photographed), much more quickly than it is understood or read. So although by reducing the number of fixations, backward eye movements and overlapping of eye spans you can increase the speed of your text coverage, this may not mean a greater reading speed as regards understanding what you read.

You can help your students to increase their scanning speed by presenting them with a series of narrow but progressivly widening passages of text which have lines down their centres.

The idea is to fix your eye on the centre of the line, gradually taking in more text with this one fixation as you progress through the passages.

Out of a series of say ten passages, the first might look like this:

Make sure you
keep looking at
the line which

> runs down the
> centre of this
> passage. Do not
> look from side
> to side, only
> at the line.

and the last might be this wide:

> If you keep concentrating
> on the line down the
> centre of this passage
> you will read all this
> very quickly. Remember
> not to let your eye
> sweep from side to side.
> Keep moving downwards.

Your students may well enjoy this exercise and they could make up the passages themselves, possibly for each other.

However, you should warn them that although they will benefit from decreasing the number of fixations they make if they began as slow readers, they should not confuse speed-reading with reading comprehension. Fast scanning is very useful in searching books and other written materials for relevant sections. But they also need to learn how to read thoroughly. It is a question of developing flexibility and the ability to recognize the most suitable strategy for the task – fast scanning or slower reading for thorough comprehension.

Note-taking from books
It is unlikely that your students will need to take notes from a whole book. They will probably wish to take selective notes for a project. This means that they will need to begin with a preview, an initial few minutes spent on a survey to obtain clues from the title, preface, contents page, index, chapter headings and summaries. Only when they have a general idea of the book's content should they begin taking notes. You should therefore do some previous exercises with them.

There are at least two overall methods for note-taking. A lot depends upon whether your students own the books concerned or whether they have borrowed them. If they own them, which is unlikely to be the case, they can go through the relevant sections with a yellow highlighting pen, identifying the main points. They can then note these down in their own words. If they have borrowed the books they can still do this, but using pencil and carefully rubbing out the marks at a later stage.

An alternative is to make notes as they read, but this is very difficult. Their tendency will be to start writing the moment they begin reading, and to copy out whole chunks verbatim. You have probably had the experience of receiving essays and projects with strings of poorly related sentences taken from books and obviously not understood by your students.

Note-taking should be an active and a selective process, but as university students often find it difficult after years of O- and A-level study, vocational-preparation students will probably need an enormous amount of guidance and practice. Keep asking yourself and them *why* they are taking notes. That way they should learn gradually that it is best to wait until they understand a passage thoroughly before they commit themselves to notes on paper.

Note-taking
- Students should work in pairs.
- Give each pair a short passage and two or three questions on it.
- One student reads the passage silently; the second student reads aloud the questions.
- The first student answers using information from the passage; the second student writes down the answers.
- They both look at the passage and questions, and check whether all the relevant information has been included in the answers. The idea of this is that they are forced to step back from the passage and to consider specific questions before taking notes.

If they do need to note down the message of an entire passage, encourage them to read it through once without holding a pen. Next they should consider it sentence by sentence, and try to put it in their own words. Lists should be reduced to overall category terms; details should be omitted. They should usually follow the author's order of headings. This, of course, is a summary. And it is not easy. Once more, be sure that they know *why* they are reducing the passage to note form. Do they really need all that information for their project? Would it be better to read it in pairs, to talk about it, to close the book and then to write it in their own words, from memory? They could look up any facts, figures or forgotten details, and add them in.

Encourage them to leave lots of space between each point they write, so that they can insert extra details, or re-order their points later.

If you have access to a microcomputer with a simple word-processing package, so much the better. Let them enter their notes from the keyboard and then they can add and amend as they like before printing the text out.

Reading comprehension
Comprehension is an active process and it is not an automatic companion of fast scanning. In fact the two rarely go together. As always, your student needs

to ask, 'Why am I reading this? Do I wish to memorize it or to find answers to specific questions?'

If you are cued into what you read, if you have some questions in your head and a helpful title for the text, you are far more likely to make the necessary connection between the words you are reading and your existing knowledge.

Try this:

With hocked gems financing him, our hero bravely defied all scornful laughter that tried to prevent his scheme. 'Your eyes deceive', he had said. 'An egg, not a table, correctly typifies this unexplored planet.' Now three sturdy sisters sought proof. Forging along, sometimes through calm vastness, yet more often over turbulent peaks and valleys, days became weeks as many doubters spread fearful rumours about the edge. At last, from nowhere welcome winged creatures appeared signifying momentous success. (Adapted from Dooling and Lachman, 1971, p. 217)

reported in New Scientist 9 February 1978

Now read the passage again with this title: 'Christopher Columbus discovers America'. Better? You may not agree with the implications in the title, but it should certainly cue you into the text!

Your students may be reading books, worksheets and handouts, leaflets or forms. The context may be study, or what could be termed functional or political literacy. Different reading material will mean different goals. You should talk about the need for flexibility with them as they may assume that reading is the same kind of activity whatever their purpose and whatever the material.

There is a technique commonly referred to as 'S Q 3 R':

- *S-survey:* Quick preview of text for general idea of content
- *Q-question:* Why are you reading it? Do you have specific questions to answer?
- *R-read:* Read through fairly quickly.
- *R-recite:* Put the materials in your own words.
- *R-review:* Go back over the text; check whether your notes and ideas are an accurate reflection. Do you agree with the author?

Pair work and buzz groups (section 2.3) could be concerned with each of these stages, with plenty of reporting back to ensure that the purpose of each stage and the procedure were understood.

This technique has obvious relevance for getting information from books. It is also a useful way of tackling shorter texts, worksheets, and passages of factual information.

It is possible to list a number of strategies that are involved in close, thorough reading of a text.

- Quickly study the headings and sub-headings
  - ★ establish main and subsidiary themes

    ★   ask the question – why do I need information on these themes?
- locate main ideas and separate these from the supporting materials
    ★   list the main ideas and underline them
    ★   leave lots of space for selected details between them
- find any definitions
    ★   this is particularly important if you are new to the subject and are learning the language
    ★   make a note of them under the relevant main-idea headings
- look for any passages with lists of examples or obvious extra details
    ★   reduce these to single words or short phrases
    ★   jot them down
- learn to recognize signal words which tell you what the author considers are important or subsidiary points, what are illustrations, and what are supporting arguments – signal words may indicate:
    ★   *emphasis* – 'above all', 'the chief factor', 'most important'.
    ★   *illustration* – 'for example', 'such as', 'specifically'
    ★   *addition* – 'first', 'also', 'moreover', 'likewise'
    ★   *change of direction* – 'however', 'yet', 'on the other hand'
    ★   *conclusion* – 'therefore', 'thus', 'hence', 'consequently', 'finally'

It might be quite fun to get your students to go through texts collecting these words and then trying to use them in sentences tied to a variety of contexts, serious and humorous. Although the cues implicit in them may seem obvious to us, your students may never have been alerted to such signals before. Recognizing these words can make an enormous difference to the ease and accuracy with which they read a text.

Note-taking

From listening and viewing
It would be a good idea to begin with a brainstorming session (section 2.3) to get your students thinking about what kinds of situations lead to written notes being taken from spoken words or visual materials. After the contributions have been organized you might have something like this:

- from a tutor's voice (exposition, briefing and plenary sessions)
- from visual aids (video, OHP, wall chart)
- from tape (students' tape-slide presentations, taped talks)
- from peers' voices (in buzz groups, syndicates, and discussions)
- from the telephone (messages, memos)
- from friends' voices (to relay messages)
- from supervisors at work (instruction to note down and to follow)
- from the media, television, radio, music or theatre (for projects or surveys)

    The next stage is to discuss the need for different styles of note-taking for different purposes. This might lead into an exploration of listening comprehension. There is listening for straightforward information, in which points are heard and noted down, and there is listening for understanding and interpretation, in which another stage is involved. The points may not make immediate sense: evaluation is required as well as attention. The first type of listening is fairly passive; the second type requires active participation. The listener has to synthesize the information and add to it from previous knowledge and experience.

Any type of note-taking from listening is more difficult than note-taking from writing, because you cannot backtrack and go over sections again. There is also a limit to the amount of information that can be held in short-term memory. Messages are received and stored temporarily. Unless they are rehearsed – that is, repeated and gone over – they will not be transferred to long-term memory. Notes from a verbal delivery therefore need to be taken at a fairly fast pace.

From lectures and exposition lessons

You might like to give your students early practice in a controlled situation before you require them to take notes from a lengthier exposition phase.

Note-taking exercise

- Divide your group into pairs.
- In each pair, one student has three minutes to explain an aspect of a leisure activity or interest to his or her partner; the listener may not take notes.
- The listener then repeats the information back.
- They then reverse roles and go through the procedure again.
- Finally they list the difficulties encountered and share ideas on what kind of notes they could have taken.

This activity should lead to a discussion about the kind of notes that might have helped.

Some people find it easier to attend if they have prepared themselves by asking questions beforehand that they hope the tutor's exposition will answer.

Incomplete handouts

You can help your students to take notes from your own presentations by providing incomplete handouts and worksheets. On these you could put the main headings and any important details, figures, and examples. Leave lots of space for your students to add information. If you use visual aids, provide the diagram skeleton on the handout, leaving the details for your students to add.

It is not a good idea to give them *all* the information: unless they make the handout 'their own' by adding to it they are unlikely to remember it, or maybe even to read it.

Note-taking decisions
Even if you provide an incomplete handout your students will have to choose
a style of note-taking.

Some of the possible decisions are:

- take down everything, including diagrams
- take down skeletal notes (main headings and points), but only write notes
  on the rest, in your own words, after listening for a while
- use a flow-chart presentation, putting arrows between the points – for this
  you need to note the speaker's structuring moves and signal words ('there
  are six main points', 'that concludes', etc.)
- draw spidergrams or brain patterns (Tony Buzan, 1974)

Teaching note-taking skills
Encourage your students to try out all of these by giving short presentations
and by letting them experiment and compare notes with each other. Figure
15.1 shows a spidergram for this section.

Whichever method is chosen there are some tips you can give:

- try out blank and ruled paper to establish personal preference
- title and date the first page; thereafter number the sheets
- underline headings
- leave wide margins
- begin headings and main points at margin edge
- indent subsidiary points
- use a numbering system for lists of points
- leave lots of space between headings, for inserts
- leave a space if you miss something, and remember to go back to it
- make up a system of abbreviations for words used often
- leave out words like 'the', 'is', 'a', 'and'
- remember to continue taking notes during discussion and questions

After you have helped your students practise note-taking, give them the
opportunity to synthesize their notes and reproduce a spoken text. This is
usually a more difficult operation.

Use situations that are credible – a telephone message, for example. People
often jot down brief points while they're on the phone. Then if they need to
leave a message which someone else will understand, they have to connect the
points in more or less continuous prose. Pairs could simulate that situation.
Notes could also be taken from video films, or you could ask your students to
watch a news or magazine programme on television and take notes ready for a
short oral presentation the next day. This would tie in well with media studies
(section 7.4). During visits (section 5.2) – say, to a magistrates' court –
students could be encouraged to take notes.

You will probably find that your students have difficulty with all types of
note-taking at first. They should improve gradually with practice, but in class
it is probably best to give them lots of support, with incomplete handouts and

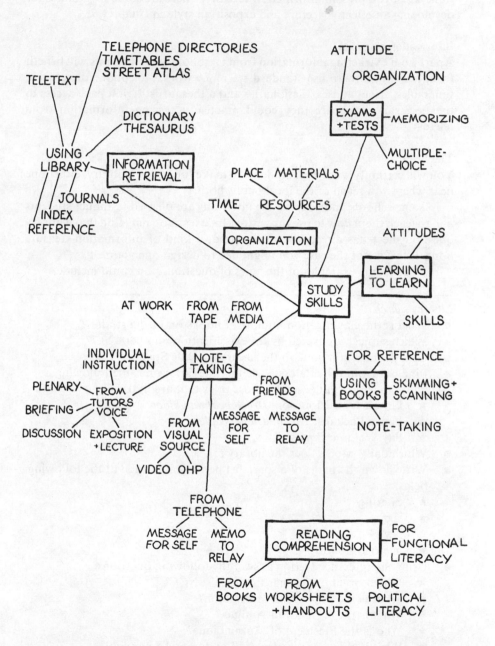

Figure 15.1   Spidergram notes on this study-skills section

carefully structured and paced presentations. Try not to jump from topic to topic when you present information verbally. There are some suggestions for developing an effective lecture and exposition style in Chapter 6.

Information retrieval
Apart from extracting information from textbooks your students will benefit from learning how to use standard reference works, telephone directories, timetables, street atlases, dictionaries and a thesaurus. If you have access to the necessary hardware they could practise accessing information from teletext.

The library
You will certainly want your students to make full use of a library, either one near where you teach or the local public library.

In some schools and colleges the librarians are pleased to induct students and to teach them how to use the various indexes. You may find that a library question sheet has already been produced, a kind of information treasure hunt. If this is not the case you might like to design one yourself.

Here are some examples of the types of questions you could include.

Library search
- What is the classification number of books on media studies?
- Which subject is covered by the classification number 420.7?
- Give the title of a book in the library by Dale Spender.
- Find out from the catalogue whether the library has the following books in stock. Put a tick by those titles that are in the library.
  - ★ Linton Kwesi Johnson: *Dread beat and blood*
  - ★ Vance Packard: *The hidden persuaders*
  - ★ Fay Weldon: *Praxis*
- Which daily papers does the library take?
- Write down the name of a specialist periodical in each of the following fields:
  - ★ catering
  - ★ jazz
  - ★ law
  - ★ microcomputing
- Using the reference section answer the following questions.
  - ★ Which organization has the initials 'NCCL'?
  - ★ What is the population of Brighton?
  - ★ What is the currency of Antigua?
  - ★ Who is the President of Mozambique?
  - ★ What is the distance between London and Liverpool?

Once your students have become accustomed to using the library you might like to encourage further exploration by giving topics for short library-research projects.

Telephone directories, street atlases, travel timetables
It is probably best not to set isolated tasks. Some of the integrated assignments that students can work on in a communication workshop context (Chapter 8) include questions to do with direction-following and route planning. While groups are working on these you could circulate and give individual help.

If you can arrange for friends and contacts to be at home or work to receive telephone calls at specific times you could encourage your students to look up real telephone numbers and make real calls. This is more acceptable than working through lists of anonymous names for numbers or than sorting names into alphabetical order.

When you arrange a visit (section 5.2) involve your students in planning the travel. This involves using maps and timetables and often working out the fares.

Always try, in this way, to set these tasks in a real context.

Coping with tests and examinations
Although your students will probably not be taking many formal examinations a number of courses do involve a test element. The City and Guilds course in Communication Skills (772) has a multiple-choice test, for example. And you yourself may wish to check your students' learning progress with an occasional formal test. In any case your students will benefit from some practice in memorizing.

Memorizing
Alert your students to the need to find methods that will suit their own individual learning styles. Some people learn best from continuous text, some from diagrams, others from listening. Some like mnemonics and word associations, others prefer regular repetition and rehearsing.

Talk to them about short- and long-term memory. Information is only held in short-term memory for about thirty seconds unless it is rehearsed. New material is likely to be forgotten unless it is linked to existing knowledge. Encourage them to seek ways of connecting the material to be learned to their past experience.

They will need to organize the material, possibly by imposing an artificial structure onto it. Say for example they wish to memorize a list of shopping items:

beer, shampoo, squash, cereal, bacon, plasters, milk, eggs

They could categorize it:

drinks	chemist	breakfast
milk	shampoo	cereal
beer	plasters	eggs
squash		bacon

Another method is to use first letters to remember a list of key words. These need to be rearranged until a word is made that is easily remembered. These methods can assist with the rote-learning type of memorizing which we all need to do occasionally for telephone numbers, dates, car and bike registration numbers. The alternative is reciting the information over and over again, with repeated self-testing.

Explain to your students that it is better to space such memorizing out over several sessions. Several short bursts are more effective than one long blast. This is because the material can transfer from short- to long-term memory during the 'rest' periods.

Tests

You could begin by giving your students a trick set of instructions to alert them to the need to read question papers thoroughly. This need applies to their work experience too. They may use machinery such that it is essential that they pay attention to all the written and verbal instructions before they touch anything.

Here is an example of the kind of trick questions you might include:

Instructions (Read all instructions before you begin)
1 Write your first name in block capitals.
2 Write your surname.
3 Write your full address.
4 Write down your favourite colour.
5 Write down the name of your favourite female singer.
6 Count the number of male students in the room.
⋮
18 How much would it cost to buy 8 tins of cat food at 35 pence per tin?
19 Give the names of three television programmes you watch regularly.
20 What is the name of the leader of the opposition to this country's government?
Answer questions 1, 2 and 3 only.

Some tutors like to include some deliberately silly questions, such as 'stand up to answer this question' or 'touch your nose three times'. This can of course be fun, but it can also arouse students' suspicions and it lessens the similarity between a real test and this instruction sheet. You will probably find that most of your students are caught out, but that they will pay more attention to initial instructions in later test situations, and also in their work on class assignments.

Multiple-choice

Your students may well take a multiple-choice test so you will wish to give them some practice.

There are a few suggestions you could make:

- Go through the paper at an even pace, answering the easier questions first.
- Leave any you are unsure about until the end.
- Guess if you don't know an answer. But stick to your first guess. Research indicates that it has more chance of being right!
- If guessing, go for the answers that have qualifiers like 'usually', 'most', and 'generally'. These are more likely to be right than ones with absolute statements with words like 'all', 'only' or 'never'.
- Even if the first answer to a given question in a given set seems correct, read all the other possibilities before you commit yourself. There may be an even better answer later, or one that says 'all of these'.
- Apart from this try to lessen the anxiety of tests by giving plenty of practice and by remaining outwardly calm yourself on the day.

If you can develop these skills alongside the work you do in social education and communications, integrating them wherever possible and reinforcing them with practical exercises, your students should increase their ability to receive, understand and use the messages addressed to them through coursework and other published materials.

They will also need to practise listening to each other to pick up the messages, stated and implied, in all types of social communication. Role-play and simulation can provide the context for this work. If you haven't already done so, you might like to look at sections 4.2 and 4.3.

15.3 Receiving the message through the media

Your students live in a society in which social and cultural values are transmitted through mass-media channels. Television, radio, newspapers and magazines all pass on explicit and implicit messages about what kinds of behaviour are valued in our society and what kinds are considered to be anti-social. Images of achievement and success are manufactured and communicated through pictures and text. We tend to react to these messages according to our existing attitudes. Hence we identify news items or features which we consider to be biased and those we accept as more objective. We are able to pick out the stereotypes and the worst examples of exaggeration and omission.

Despite this ability to discriminate, we are all influenced to some extent by the established 'consensus' attitudes held in our society. This widespread acceptance of 'commonsense' views, of a shared framework for interpreting reality, leads to assumptions. One such assumption is that television news is generally impartial and trustworthy, particularly that produced by the BBC. But close study of the media, of the way meaning is constructed and presented for the public, can reveal the ambiguity and relativity of many of the messages that are put over as unchallengable basic truths.

If you have studied or are particularly interested in media analysis or if you teach on more advanced communication and media courses, you will be aware of the contribution semiotics has made in analysing signs and alerting us to the social production of meaning and the process of myth-making. If you are a specialist in this area, it may seem difficult to you to conduct a serious study of the media without reference to concepts such as the 'multi-accentuality of signs' and the 'relationship between connotation, myth and ideology'. There are however ways of alerting your students to the power and influence of the media without using the kind of terminology that would certainly confuse and probably alienate them. If you have not yet encountered semiotics and would like to learn more for your own interest and to provide a background for your teaching, have a look at some of the books recommended in the resources list (section 15.5): these include introductions to this increasingly popular system of analysis.

Your students will probably not be aware of the contribution the media makes to the shaping of their behaviour, tastes and attitudes. Their own identity and self-image, the way they see themselves in relation to their peers, parents, tutors, and supervisors at work, will be affected by their exposure to the news channels and to the images of youth presented in films, novels, music videos and theatre.

These will affect, if not determine, how they define success and achievement. The media encourages and discourages certain types of behaviour, and gives positive value to some life-styles and negative value to others. Probably the biggest influence on the way your students will see themselves is that of television programmes, videos, and the magazines produced for the youth market.

There is little doubt that they receive these messages. You can help them to interpret them and make sense of them on their own terms.

Take common media messages and explore them with your students to see how the message is created, built up by collections of images, verbal and visual. Help your students to identify the more biased, subjective texts. Look at emotive language and at the ambiguity of visual images. Your aim should be to prevent your students from feeling too much pressure, either to conform or to react negatively.

Detecting bias

A common but much criticized analogy used in describing the media is of a 'mirror held up to society', an impartial record of reality. Criticism of this centres on the argument that the media itself plays a major role in creating this reality in the way it selects and presents information and interprets it. The media is not a passive mirror but an active, creative part of society and social meaning.

In order to communicate we need to share common frameworks of interpretation. The way we perceive events is at least partially determined by our previous experience and by the categories our language makes available to us. The media plays a major part in manufacturing and reproducing cultural images which help make up this shared 'reality'.

It is of course a very complicated process which neither we here, nor you in the classroom, can do justice to in the time and space available and at the level which concerns us. Nevertheless it should be possible to give your students insights into this process. You can look at the ways in which information is selected and presented and you can discuss the influence of this presentation on attitudes and values and ultimately on behaviour.

The ideas you discuss are abstract and may well be new for your students so you must make sure that the vehicle for them, the material you use, the topics and the contexts are all familiar.

News selection

One way in which the media helps to create our view of reality is by a process of selection. Certain types of event are publicized and highlighted; others are ignored. You could explore the idea of 'news-worthiness' with your students by conducting small-scale research projects on newspapers and television news programmes. There are ideas for this type of activity at the end of this section.

Here are some of the questions you and your students might ask.

Discussion of news selection

● How accurately does the selection reflect the real world?

● Is there a 'real world' to be objective about? Or do we all have our own 'real worlds' in which events are interpreted according to our own experience and gradually developed set views? Is our perception rather like looking through different camera lenses and filters?

● Which assumptions are taken for granted by the media? For example: 'all stealing is a crime and shouldn't pay'; 'women should put their families and in particular their children before all else'; 'strikes damage the economy'; 'adults know better than children'.

● Is it inevitable that young people's reality will differ from that of their parents?

● If all the owners of newspapers, the Government, television controllers and journalists were under twenty years old, how would the selection of the news be different from the selection we have now?

Impartiality

Once you have looked at news coverage, the deliberate and less conscious highlighting of certain types of events and the exclusion of others, you can turn to an analysis of the news items themselves.

Language in newspapers

- Look at the language of newspaper copy. How are people and events described? Your students could collect words that describe the same set of people or events but that have differing connotations. Consider, for example,

  freedom fighters; soldiers; guerillas; terrorists

  or

  young people; teenagers; adolescents; youths; hooligans.

  What is different about each label? What are the assumptions, values, and messages implicit in them?
- How are certain groups in society – e.g. women, black people, young people, the unemployed – represented?
- Is the language sexist or racist?
- How does the use of such language help to form attitudes?

You may find your students resistant to some of the ideas that will probably emerge in discussion. It is, after all, difficult to adjust to change and they will probably not have challenged the idea of 'commonsense' and accepted shared reality before. The idea that language affects attitudes may be real to them, in their own experience of prejudice, for example. However they may not previously have analysed what is going on in terms of attitude formation, as for example when women are left out by terms such as 'chairman' or phrases such as 'all men are born free', or when an encounter between police and black citizens of similar age is described as a confrontation between police 'officers' and black 'youth'.

We all take a while to accept new ideas so it is probably best not to argue too strenuously with unconvinced or suspicious students. After they have worked on a few projects they will probably attune themselves gradually to a new way of looking at communication and language.

Alert your students to the way stereotypes are built up, to the way the news tends to present opposites. Examples include: government/unions, police/criminals, and workers/scroungers. What is the purpose of this? How does it determine our attitude to what is acceptable social behaviour and to what counts as achievement? Should we accept the dominant view of reality by reading media messages in the way they are intended or should we challenge the assumptions?

Look also at the visual images, at press photographs and pictures in advertisements. How do these contribute to the verbal message? How are people dressed? What are their facial expressions, their postures and their gestures? Are there deliberate juxtapositions of social groups – pickets and managers, football supporters and police? If there are, what messages are intended? How are these images presented as social reality? Could they be presented in a different way? How do pictures and captions work together? There are suggestions for exploring these ideas in the sample lesson plan (section 15.4).

Remember that your primary purpose is not to teach the theory or even the tools of media analysis; nor is it to incite your students to reject all the values that our society transmits through its media. Your aim is to help your students to recognize the influence the media exerts upon them. That way they should be able to receive the messages consciously and to discriminate between what on the one hand is relevant and significant for them and what on the other hand will only contribute to a negative self-image or create anxiety for them if they do not present their own challenge.

A carefully organized, enthusiastic exploration of the media should help students to understand and come to terms with what society seems to expect of them and what they believe they can realistically offer and achieve. The goal is a sufficient degree of self-determination, confidence and ability to discriminate and to decide for themselves.

Suggestions for media projects

Media studies usually involves an exploration of ownership and control, of the process by which news is selected and manufactured and of the effect of news presentation on social behaviour. These are almost certainly beyond the scope of small-scale classroom projects. It is probably best to concentrate on the way images and content are presented in television news, radio, newspapers and journals.

Compare news sources

- Compare two daily newspapers (the *Mirror* and the *Guardian*, perhaps) or two different news channels (e.g. BBC and ITV news).
- Look at which news items are selected, which are given prominence.
- Examine headline size and the relation between headline and copy. Look at the location of articles, such as on page one or at the bottom of a centre page, or at the beginning, centre or end of the running order of television news items. How many pictures are used and how are they juxtaposed with text?
- Look at a particular television news programme over several days. Then analyse it under headings that you have agreed with your students, perhaps as the result of a brainstorming session. Give out or group-design a questionnaire and compare the news script with the visual images, the pictures used, the layout of the news desk, the appearance of the newsreader.

Compare two forms of communication
- Take one day and look at newspaper and television news coverage (daily paper and breakfast television). Ask the same sort of questions – which news items are selected; which are taken as lead stories?

Internal comparison of one newspaper
- Look at images of women – in news stories, on the women's page, in cartoons. Is there consistency in the attitudes communicated?
- Look at images of youth – in stories, perhaps. How many refer to young people; what language do they use? If there is a special section for young readers, what does it assume regarding the interests of young people?

Compare different channels of communication
- Take one subject (like 'police', the 'unemployed' or 'mothers'). Look at how it is presented in television news and newspapers, and compare this with its representation in fiction, plays, comedy shows, and advertisements.
- What does this tell you about the construction of images? Look for stereotyping and assumptions about consensus attitudes.

Compare students' own experience with media coverage of local events
- You could link this with a visit, to a magistrate's court, perhaps. Students could take notes and compare their own record with the reporting in the local paper.

An area of interest
- This could be for individual projects. Students could compare media coverage of a topic (like environmental pollution, local unemployment, or crèche facilities) with their own research.

Television news
- Lead a discussion on the major categories of news topics. You would probably come up with domestics news, foreign news, the economy, politics, sport, occasional stories on disasters, celebrities and so on.
- Ask your students to watch television on an agreed night or to read a particular paper on agreed days. Add up the number of stories that fall into each category. This could lead to a survey report involving pie charts and histograms.

Relation between visual images and copy text
- Select a page or a story in a newspaper.
  - ★ What do the visual images contribute? Could you spot the storyline

from the pictures alone? If you used different pictures, would it
alter the meaning of the words?

★ Look at the elements that help news photos signify. What makes
them newsworthy (e.g. topicality, glamour, conflict, celebrity
presence, humour)?

★ Look at the body language – facial expressions, gestures, postures.

★ What of the context – picture background, any physical objects
deliberately included?

★ Examine technical aspects – are the pictures blurred, sharp, close-
up or distant shots, light or dark?

★ Consider the photo's position in the paper – juxtaposition,
position on the page, caption.

★ Explore the ambiguity of the visual cues. Look at how the written
caption or the spoken commentary influences the interpretation of
the visual image.

● Ask your students to bring in selected newspaper pictures with the
captions stuck on separate pieces of paper. These contributions should
then be jumbled and the exercise is to rematch the pairs. Then lead a
discussion on all the issues involved.

● Alternatively you could bring in the pictures and your students could
write the captions. They could then look at the original ones and
consider any differences.

● You could also ask your students to pick a local topic they would like
to study (for example, housing or unemployment). Once the whole
group has agreed on a topic, get small working pairs or trios to decide
on a particular news 'slant' they want to emphasize. These teams then
take three of four still photographs to illustrate their 'angle'. They
could also write accompanying text, or tape a commentary with the
addition of selected music.

Written language in newspapers
● Look at the use of rhetoric (language used to persuade or influence).
Identify catch phrases ('hold the country to ransom', etc.) and discuss
their influence. Search for examples of the use of sexist or racist
language.

Content analysis
● This is probably beyond the scope of your time but you could alert
your students to how this is done. Take a large sample of stories and
then classify them under different headings, to look at the weightings,
preoccupations and omissions. (See the work of the Glasgow Media
Group, 1976 & 1980, and Fiske, 1982.)

Keep a daily log
- Students could each take one week and record how much time he or she spends on the media in its widest sense – include television, newspapers, radio, books, cinema, theatre, music. They could then conduct a survey using their friends as subjects.

Local newspaper or radio station visit
- Try to establish a visiting relationship with the staff. Arrange a visit so that your students can observe the stages of news production. They may even be able to accompany a reporter on an assignment.

Simulation
- Students work in editorial teams to produce a radio news bulletin on tape or a television one on video. This could involve editing and re-writing stories or writing and recording a linked commentary for a video. Rather than write all the stories you could use a local newspaper as a source of copy and rewrite this. (See the reference for Radio Covingham Simulation, page 81).

Select a theme
- Students could then go out and take photographs to illustrate the theme. Two groups should then take the same set of photographs and one write a commentary to present the subject in a favourable light and the other to show it in an unfavourable light.

Select an issue
- In groups your students could take an issue that they feel affects them personally. It might be a local protest or a youth fashion cult. They should then bring in pictures and write captions. After a discussion of bias, etc., each student or student group could write a short article using the pictures.

Advertisements
- You and your students could bring in a selection of advertisements.
  - ★ Separate the written text from the visual. In buzz groups attempt to relink the two.
  - ★ Lead a discussion on how advertisers seek to persuade and influence. Consider how women, black people, children and other groups are presented.
- Ask your students to select a product and produce pictures and written text to promote it.

15.4 Sample lesson plan

Length of session: 2 hours (be flexible about phase timing).
Group size: 15.

Resources
- Two copies each of three different newspapers for the day of the lesson. (Suggested range: *Guardian, Mail, Mirror.*)
- Large cards, scissors, paste, felt pens (three sets).

Aims
- To raise students' consciousness of the role of the media in determining and/or reinforcing social attitudes and stereotypes.

Objectives
- Students will compare different newspapers' presentation of three social groups.
- Students will identify the ways in which the media sends messages.
- Students will distinguish fact from opinion.
- Students will practise communicating effectively in speech and writing.

Method
Phase 1: Introductory activity (5 minutes)
a Write three words on the board: women – youths – unemployed.
b Ask students to spend three minutes writing down the first ideas that come into their heads.

Phase 2: Introductory discussion (10 minutes)
a Invite and write up students' ideas on board under the appropriate headings.
b Check how consistent and similar the contributions are.
c Lead a discussion on how students think social attitudes are formed.
d Explore the idea that social consensus influences them. How far do their ideas fit in with prevailing social attitudes?

Phase 3: Group activity (45 minutes)
a Divide the students into three groups.
b Give each group two copies of a different newspaper.
c Brief each group separately; while they wait for this they can browse through the paper.
d In your briefing ask them to find as many references to each of these three categories (women, youth, unemployed) as they can. References could be in articles, cartoons, news stories, pictures.
e Ask them to cut these out and stick them to the large cards – one sheet per category. At this stage they need not evaluate or comment on the material.

Phase 4: Whole-group activity (15 minutes)
a   Display the three sets of cards for each subject category.
b   In the whole group lead a discussion comparing and contrasting the images. Points to bring out: are the subjects presented differently in different sections of the papers (fashion, sport, overseas, etc)?
c   How do the three newspapers vary in their approach?
d   Are there examples of sexism, ageism, racism?
e   Do the students believe that readers of particular newspapers have existing attitudes reinforced or are they subject to fresh influences?

Phase 5: Individual activity (written) (30 minutes)
a   Ask each student to select one of the three subjects and to use the evidence presented on the cards to write a brief report on the way the three different newspapers present a view which might affect attitudes.
b   If you have students for whom this task is too difficult, provide a range of alternatives: incomplete worksheets, cloze-procedure worksheets using newspaper articles, etc.

15.5   Resources list

Tutor's background reading

General
Fiske, J. 1982 *Introduction to communication studies* (Methuen)
Fiske, J. and J. Hartley 1978 *Reading television* (Methuen)
Glasgow Media Group 1976 *Bad news* (Routledge and Kegan Paul)
Glasgow Media Group 1980 *More bad news* (Routledge & Kegan Paul)
Gurevitch, M., T. Bennett, J. Curan, J. Woolacot (eds). 1982 *Culture, society the media* (Methuen)
Hartley, J. 1982 *Understanding news* (Methuen)
    There is a useful list of projects in Chapter 10.
Packard, V. 1981 *The hidden persuaders*, revised edn. (Pelican)
Tuchman, G. 1978 *Making news: a study in the construction of reality* (New York Free Press)

Visual
Thompson, P. and D. Davenport 1980 *The Penguin dictionary of visual language* (Penguin)

Women
Adams C. and R. Laurikietis 1980 *The gender trap: Book 3 Messages and images* (Virago)

Race
Hartman, P. and C. Husband 1974 *Racism and the mass media* (Davis Poynter)

Husband, C. (ed.) 1975 *White media and black Britain* (Arrow)

Classroom materials
Get from the British Film Institute a catalogue of their teaching packs and slides packs. British Film Institute Education Department, 81 Dean Street, London W1U 6AA.
Adams, C. and R. Laurikietis 1980 *The Gender Trap* Books 1, 2 and 3, revised edns (Virgo Press)
Book 1: 'Education and work', Book 2: 'Sex and marriage', Book 3: 'Messages and images'. Comprehensive and useful books with discussion and activity materials based on sex roles.
Barret, R. and G. Green 1983 *Day-to-day English* (Longman)
5 sections, each with a range of assignments: 'Headline news', 'Sending messages', 'Planning a holiday', 'Invention and communicating', 'Word perfect'.
Buzan, A. 1974 *Use your head* (BBC Publications)
Comprehensive ideas for exercises on a wide range of study skills.
De Bono, E. 1976 *Teaching thinking* (Temple Smith)
De Leeuw, M. and E. 1965 *Read better, read faster* (Penguin)
Further Education Unit 1981 *How do I learn?* (FEU)
Good, M.R. Jenkins, S. Leavers and A. Pates 1981 *Basic education 16–19* (National Extension College)
Tutor's resource manual, adapting the student-centred approach used in adult education to the 16–19 age group. Short chapters on 'Learning and memory', 'Curriculum models available to copy', 'Assessing students' progress', 'Groups', 'Making your own resources'.
Hopson, B. and M. Scally 1982 *Lifeskills Teaching Programmes No. 2* (Lifeskills Associates)
Tutor's notes and teaching ideas, including study-skills techniques and discussion of learning from experience.
Inner London Education Authority *Learning in a city* (ILEA Learning Materials Service, Publishing Centre, Highbury Station Road, London N1 1SB)
Workpack of students' materials with tutor's notes on study skills and learning styles.
Krupar, K.R. 1973 *Communication games* (New York Free Press)
Group-interaction games, dealing with aspects of verbal and non-verbal communication.
Robinson, D. and R. Power 1984 *Spotlight on communication* (Pitman)
Student's book with assignments and tasks in an appropriate range of contexts, social and vocational, including form-filling, interpreting charts and graphs, information retrieval, non-verbal communication.
Underhill, A. 1980 *Use your dictionary* (O.U.P.)

16 Values and choices

16.1 Teaching about moral issues

Moral education is an area not unfamiliar in schools, though it is relatively rare in the further-education curriculum. True, some of the topics chosen as examples of teaching ideas in this chapter are issues that tutors in other fields (notably general studies) have often dealt with in the past. Other objectives which you need to pursue if you are to do justice to the area are uncommon in further-education courses: expecting tutor and students to identify and justify moral rules and principles, for example, or helping students to formulate their own codes of behaviour.

Suggesting that you help your students 'formulate their own codes of behaviour' is deceptively straightforward; they *already* operate according to certain values and moral rules. You and they have to discover what their personal value systems are; then evelute these according to certain mutually agreed criteria; and finally test them out by applying them to a range of examples.

Is there anything distinctive about moral reasoning? What are the teaching skills involved? How do you as a tutor distinguish between whether students are 'doing it wrong' (i.e. lack some of the skills necessary to formulate and apply principles) or whether they have 'got it wrong' in the sense of contemplating actions that many would find unacceptable, or that go against principles that they claim to hold? Seeing stealing as an alternative to unemployment is one such example discussed in Chapter 13. A related but different problem is when students defend opinions that you find personally offensive, such as racist views. What do you do in such instances? Exactly what can one afford to be neutral about?

Moral questions and the 16–19s
Why are moral issues included in the core curriculum? Most schools include discussion on moral issues as part of areas like social or religious studies. What makes it worth emphasizing these again for the 16–19 age group? Finding answers to this question will help you clarify your ideas about what objectives are worth pursuing, what topics worth taking up.

There are several reasons why moral issues and personal values become important at this stage.

- Newly acquired adult status carries untried rights and responsibilities. The students' range of relationships is widening, their field of action is becoming correspondingly greater.
- There are often contradictions in the expectations of this wider range of social contacts. With greater independence comes conflicting pressures. The task of building one's own personal value system becomes more complicated.
- The speed of social change presents them with new problems to which old solutions cannot be applied. At this stage of their lives students must negotiate a delicate balance between adapting to expectations and selecting (more or less consciously) where to conform, while also innovating to meet situations that have not arisen before.
- Older students are often well equipped and willing to engage in reflective discussion and intellectually prepared to be objective about themselves, though not always in a conventionally formal language. Preoccupations about how to treat others and how they wish to be treated are strong.

'Doing' morality

Morality is a practical activity. As with other activities that come under the umbrella of social education, making sense of it requires the use of concepts and processes from various disciplines: philosophy, psychology and sociology. A tutor could ignore these differences and just go ahead and 'do it' – that is, plunge straight into one of the activities suggested in the ABC core and use his or her own judgement and experience to discuss the rights and wrongs of the examples. The difficulty with the *ad hoc* approach is that:

- it won't necessarily help students develop their own ability to argue a case, or to generalize from a familiar example to an unforeseen or more complicated one
- it does not equip the students to make a critical assessment of the tutor's reasons or actions
- without some model of what is involved, the tutor is not equipped to analyse mistakes or inadequacies in the students' reasoning

Finding a model for making moral decisions

Having stressed the need for an understanding that goes deeper than the commonsense or rule-of-thumb approach we do not want to give the impression that no tutor should discuss moral questions until he or she has become a theoretical expert. As we made clear in the introduction to this book, in our view this is not how teaching works. Teacher education itself is bedevilled by the static model – 'learn first' than 'go and do'.

Research into moral education has one of two starting points: the rational approach which makes a philosophical analysis of moral concepts, principles and procedures, or the inductive approach (used in much of the Schools

Council Moral Education Project material) which begins with the students' own accounts of moral problems. If you want to go deeper into any of these approaches, look at the sources recommended in the resources list (section 16.5). Our own approach favours the second method. We hope that the discussion that follows will give you ideas useful for planning sessions and for illuminating what happens when moral choices are to be made.

The need for ground rules
In your discussions with students you will be asking them to reflect on their own actions, evaluate the actions of others and choose a course of action for a particular circumstance, taking into account the effect their actions will have on others. Because it is a practical activity the manner in which you handle the group will be available for evaluation in just the same way as other actions that may be discussed. Your subject matter can be used reflexively to judge how you behave towards your students. Concepts like consideration for others and fairness have to be *exhibited*, not just talked about. For this reason there should be explicit and mutually agreed rules which govern your discussions.

What does making a moral judgement involve?
Rather than presenting students with an answer to this question and asking them to apply it to particular instances (the rational 'front-end' model) it is more useful to begin by talking about problems as students see them, and to derive the principles and ideal procedures from their discussions. This allows the students to go at their own pace and level, and will give you a much clearer picture of the kind of reasoning they are using.
    Reasoning about moral issues has these elements:

● a perceptive awareness of one's own feelings and those of others
● some fundamental ordering principles such as consideration for others
● the ability to formulate rules based on these
● the ability to select relevant information and use these rules to draw up courses of action
● the foresight to see likely outcomes and their effects on others

Levels of reasoning
You will need criteria to help you assess the various styles of making judgements that your students use. Developmental psychologists (notably Piaget, 1932, and Kohlberg, 1961) see the variety of styles as stages in the development of the child's ability to use moral reasoning. As with other aspects of psychological theories about intellectual and emotional develop-ment, the value of these insights is that they give you a picture of the logical steps through which such thinking develops. Tutors working with older students tend to discount such theories as only relevant to those working with younger children. It is more helpful to see the chronology they describe as that of a logical sequence rather than as a person's growth measured in years –

people of very mature years are capable of showing all the signs of a fairly simple level of reasoning, just as children's powers of reasoning are frequently underestimated – one undesirable influence of the theories.

In general, progress begins from the simple level at which rules must be obeyed without question. The next stage is marked by an awareness that there is some choice – rules are still there to be obeyed but you do it for some reward, such as social approval. The most mature or sophisticated level is that at which the individual chooses to observe certain rules out of a reciprocal respect for others.

Choosing your teaching objectives

You probably won't want to run a sequence of sessions devoted solely to discussing moral issues. You are more likely to include them as another aspect of one of the topics suggested elsewhere in this book. When your students are talking about work experience, for example, or looking at age limits and legal responsibilities in relation to drinking, driving or borrowing money. Personal relationships contain a strong element of moral responsibility.

The teaching suggestions included in this chapter list ideas which could form whole sessions or parts of sessions. The longer your teaching session, the more reasonable it seems to see this activity (learning how to make moral judgements) as forming part of the session only. The basic pattern for each of these teaching ideas is of an active strategy (it might be role-play or a game) followed by a discussion. In both kinds of activity you will be looking to develop some of the abilities listed below.

The abilities necessary for solving moral problems
- *Reasoning ability*
  - ★ Can the students consider a body of evidence and form a hypothesis?
  - ★ Are they able to test it out by making up further examples?
- *Formulating rules and principles*
  - ★ Can they derive these from a variety of instances?
  - ★ Can they analyse social situations?
  - ★ Can they select relevant information?
- *Creative problem-solving*
  - ★ Are they willing and able to see a variety of solutions?
  - ★ Do they appreciate the contrast between convergent and divergent styles of thinking? (Of course it's not necessary that they use those terms, just that they have some experience of using each style.)
  - ★ Can they accept and use each other's criticism in a problem-solving activity? Try using games as a way of testing this out, such as one of de Bono's lateral-thinking exercises. Criticism is less damaging when the content is value-free. Brainstorming works by building into the problem-solving session a period during which no criticism is allowed.

- *Reflective and productive discussion*
  - ★ Can they work effectively as a large group to examine controversial issues? Do they see discussion as a useful tool?
  - ★ Can they handle disagreements for themselves? Can they tolerate frustrations when no solution seems likely?

Establishing ground rules
- Derive a list of ground rules with students. Examples include:
  - ★ no two people speaking at once
  - ★ no personal criticism
  - ★ fair sharing of speaking time
  - ★ no disagreement without reasons
- Display the list and nominate someone to keep a check on whether they are being kept. After a while students won't need the list and will be able to monitor themselves – and you.

- *Sensitivity to others' feelings*
  - ★ A necessary part of foreseeing the consequences of one's actions is the ability to empathize with others. This may seem a sophisticated ability yet there are some very practical ways of checking whether the foundations exist. Can students express a wide range of emotional states with words, intonation, gesture, body position and facial expression? (It may be helpful to read the section of Chapter 14 on paralinguistic and non-verbal communication.)
  - ★ Role-play is the best stategy for helping students to see things from others' points of view.

These abilities are the components of moral reasoning. There are two possible reasons why you might want to isolate one of the components and work on it with your students:

- Where a group fails to come to any conclusion that satisfies them or you. Which part of the process has not worked?
- Where a group discussion might falter if they were presented too early with a complex problem. This may be because group members are not good at handling controversy, or lack confidence in their own ability to solve difficult problems. A step-by-step approach will control the level of difficulty at each stage.

16.2   Your role as tutor

Elsewhere in this book we recommend that for some discussion purposes tutors should encourage students' own attitudes to emerge freely. 'Facilitator' is a clumsy word, but it usefully defines a particular role that a tutor may take.

As such you should be careful not to impose your own views on students, resist allowing your own ideas to intrude while students are discussing and avoid making judgements on what is being said or done. Instead of these more traditional functions of teaching you may want to concentrate on the interpersonal relations in the group, making an assessment of the way in which its members work together in order to create the best conditions for allowing the students' own ideas to emerge.

When discussing moral issues with students, however, neither of these roles seems totally adequate. Certainly it is important to protect the diversity of views that students from varied cultural and religious backgrounds may hold. Yet merely to 'facilitate' (i.e. encourage) their expression may seem irresponsible, particularly where such views may offend or go against the interests of other students.

In the 1970s the Schools Council Humanities Curriculum Project Team coined the phrase 'neutral chairman' to define the role they wanted teachers to take when they discussed controversial issues. While this usefully contrasted with what was then the more familiar traditional teacher's role in the single discipline areas, it does not sufficiently distinguish the different things a tutor may do in the course of a discussion. 'Impartial but active' (Wilson, 1975) is a more helpful phrase.

Neutrality should not be taken to mean that the tutor has no evaluative role. However careful you were not to disclose your own opinions, and however successfully you managed not to communicate anything by your tone, posture or facial expression (and how unlikely that seems!), you would be unable to prevent students picking up some clues about what you thought. After all, developing this awareness is one of the things you are trying to teach them.

Acting as chairperson you will have to select and order contributions, pose questions and prompt particular lines of enquiry. Older students are likely to want to know your own opinion in any case. They have a right to see whether you can defend it with the same arguments you are asking them to use. Most importantly, you cannot abdicate from expressing your own views if you find a majority view which you believe must be challenged. All prejudices come into this category. Sexist and racist prejudices are the prime examples of views that it is part of a tutor's responsibility to challenge, because it is part of your job not to deny opportunity to anyone by discriminating unfairly. The challenge has to be in a form that removes the element of personal confrontation, however, as this can simply reinforce the belief.

Our suggestions for meeting these difficulties are these:

● Maintain a clear distinction between instances when you are judging the discussion ('you've talked too long', 'you're being unfairly personal') and those when you are judging the content. (You could ask different students to take on each responsibility.)

- Stick to the ground rules and encourage students to take over this monitoring role from you.
- Time the disclosure of your own views carefully.
- Encourage the students to learn a pattern of questioning which they can initially use on you to discover the grounds for your beliefs.

16.3   Current and future problems

Differences of opinion

Discussion of older people's opinions
- What evidence do students have that older people often disapprove of them?
- What are these judgements based on? Dress? Language? Behaviour? Media reports? Are these sound evidence of someone's values or opinions?
- What makes older people believe they have a right to do this?
- Does experience of some problems necessarily make older people better able to make moral judgements?
- What are the 'ingredients' of sorting out a moral problem?

Moral reasoning
- From a general discussion, students can arrive at their own definition of the elements of moral reasoning. They could be given a narrative example to use to help in their analysis. Here is one idea:
  - ★ Two girls (Kath and Em), who are close friends, see an advert for a Saturday job in a shop window. The manageress is a friend of Kath's mother. Kath says she is not interested. Next day Em goes in and sees the manageress who promises her that she can have the job, and arranges for her to start the following week. Later that day Kath goes into the shop to buy something and is approached by the manageress who says no one else has applied, and offers her the job instead. Attracted by the money, Kath accepts.
- Who is at fault here? What exactly has she/have they done wrong? What should she/they have done?

Personal relationships
- Ask students to draw up a list of rules that close friends should observe.
- Is the code for close friends different from that for boyfriends or girlfriends?
- Ask for examples of things it would be *wrong to do* to a close friend. Examples might include:
  - ★ 'steal' another's boyfriend or girlfriend

    ★   go out (for one occasion only) with another's partner
    ★   tell a friend that his or her own partner is two-timing him or her
    ★   lie to protect one's own best friend
    ★   inform on one's own friend in order to protect others

- Groups can add to the list. Alternative ways of doing this would be to turn the items into opinion statements and ask students to mark them agree/disagree, or to rank them in order of seriousness.
- All examples of problems involving peer-group values can be used to explore the differences between the levels of reasoning described earlier.
  - ★ Turn the above list of friendship rules into narrative examples. Give small groups a different example each. Ask them to say what they would do in each case. Compare and evaluate the solutions according to the 'levels' of reasoning.

Religious and cultural differences
- What courses of action are open where problems arise between friends which may be due to a clash of religious or cultural values? Your students may have examples of these. Issues may centre on parents imposing sanctions about 'suitable' friends, daughters going out alone with boys, family observance of religious rules, etc.
- What are the rights and wrongs of helping a friend disobey their parents' cultural or religious rules (e.g. helping a girl to go out alone with a boy without her parents' knowledge and against their known wishes)?
- Would it be right to contrive to get a friend to break a religious rule in ignorance (e.g. to drink alcohol, eat forbidden food, break a fast)?
- What religious or cultural prohibitions do your students observe or know about? What do they think are the reasons for these?

There is obviously considerable scope for extending investigation into these topics. Tutors who teach racially mixed groups may see this as one of the main areas they want to explore.

Parents and children
- Family life is a source of many useful examples of moral issues.
  - ★ What are the commonest sources of arguments about rights and wrongs at home?
  - ★ Collect examples and organize them into categories. These may include: duties children owe to parents; responsibilities parents feel for children; changes in views about moral behaviour; clashes in religious or cultural values, where children born in the UK do not share parents' beliefs. (Get students to nominate their own definitions of the categories and use *their* words for these, even if they are less precise than your own.)

- Ask students in small groups (threes or fours) to choose a category and devise a role-play that illustrates one example of a conflict.
- In feedback discussion, highlight the viewpoints of the parent(s) involved. Explore the feelings of the parents in detail. Then ask groups to reform, switch roles and play out a different outcome to the conflict. Does understanding someone's point of view help one find a better solution?
- What rules would students draw up for their own children?

Future trends in marriage and life-styles

This is one area where it is possible to find a clash between students' values and changing trends. Some of the traditional values they may express about marriage may contrast sharply with survey findings about the reality of current family life. Below are some examples of ways in which survey findings can be used to identify value clashes and moral problems which students may meet in the future.

Marriage

Asking about marriage (Guy, 1983) summarizes results of surveys undertaken by marriage-guidance councils with over 4000 people. Sections include responses from school and college students contrasting cultural views about marriage, and a description of the effects of unemployment on marriages. Ethnic and regional variations in opinions are strongly marked, and have to be taken into account.

Divorce

Do your students have traditional beliefs, such as a commitment to life-long marriage? Do older people that they know share these beliefs? If such beliefs are still common, why do so many people change their minds? For example,

- of three marriages, one is a remarriage for one partner
- of six marriages, one is a remarriage for both
- there has been a 500 per cent increase in divorce over the last 20 years
- of five children born, one now has parents who will divorce before he or she is 16

Beliefs about marriage

- Where do students get their values from? An idealized media picture of marriage? Why is the ideal important?
- Are values (e.g. fidelity, marriage till death) out of step with the facts?
- Are values the same thing as moral beliefs? This very abstract issue needs to be explored through a concrete issue. Take the list of rules for treating friends produced earlier. Do students expect to use the same 'code' in their marriages?

Family life
The report of the Study Commission on the Family contains findings that make it clear that current welfare policy is based on an outdated definition of the family which assumes that a wife will remain at home dependent on her husband's earnings, and that the care of dependent children remains financially and domestically a shared task of the two parents. In fact,

● one-person households have doubled over the last 20 years
● married women now make up one-quarter of the labour force, outnumbering *un*married women 2:1.

There is no 'typical' family any more. The single-parent family is not a new phenomenon (thousands of women brought up children on their own after both world wars), but there has been a considerable rise in numbers:

● 1971: 570 000 one-parent families in the UK
● 1980: 890 000 one-parent families in the UK

And the variations are greater than before:

● 36% are divorced mothers
● 23% are separated mothers
● 12% are lone fathers
● 16% are single mothers
● 13% are widows

Bringing up children
● What are students' views about bringing up children?
● Do these conflict with trends?
● How should the responsibility be shared?
● Are the children of these new-style families going to have different values?

Role-play, case study, or a survey would all be suitable alternative strategies.

Looking after the elderly
The most dramatic change is in the increasing numbers of old and very old people who now survive. (Most single-person households are old people living alone.)

● 1901: 1 in 20 of the population was over 65, 1 in 76 over 75
● 1981: 1 in 7 of the population was over 65, 1 in 16 over 75

The elderly are a section of the population more vulnerable than most to the effects of poverty, ill-health and bad housing. Whose responsibility should it be to care for them? In future more of the elderly will be divorced, while there are many fewer daughters who remain unmarried and therefore free to look after them. Your students could consider both the personal and the political aspects, discussing not only personal responsibilities towards parents and other family members, but possible policy solutions, such as more financial support for one-parent families, or new kinds of social or community care for the elderly.

Reconstituted families
● Give students contrasting case studies to consider.
  ★ A mother lives alone with two children aged 12 and 15. Her divorced husband's mother (the children's favourite grandmother) falls ill and asks to stay with them.
  ★ A husband remarries and has a second family. His own father becomes unable to live alone. The husband raises the possibility of his father coming to live with his present family. His second wife is reluctant to consider the suggestion as the old man is not *her* children's grandfather.
● Ask students to describe the feelings of all the participants before they decide on a solution. Small groups then exchange solutions, describe possible consequences and evaluate alternatives.
● Ask students to draw up a social policy to cope with the problem of an ageing population, increased variation in family patterns, and higher participation of married women in the labour force. (They can be given these facts as briefing material in a syndicate exercise.) Ask them to distinguish between their practical solutions and the values on which they rest (e.g. about the role of women, and about responsibility towards parents and children). Compare resulting policies and likely changes in values.

Moral issues that may arise at work
At work the application of one's own principles may become more complicated ause of conflicting loyalties.

Examples to discuss
● Here are some possibilities:
  ★ informing a supervisor of a workmate's mistake or dishonesty
  ★ a conflict of loyalties in relation to trade-union membership and industrial action
  ★ the problem of workmates whose actions go against one's own principles (unfair treatment of racial groups or women, 'perks' or 'fiddling', for instance)
● What are the feelings of those involved? Refer back to the list of principles and rules your students drew up for their own friendships (page 296). What problems would the newcomer have if he or she tried

to stick to his or her principles in each case? Ask groups to play out alternative courses of action.
- Students already on work experience may have examples of their own. A general prompt question such as 'What sort of difficulties can a newcomer have in deciding between right and wrong actions?' may elicit problems from their own experience.

Some jobs regularly involve those who do them in moral decisions as part of their work. Such examples may be more dramatic but they can be used to highlight the processes of reasoning involved. A code of medical ethics exists to help doctors apply principles consistently and to protect patients. Other jobs are left to develop their principles 'on the job'. Do your students think his is good enough? Consider these examples.

Moral decisions
- A doctor is consulted by an under-age girl wanting contraceptive advice. Should she inform the girl's parents? (Medical ethics protect the girl's confidentiality, but there has been one test case where a Roman Catholic parent contested this right.)
- A nurse has contact with a patient whose illness is terminal but who does not yet know this. Should the patient be told? How? By whom? If not the patient, who should know?
- Social workers disagree over the case of a neglected child. Should the child be taken into care against the parents' wishes?

These examples combine moral issues with the question of individual rights (patients' rights, children's rights and parents' rights). This may be an area that will overlap with teaching about political literacy.

Moral problems connected with unemployment

Disapproval directed at the unemployed
- This can be investigated with a sentence-completion exercise from various viewpoints. 'Unemployed people are . . .' (Complete as a pensioner, housewife, politician, policeman, etc.)
    - ★ Compare the opinions.
    - ★ Introduce the idea of the Puritan work ethic.
    - ★ What else affects attitudes to the unemployed?
- Present to students a selection of controversial examples of behaviour of the unemployed. Working in pairs they should prepare, then deliver, brief timed arguments in defence of or against the behaviour. Examples can include:
    - ★ the view that those who work in the black or home economy (e.g. handymen, carpenters, baby-minders) should not draw benefit

★ the view that those work directly for cash and do not pay income tax or VAT are not entitled to use the NHS, free schooling or the other things that taxes pay for

★ the view that all unemployed people should do a period of voluntary work as their contribution to society

★ the view that if there is no hope of a job, then any way of making money is acceptable

---

Ask students to look for any contradictions there may be between their own opinions about the unemployed and any plans they may have for coping with it themselves. They can work from the programme of possible activities they have already produced, as a result of activities suggested in Chapter 12.

16.4   Sample lesson plan

Length of session: 1 hour.
Group size: 20.

Resources
● Paper and pencils.
● Students should know how to do a spidergram (Figure 15.1).

Aim
● To clarify students' values about close friendships.

Objectives
● To identify the qualities of good friends.
● To list students' own codes of behaviour between friends.
● To describe common problems that arise when these rules are broken.
● To compare solutions to these problems.

Method

Phase 1: Listing ideal qualities of friends (15 minutes)
a   Ask students to form small groups (threes or fours). These should *not* contain close friends.
b   Draw a circle in the centre of the board and write 'Choosing a good friend' in it. Ask one student in each group to copy this. Give each group five minutes to complete a spidergram that identifies all the qualities they look for in a close friend.
c   Collect items from the groups and pool these to complete your own diagram on the board.
d   Discuss the ideas that have come out of this: what values are important in friendship?

Phase 2: Identifying common problems (15 minutes)

a   Now ask groups to write a list of the five most important rules of friendships. (Set a time limit.)

b   Ask each group to make up a brief 'problem' story that starts when one of these rules is broken. This should be fair-copied onto a separate sheet of paper. (Circulate while this is going on to make sure the final wording is in a form clear enough to be understood by other students.)

Phase 3: Comparing solutions (25 minutes)

a   Groups exchange problems and are given 5–10 minutes to decide on a course of action for meeting the problem.

b   Problems and solutions are read out and justified by groups of 'solvers'. The 'problem-setting' group is given first chance to comment on their solution before it is thrown open for general comment.

Follow-up

This exercise can be used as a starter for linking with:

● ideas about rules for treating your partner in marriage
● examining and comparing these rules with those that apply in friendships at work
● investigating gender differences in the nature of friendships
● exploring literary accounts of friendships.

16.5   Resources list

Tutor's background reading

Papers in Taylor's *Progress and problems in moral education* define and illustrate a variety of approaches to teaching about moral issues, and different standpoints on teacher neutrality. For an extended account of Stenhouse's views on this see his own book (1970), written for teachers using the Humanities Curriculum Project.

Several publications were produced to support the Schools Council Moral Education Project. (The 'Lifeline' series of materials from this, published by Longman in 1972, are for the older age group of 13–16 year olds.) The project Director, Peter McPhail, has produced a more recent book on social and moral education, which looks at students' opinions about the moral issues they see as most important. McPhail contrasts earlier findings of research in the 1960s with those subjects that students of the 1980s take most seriously. The list of issues presented in the concluding chapter of his book includes:

● (un)employment
● education for leisure
● education for work creation/self-employment
● economic pressure to go on living at home

- nuclear issues
- political polarization and disillusionment
- marriage; divorce; having children

The list is interesting for two reasons. Firstly, it provides a starting point for teachers who want to identify topics that will interest their students. That is a very simple practical point. Less obviously, but possibly more useful in the long term, is the way in which such a list shows how some concerns that the moral educationists identify overlap with those now seen to be part of the political-literacy field.

Many of our teaching suggestions for political-literacy lessons (see Table 17.1 on page 313) have their roots in a moral issue but extend into the area of the political. This may happen because individual rights are protected by laws, or because particular values that different groups hold are reflected in policy. For tutors who take an issue-based approach to constructing a programme of topics, the overlap can be helpful in encouraging you to link topics and lead students out from their initial interest to new areas. It is also important to keep a clear idea of the dissimilarity of the two approaches where this is reflected in contrasting procedures, different concepts and a distinctive vocabulary. However controversial (and therefore potentially stimulating) a topic may be, there can be an awful, mushy sameness about teaching that has no clear sense of direction in the way it develops the quality of students' thinking.

de Bono, E. 1971 *The use of lateral thinking* (Penguin)
de Bono, E. 1976 *Teaching thinking* (Maurice Temple Smith)
Guy, C. 1983 *Asking about marriage* (National Marriage Guidance Council)
Kohlberg, L. and E. Juriel, 1961 *Moralization research: the cognitive approach* (Rinehart and Winston)
McPhail, P. 1982 *Social and moral education* (Blackwell)
McPhail, P., H. Chapman and J.R. Ungoed-Thomas *Moral education in the secondary school*: Teachers Book for the Schools Council Moral Education Project 13–16 (Longman)
Piaget, J. 1932 *The moral judgement of the child* (Routledge and Kegan Paul)
Stenhouse, L. 1970 *Humanities curriculum project teacher's book* (Heinemann)
Study Commission on the Family 1983 *Families in the future* (3 Park Road, London NW1 6XN)
Taylor, M. (ed.) 1975 *Progress and problems in moral education* (NFER)
Wilson, J. 1975 'Teaching and neutrality' in Taylor

Classroom materials
Chapman, H. 1972 *Proving the rule?* (Longman)
5 student booklets using an imaginary character and his family as a focus for these issues: 'Rules and individuals', 'What do you expect?', 'Who do you think I am?', 'In whose interest?', 'Why should I?'

Cheston, M. 1984 *It's your life* (Religious and Moral Education Press)
Sections include: 'Yourself', 'Surroundings', 'Relationships'. Contains student materials and background information.
Crampton Smith G., and S. Curts 1984 *It's your life* (Longman Resources Unit)
Student material, with discussion topics including advertising, smoking, laws, babies and parents, race, sex and birth control, roles, drinking. Includes strip cartoons as a stimulus for discussion, and an information file with background facts.
Jones, A., J. Marsh and A.G. Watts *Living choices* (CRAC)
Student's workbook (separate tutor's notes). Sections on: 'Family life', 'Group living', 'Living on one's own', 'Choosing partners', 'Bringing up children', 'Relations between generations', 'One's future'.
McPhail, P. 1972 *In other people's shoes* (Longman)
3 sets of cards presenting situations as discussion starters, grouped under: 'Sensitivity', 'Consequences', 'Points of view'.
Ungoed-Thomas, J.R. 1972 *What would you have done?* (Longman)
6 student booklets using particular historical events for the topics of commitment, persecution, compassion, addiction and prejudice.

17 Getting involved

17.1 Why teach political literacy?

One short answer to that question is because you can't avoid it. Social education, as Porter (1983) points out, is 'inextricably linked' with political education, dealing as it does with social issues, the workings of social institutions and the effects of these on individuals' lives. As regards aims, they jointly share a concern for:

- developing with students conceptual frameworks which they can use to make sense of their experience
- making students more effective participants in social processes
- emphasizing certain process aims related to holding discussion and debate on controversial issues, developing the ability to make reasoned arguments and critically to examine evidence and courses of action
- working with students to clarify their own and others' values and principles
- acknowledging the importance of making a tutor's value commitment in relation to the aims explicit – to themselves in the first instance (in order to devise coherent programmes) and possibly to students too (if it is appropriate to the pursuit of particular learning objectives)

You will arrive naturally at political topics via other areas of the course. Many of the questions about moral values raised in Chapter 16 have a political dimension, and the two areas share process objectives in relation to conducting arguments. Questions of legal status and rights also overlap with political concerns, frequently because students need to be able to perform many of the activities associated with effective participation. This is primarily because you will want to ensure that students have the necessary information about which rights they can lay claim to (or that they know how to find this out) and that they possess the necessary communication skills to invoke them. This may involve using the appropriate linguistic register and being sufficiently assertive.

Any extended projects that students carry out in their own neighbourhood may uncover local political issues. The actions of local government or local pressure groups may be relevant to the question they are looking at. What local issues are provoking interest during the period of your course? What are the major parties' policies about these issues? What were their policies at the last election? Are there any elections pending?

Young people's political attitudes
A more general justification for including political literacy in the curriculum is provided by the weight of evidence that shows how widespread politically apathetic attitudes are amongst the younger age groups, and how inadequate is the general level of informed political opinion.

Two recent national surveys polled opinions and attitudes in teenages and found a general impression that politics was 'too complicated to understand' and a feeling that they were disenfranchised because 'nobody listens' and 'nobody understands' their point of view.

The first remark was a response from the majority of the 4000 fifth-years who completed questionnaires in a survey carried out by Stradling in 1975 on 15- and 16-year olds in 72 schools. The questionnaires looked at their level of political knowledge, their attitudes to politics and their ability to analyse political issues. Stradling found widespread ignorance of where political parties stood on major issues and a woeful lack of the basic information necessary for informed political choices. (42 per cent of those surveyed agreed with a statement that said the IRA is a Protestant organization.)

In 1981 the Youth Service Review Group commissioned the National Youth Survey to canvass opinions from 635 14–19-year-olds, on a wide range of topics which included politics. Three-quarters of them admitted to being politically apathetic – the proportion was higher at the younger end of the age group. Class differences became significant in relation to participation skills, middle-class respondents being more likely to see themselves as politically effective. Ethnic-minority groups were marginally more positive in their views about the potential support for their interests that party politics could offer. (The survey suggests that this is connected with an awareness of the need for racial discrimination laws to be effective.) Interestingly FE students were as a group less apathetic than the majority, but possible reasons for this are not offered, and without knowing more about which courses they were on, whether they were day-release employed or full-time students it would be unwise to speculate on relevant factors.

One might say on the basis of such findings that, for a group of people who are on the threshold of joining the electorate, these respondents (taken as a representative sample) are an age group that is remarkably apathetic and ill-informed. How far back do the roots of this disaffection go?

Political attitudes in children
One study of much younger children examined the early stages of political thinking in discussions with 7–11-year-olds. One or two of the positive conclusions to which Olive Stephens (1982) comes throw an interesting light

on the points that are worth taking note of as you formulate your aims for activities with the older age groups.

- At this early age the children gained a great deal of information about current political issues from the media, predominantly television.
- Even at this age there were clearly marked gender differences in performance: girls tended to be less articulate and confident in discussions in mixed groups, and they were interested in a narrower range of issues, which they tended to interpret in subjective terms.
- In their discussions children showed clear positive signs of an ability to form hypotheses, to consider evidence, to begin to make a reasoned analysis of an issue and to argue for alternatives. All these facets of their discussions were found even in those who, according to a literal interpretation of stage theories of cognitive growth, should have been too young to attempt such things.
- Because of the signs of the early development of these abilities, Stephens supports the idea of consciously developing the ability to think logically and formulate and defend arguments, even as early as the primary stages.

The roots of political apathy

It seems a fair (though untested) assumption that many of these alert and interested 7–11-year-olds may in time join the apathetic and disinterested group of 14–19-year-olds, and that the reverse may also be true – that many of the older groups were more prepared to see political issues as another area in which they could learn something useful when they were younger. What factors might be relevant to the changes?

The older group may be reflecting cynical or disenchanted opinions about politics that they have absorbed from their families and older people. *Young people in the 80s* (DES, 1983) hints at this as relevant, but says it collected no evidence that might have supported it one way or the other.

The impression that they were disenfranchised ('nobody listens to us') is borne out by much of the historical-sociological evidence of Chapters 10 and 11 in this book: their dependent status has been over-prolonged. In many aspects of life at home and at school the passive and subordinate aspects of their role have not developed their ability to participate effectively in areas of life dominated by older people.

The feeling that politics is too complicated to understand is an admission of defeat in the face of complexity they are now more aware of but which, given that awareness, they lack the confidence or methods to disentangle. Stephens was persuaded by her conversations with 9-year-olds that there were clear indications of developing rationality in the way they approached problems. Yet in this area of political judgement (as in many others, it must be said) the education of the older age groups seems to have failed to equip them with systematic ways of sorting out complex problems that involve fact and opinion. The surveys of young people found that they lacked the strategies or the confidence to feel that they could sort out complicated real-life political issues, and had no strong convictions or perceptions of how their own lives were affected by these matters. Consequently they lacked any willingness to become involved.

So many negative judgements need balancing by some reservations: they were made on the basis of questionnaire evidence, which is a formal and impersonal method particularly for the younger group. Whether your own students show the same attitudes is for you to find out. You could construct a simple questionnaire to discover their attitudes.

Helping to develop students' political thinking
It would be unjustified to conclude from the survey evidence that these young people were not operating with any conceptual apparatus at all when talking about political matters. It is important to remember, as Stradling *et al.* point out (*Teaching controversial issues*, 1984), that any discussions about issues that you have chosen for their relevance to students means that you will be intervening in a learning process that is already going on outside the classroom.

Surveys may have uncovered apathetic attitudes to 'politics' as young people generally perceive it to be, but this does not mean that they will not have strong feelings or previously formed opinions of their own about the particular issues that you and they choose to consider. This has particular relevance to your choice of strategies and in relation to your role in the classroom.

Styles of reasoning
It does mean that you have to begin by interpreting the kinds of reasoning that students are using already before imposing or offering this model. Is their reasoning inadequate or partial or are they simply not using the right style of language? If they do not use the appropriate word, does this mean they do not have the concept? It is worth noting that both Stradling and Stephens refer to Bernstein's theory of restricted and elaborated codes when dealing with this question. This theory has itself been the subject of much controversy (see for example Labov, 1972), because of its assumed connection with arguments that working-class language is a sub-standard style of communication.

This is not an appropriate place to go into that particular debate (itself one of the most politicized of educational controversies). There is more discussion about the efficacy of varieties of non-standard English for different purposes in section 14.3. The most important thing is that you use flexibly the concepts and procedural rules outlined below, and that you are prepared to accept that students may express arguments and justifications in terms and forms other than those provided. You should keep an open mind about whether their reasoning is justified or logical until you have been able to cross-check students' understanding by repeated and reworked examples.

Discussing political issues
In discussing a political issue (for example, investigating local-authority policy on unemployment), you will want students to be able to:

- consider and analyse a complex issue
- weigh evidence (looking for partiality and omissions)
- state relevant principles and values
- defend a point of view with reasoned argument
- arrive at conclusions
- choose between or formulate courses of action

Two other general points are worth making. The first relates to students and the media. Stephens and Stradling both agree that young people get most of their information about political events from the popular press and 'non-serious' television current-affairs coverage. You will want to make them more than merely passive recipients of these messages. Much of Chapter 15 is relevant to this aim.

Finally, bear in mind the evidence of how differently boys and girls respond to political topics. Each sex seems to choose topics consistent with the values underpinning their different social roles. Boys go for issues like war, inflation and unemployment; girls for 'welfare' issues (old people, Third World starvation, poverty). You may well want to challenge this pattern and broaden each group's range of interest. First however you would have to find out whether your students conform to this pattern and then examine some of the implications with them.

Gender differences in discussion
- Give students a list of current topical issues to choose from (unemployment, public-expenditure cuts, nurses' pay, etc.). Is there a difference between boys' and girls' choices? If so, is this natural? Learned? Desirable? Do women politicians follow the same pattern?
- Evidence also shows that there are gender differences in discussion performances. Ask students to observe whether girls perform differently from boys in mixed discussions. Try a fishbowl exercise (section 2.3). If there is a difference, is it due to language (e.g. choice of words) or to patterns of interaction (hesitation, unwillingness to interrupt, aggression rather than assertiveness, for example)?
- Help students to see that patterns which they may have discovered are not accidental by testing to see whether they occur elsewhere. See if they can observe other lessons, staff discussions, etc.
- Help students to change or adapt their discussion style to accommodate or alter these differences: encourage groups to value tentativeness, for example, and to create the space for it to exist.

17.2   Objectives in teaching political literacy

Politics is 'the process whereby conflicts of interest and values within a group are conciliated' (Stradling and Porter in Crick and Porter, 1978). Political literacy is the development of the ability to understand and engage in this process. Its overall aim is the development of the relevant knowledge, skills and attitudes that are necessary if students are to participate in society in an informed way. It is *not:*

- content-based teaching about the British constitutional system
- deductive teaching about fundamental and abstract political concepts

The ABC core identifies four curricular areas necessary to the development of political literacy:

- Developing a procedure for analysing the issue using a basic political vocabulary which identifies causes of disagreement, sources of information about the dispute, evaluates policy alternatives and ways of reaching them (9.1).
- Understanding the functioning and decision-making processes of formal and informal groups (9.2)
- Giving students experience of being a participant in a formal decision-making group (9.3).
- Having an informed understanding of national politics (9.4).

These aims can be achieved through an issue-based approach to teaching political literacy. This is associated with much recent curriculum development work, notably the Programme for Political Education, which published a set of papers outlining a rationale for political education with examples of curricula and some lessons (Crick and Porter, 1978). Of the various approaches described, issue-based teaching seems most suitable for the vocational-preparation areas, partly because of the high value it places on participation and because it meshes most easily with an integrated course structure which emphasizes experiential learning.

The issue-based approach

There are two possible ways to identify the issues you will use:

- asking students to identify those issues that interest them
- selecting issues yourself because you see them as particularly important for your students

Which of the two methods you use (or which combination of the two you arrive at) will be influenced by various factors apart from your own preference, including the length, organization and frequency of your teaching time with students.

Asking students to identify issues
This would combine well with various other forms of negotiation over course content during the induction phase. It has the advantage that it offers the quickest way of winning students' interest in topics.

The simplest method is to give the students a list of opinion statements with which they can agree or disagree. Areas of consensus or disagreement in the group can then be identified and discussed. The list can include those issues in which (according to those surveys already cited) young people most often declare themselves interested:

- unemployment
- inflation
- nuclear issues
- relations with the police; law and order
- welfare issues (e.g. health, education, poverty)
- problems of various groups (e.g. old people, ethnic minorities)
- public opinions about young people as expressed in the media
- industrial relations
- perceived usefulness of party-political activities
- new adult legal and political rights

Selecting issues
- Turn these issues into statements of opinion (e.g. 'There should be more nursery places so that all mothers who want to can go out to work'). Ask students to mark them 'agree/disagree'. Then choose the three *they* think most important. Small groups can confer to agree on a short list of issues.

The situational method
Another way of identifying starting points is to work from those issues that arise in connection with topics which have already been identified elsewhere in this book. Table 17.1 lists a selection of these. The list is not exhaustive: many other starting points could be taken up.

Giving students a method of analysing issues
Political activity centres on conflict between people. The conflict may be over inequalities in access to resources, or in the distribution of power; it may be over the goals the group is to pursue or the values on which these goals are based. It may centre on the methods by which the group pursues its ends, or be produced by the results of their decisions. This in turn is affected by whether membership of the group is voluntary or involuntary.

These aspects can be expressed as a checklist of questions:

Table 17.1   Issues relevant to the teaching of political literary

Page no.	Issue	Aspect of political activity
Ch. 10 p. 156	Sources of family conflict	Conflict in small group
Ch. 10 p. 162	Inequalities of financial support for school-leavers	Policy-making simulation: evaluation of policy
Ch. 10 p. 163	Tasks of running a school for themselves	How institutions work, and make rules
Ch. 11 p. 178	Setting up formal group committee	Planning and carrying out group procedure
Ch. 12 p. 196	Purposes of YTS	Evaluation of policy
Ch. 13 p. 221	Reactions of young people to unemployment	Varieties of political and non-political activity
Ch. 13 p. 232	Restructuring work, to cope with unemployment	Policy-making simulation; pressure groups
Ch. 14 p. 249	Loading words to convey attitudes	Analysing social basis of language
Ch. 14 p. 249	Analysing passages for emotional content	Analysing social basis of language
Ch. 14 p. 250	Distinguishing fact from opinion: sexist language	Analysing language for prejudice and stereotypes
Ch. 14 p. 254	Non-standard varieties of English	Language as part of cultural identity
Ch. 15 p. 281	Distinguishing selectivity for the purposes of argument	Bias and the media
Ch. 15 p. 282	Analysing press reports for examples of labelling	Bias and the media
Ch. 15 p. 282	Constructions of stereotypes	Bias and the media
Ch. 15 p. 283	Media projects: *Comparison of news slant	Identifying political voice of particular papers
	*Internal comparison within one newspaper	Differing images of social groups
	*Following one controversial subject through media presentations	Identifying the building of consensus
	*Compare own experience with media coverage of local event	Comparing personal experience and press interpretation
	*Looking at rhetoric and catch phrases	Language use to persude or influence
	*Select an issue and represent a viewpoint using text and images	Reading pictures for messages

- What opinions are expressed? What form do they take?
- Do I have all the information necessary to understand it?
- What is it about (i.e. what are our goals, resources and values)?
- What are the beliefs of those involved (as these reflect values and goals)?
- What are the likely outcomes? Will I be affected?
- How will others be affected?
- What concepts are relevant to an understanding of the issue?

We have provided this checklist for *your* use, but there is no reason why students should not work with one, using it as a prop in the early stages to organize their discussions. You would want them to arrive at suitable questions rather than be presented with this list (following the inductive approach) and this could be one of the tasks of the early sessions (see the sample lesson idea in section 17.3).

In the same way, while they accquire the vocabulary for political discussions you may find it useful to remind yourself of the range of concepts and terms that will be appropriate:

power	authority	law	compliance
force	influence	justice	consent
reason	pressure	representation	dissent
rights			

Using the politics of everyday life
Understanding political activity involves being able to analyse how people act in groups (and two or more constitutes a group). Some of the topic suggestions in Table 17.1 identify groups to which students belong as part of their everyday activity: family and school.

Proponents of the spiral curriculum structure for teaching political literacy (see Stradling and Stephens, in Crick and Porter 1978), suggest that starting at the level of everyday experience may be a better way of approaching complex issues. Simple examples that need a minimum of background information may be suitable to use while students are still acquiring the vocabulary and developing the concepts they will use.

The spiral curriculum originated with Bruner and is the expression of his belief that no idea is too complex to be taught at a simple level. While conflict in family and friendship groups has the advantage of being rooted in concrete everyday experience, this does not necessarily mean the issue is in itself simpler to understand than a more complicated political controversy would be. Its usefulness lies in its familiarity.

17.3 Sample lesson plan

Length of session: 1½ hours.
Group size: 20

Resources
- OHP/flipchart
- Students need paper.

Aim
- To provide students with a systematic way of analysing political disputes.

Objectives
- To discover students' present level of understanding of political disagreements.
- To examine one example of such disagreement in everyday life.
- To identify concepts that can be used to understand this.
- To devise a checklist of questions that can be used to study other examples.

Phase 1: Collecting examples of political disputes (15 minutes)
a   In a previous session students need to have identified topics in which they are interested. If your session is longer than 1½ hours this can done here.
b   Introduce the chosen topic – what examples of disputes are currently in the news? (Try to get one example for each of the students' identified areas of interest.)
c   What is difficult about sorting out what is going on and who is in the right? What have these disagreements got in common?
d   Suggest that looking at a simpler example may be helpful.

Phase 2: Briefing for role-play on family 'politics' (10 minutes)
a   Set a role-play scene. Friday morning, breakfast time. Family members are arguing over the use of the living room on Friday night.
   ★   Father wants to play cards with friends.
   ★   Mother wants to watch final episode of a serial on television.
   ★   Daughter wants to invite friends round to listen to records.
   ★   Son wants to bring his girlfriend round and to have some privacy.
b   What is 'political' about this kind of family argument? What does it have in common with those mentioned above?
c   Explain that a role-play will help highlight the kinds of reasons that cause such disagreements. Divide students into fours and cast roles.
d   Display a list of justifications they may want to use:
   ★   'I can make you do what I want because if you don't agree I can . . .', followed by a threat (force)
   ★   'You must do as I say because my wishes are most important here' (authority)
   ★   'If you don't do what I want I can . . .' (power).

★ 'I'm paying most money into the family kitty and deserve first choice' (right).

★ 'I work hard all week and deserve to spend Friday night as I want' (justice, fairness).

★ 'I do work that contributes to the running of the home and deserve to have my way' (right).

★ 'You get your own way more than me – it's my turn now' (justice).

★ 'I should get my way because what I want to do is more important' (value)

Give everyone two minutes to choose the reasons they want to use.

Phase 3: Acting-out (10–15 minutes)
a   Students role-play the argument in groups. Circulate to check what sort of reasons are being given.

Phase 4: Debriefing (20 minutes)
a   What has been going on in these arguments? The list of justifications is explored, new ones that come up added.
b   Introduce the concepts given above in brackets. The group discussses the meaning of each one, and matches them to the justifications.

Phase 5: Clarification (15 minutes)
a   Now ask students to work in pairs. Each pair must frame a limited number (say three) of questions that can be used to help clarify the argument. Their questions should use the concepts. (You can start with examples, e.g. 'Who has most power?', 'Who might use force?', 'Who has a right here?'.)
b   Pool the questions and agree on a checklist.

Follow-up
●   Continue the role-play to see what solutions people find. Study the different outcomes of disputes.
●   Choose a particular issue to study in depth, using the checklist of questions.

17.4   Resources list

Tutor's background reading

Olive Stevens' *Children talking politics* is an account of research into the political understanding of 7–11-year-olds. Her conclusions support the view that young children's levels of understanding are often underestimated, and confirm the importance of small-group discussion for developing under-standing. Although based on experience with primary school children, many of her comments (about the importance of teaching thinking and reasoning skills, for example) apply equally to the teaching of older students.

We have drawn on the findings of two large-scale surveys of the political attitudes of older students. Stradling's survey of over 4000 fifth-formers assessed their level of political awareness. This included their ability to analyse everyday issues, their information about contemporary political affairs, their attitude to politics, and their potential ability for acting effectively to participate in political activity. *Young people in the 80s* (HMSO) deals with a wider age range and surveys political attitudes along with many other topics. The report usefully distinguishes the responses of different ethnic groups where this is significant.

The collection of papers published under the general heading of the *Programme for political education* (Crick & Porter) covers a comprehensive range of curriculum aspects. Papers give outline aims for a political literacy programme, and examples of how teaching political literacy can overlap with other subject areas.

Porter's paper 'Political literacy', in Heater and Gillespie, traces the origin and definition of the term and reviews at length current debate about this new area of teaching.

Crick, B. and A. Porter 1978 *Political education and political literacy* (Longman)
DES 1983 *Young people in the 80s: a survey* (HMSO)
Heater, D. and J. Gillespie (eds.), 1981 *Political education in flux* (Sage)
Labov, W. 1972 'The logic of non-standard English' in *Language in education* (Open University/Routledge & Kegan Paul)
Porter, A. 1981 'Political literacy' in Heater and Gillespie
Porter, A. 1983 *Teaching political literacy* (London University Institute of Education/Tinga Tinga)
Stevens, O. 1982 *Children talking politics* (Martin Robertson)
Stradling, R. 1977 *The political awareness of the school leaver* (The Hansard Society)
Stradling, R., M. Noctor and B. Baines 1984 *Teaching controversial issues* (Edward Arnold)

Classroom materials
Amnesty International *Teaching and learning about human rights* (Amnesty International, British Section, 5 Roberts Place, London EC1)
Series of 11 project folders including 'Rights and responsibilities', 'The UN Universal Declaration of Human Rights', 'Prisoners of Conscience', and related issues. Includes ideas for acting games and dramatic sketch.
British Youth Council *A Roof over Your Head* (BYC, 57 Chalton Street, London NW1 1HU)
Pack of discussion material on wide range of aspects of housing including accompanying notes on suggestions for use.

Cohen, R.N. 1982 *Whose file is it anyway?* (NCCL)
Discussion booklet on the case for open record keeping in various areas: medical, education, housing, social work, credit references. Sections include case-study examples and relevant legislation. (Tutor's resource material.)

Coote, A. and T. Gill 1981 *Women's rights*, 3rd edn. (Penguin)
Comprehensive guide to rights. Chapters on work, money, sex, marriage, divorce and separation, children, housing, goods and services, immigration, the law, equal opportunities legislation and tribunals. (Tutor's resource.)

Coussins, J. 1979 *Taking liberties* (Virago)
Pack of 18 student workcards on equality between the sexes, covering legislation and range of social and political topics.

Edmonds, J. (ed.) *Rights, responsibilities and the law* (The Cobden Trust/ NCCL)
Bibliography of teaching materials. Sections on: civil rights, the police, courts, prison, young people's rights, women's rights, at work, minority rights, privacy and censorship, consumer rights.

Gordon, P., J. Wright and P. Hewitt *Race relations rights* (NCCL)
Comprehensive information on the law, community relations, employment (useful case-study examples), education, housing, incitement to racial hatred, racism in the media. (Tutor's resource material.)

GUST 1981 *Give us a say in things* – (National Youth Bureau/GUST)
Practical guide to youth participation. Sections on: how participation works in families, youth work, and schools. Case-study examples include participation by young people in FE; junior town councils; at work.

Lowe, M. *Women's rights* (NCCL)
Information sheets and discussion notes on abortion, education and training, equal opportunities at work, the Equal Pay Act, rape and domestic violence, social security, taxation, women, work and childcare. (Tutor's resource material.)

Madge, N. and J. Loxley 1978 *Troubled by the law?* (National Youth Bureau, 17–23 Albion Street, Leicester LE1 6GD)
Factual information and practical suggestions. Sections on the police, juvenile courts, and being in care.

National Council for Civil Liberties *Know your rights* (NCCL, 21 Tabard Street, London SE1 4LA)
Pocket-sized wallet of factsheets on: organizing a march, leafletting, selling newspapers, flyposting and collecting, picketing, search of premises, search in the street, sureties, legal aid, homosexuality, bail, arrest, mental health, complaints against the police, police questioning. (Tutor/student resource material.)

Rae, M., P. Hewitt and B. Hugill 1981 *First rights* (NCCL)

Stradling, R. *Sierra cobra* (The Hansard Society, 16 Gower Street, London WC1E 6DP)
Simulation for students (from CSE to FE) showing how policies and decisions

of Third World countries are influenced and constrained by the actions of superpowers, neighbouring countries, trading partners and multinationals.

Stradling, R., M. Noctor and B. Baines, 1984 *Teaching controversial issues* (Edward Arnold)

Teacher's book with lesson ideas, activities and underpinning strategies. Discussion on what makes an issue controversial, pedagogic issues concerned with the tutor's role, and student' beliefs and attitudes. Gives strategies for teaching the topics of: unemployment, sexism, Northern Ireland, nuclear issues, the Third World.

Suddaby, A. 1984 *The nuclear weapons and warfare collection* (Longman)

Seven units, each containing documentary evidence and textual extracts to stimulate discussion. Units included on: 'Hiroshima and the effects of nuclear weapons', 'The nuclear arms race (the weapons roliferation and disarmament), 'Deterrence and defence in nuclear war', 'Nuclear issues in Europe, America and Great Britain'.

Appendix 1 Induction

What it is and what it's for

- It provides a relaxed, gentle, friendly introduction to the course.
- It gives time (2 to 3 weeks usually) for your students to find their way around, identify tutors, meet each other, come to terms with what will be available on the course and with what is expected of them.
- It introduces the integrated nature of the course by pinpointing the links between the core and vocational areas.
- By introducing the concept of negotiation from the onset it involves your students in planning their own programme.
- It introduces the profile and, if you are using it, the log book.
- It gives an opportunity for you to find out your students' perceptions of their own needs, hopes, and expectations.
- It allows for some tutor-initiated assessment, in communication and number, for example.
- It gives an introduction to the core areas – communication, number, planning and problem solving, and practical skills.
- It introduces students to the workplace and the vocational context.

Further periods of induction may be needed during the course as your students move from classroom based learning to workplace.

Pointers to good practice

- Plan thoroughly; organize the programme in detail.
- Ensure that all tutors and supervisors are available to meet the students.
- Provide for lengthy individual tutorials.
- Have all the paperwork, profile forms, etc. ready for use from the first day.
- Give your students a clear booklet or handout describing the main elements of the course, the opportunities, choices, and regulations; and information on their rights and on health and safety procedures.

Necessary conditions

- Team meetings – held before and during the induction period, to plan the programme, agree its objectives and review its progress.

- Adequate resources – suitable rooms; all tutors available, and some with sufficient time to meet students individually.
- Liaison with the supervisor on the job and with contacts on work-experience placements.

Notes of caution

- Negotiation is difficult and uneven when you know so much more than your students about what is available and what the course aims are.
- Asking your students to assess and express their own needs and abilities is an excellent basis for negotiating the programme, but be prepared for a mismatch between their perception of their starting points and yours.
- Think in advance about what you will do if they say they are good at something and you discover that in your terms they are not. How will you negotiate an agreed way forward?
- It isn't easy to find a balance between a pre-planned syllabus and timetable and negotiated student programmes. Consider carefully which parts of the course can be negotiated and which are fixed.

Appendix 2   Counselling and guidance

What they are

- They form a range of activities that involve tutors in giving help, support and advice to students. This is now a recognized tutorial responsibility in vocational-preparation courses and is complementary to the more familiar teaching role.
- They can be given one-to-one or in small groups.
- They can take place at a fixed time (pre-arranged interview, weekly session to fill in profile, group tutorial) or be a mode that the tutor can 'switch into' when the need arises and when conditions permit.
- They provide a methodical approach to helping students understand and deal with sensitive issues (e.g. sexual relationships, fears of unemployment) or particular problems (e.g. study problems, career problems, difficulties with personal relationships).
- They are accomplished through a particular style of conversation and questioning.
- The counselling-and-guidance function is performed through successive phases:
  - ★ establishing contact
  - ★ identifying the problem
  - ★ exploring its effects and possible causes
  - ★ examining alternative courses of action
  - ★ bringing the dependence to a close

You as tutor have to be sensitive in timing the move on from each phase, not forcing the pace, but ensuring that the development does happen.

Pointers to good practice

- Essential tutor skills are:
  - ★ self-control, to do more listening than talking
  - ★ the ability to listen with concentration, to retain details, carefully to observe all aspects of speaker's behaviour
  - ★ self-control to resist offering explanations too soon or passing judgements
  - ★ patience to wait until sufficient material has been discussed for an interpretation to offer itself

★ the ability to offer an interpretation or advice to a student with imagination and sensitivity

★ the skill to deploy all these abilities in order to see things from the student's point of view

● Counselling or guidance skills are likely to be used during any of these activities:

★ discussions between tutor and student about progress on the course, in order to complete the profile

★ group sessions to discuss sensitive issues (e.g. family relationships, as part of course work)

★ interviews with students who have referred themselves with a particular problem

★ interviews with students who have been referred because another tutor or supervisor believes they have a problem that needs particular help

(Note: In the case of these last two instances you may need to look at the behaviour that was the cause of the referral from several points of view before deciding *whose* 'problem' it is.)

● This extended responsibility makes extra demands on tutors, who should have access to trained specialists (e.g. a college counsellor) to discuss their own needs.

Necessary conditions

● A relationship of mutual trust and respect has to exist between the student(s) and the tutor.

● Students must feel confident that confidentiality will be respected. (You may find yourself involved in a clash of responsibilities.)

● There are other practical needs:

★ appropriate rooms – e.g. quiet space such as a carrell in a communications workshop in which to fill in a profile, or a private room to use for confidential conversations

★ tutorial periods – special time that can be set aside for these meetings

★ list of local agencies and specialists – to whom students may be referred or which can provide tutor with information that students need

Notes of caution

● Be a sympathetic ear for your students, but don't allow them unrestricted access that invades your privacy or interferes with your obligations to other students.

● Be honest and realistic about those things that you yourself find difficulty in talking about. Either find a way of overcoming this or refer such cases to others who *can* more easily discuss them.

- You need discrimination and knowledge to distinguish between those students *you* can help and those more difficult cases that should be referred.
- You need to be able to resist the temptation to exploit the power created by a relationship of dependency.

Appendix 3   Work experience

What it is and what it does

- It is a period of time when the student is able to be 'at work' while not yet employed.
- It may be organized as continuous throughout course (e.g. day-release), or as block(s) at certain stage(s) of the course.
- If it accounts for only a small proportion of the total hours of course time, its aims could be:
  - ★ to reinforce work skills learnt in school or college, by providing a real context in which to practise them.
  - ★ to serve as the culmination and a test of a period of course work
  - ★ to test a student's choice of job area after a period of vocational sampling within the course
- If it forms a major part of the course (as in YTS Mode A), work experience becomes the main vehicle for achieving vocational preparation objectives:
  - ★ to provide a non-educational context for developing numeracy and communication abilities and for increasing social confidence
  - ★ to provide some periods during which trainees can assess their own progress and choose the next stage
  - ★ to identify a range of jobs beyond the present one for which the experience will be useful

Pointers to good practice

In addition to the more obvious aims:
- Students see work experience as providing a more adult environment and a welcome alternative to school or college. With or without justification, they may also see it as a trial job opportunity.
- Tutors see it as a way of acclimatizing students to the different demands of working life. It serves as a way of making education effectively part-time and thus remotivating the disenchanted.
- Tutors/supervisors should produce clear written identification of which objectives out of the range of possible ones their own scheme is designed to meet.
- These objectives should be communicated to students and workplace supervisors.

- The work-experience period should be an integral part of the overall course design, not just 'stuck on' to the end.
- There should be an induction period so that students can appreciate what will be involved and become accustomed to their new role.
- Students should perceive clear links between what is done at work and topics in the main course content.
- Coursework should be organized to provide back-up practice for work tasks.
- There should be regular meetings between the school or college tutor and the workplace supervisor.
- A range of work-experience placements should be selected to match the range of local labour-market opportunities.
- Students should have regular opportunities for feedback discussion on what has been happening in their placements. There are advantages in holding these 'off-site' so that the students/trainees can feel free to be critical.
- Students should be adequately briefed about Health and Safety. The question of insurance cover should be explored.
- Experiences should be recorded in some form (e.g. a log book) that can be accessible to tutors, and perhaps to other students who may go in to placement in future. Readership for this should be decided in advance.

Necessary conditions

- Time – for the organizing tutor to find placements and then monitor them properly.
- A suitable range of opportunities – to provide a wide choice with the job families selection.
- Consideration for local employers – so that they are not overburdened by requests for placements.

Appendix 4 Profiling

What it is and what it does

- A profile is a full record of your students' progress and achievements while on your course.
- It is a complete description of their learning, their abilities and strengths, as these are revealed through syllabus activities.
- Profiling involves your students in their own progress record from the beginning; it is negotiated with them, seen by them, and contributed to by them.
- It strengthens the bond between you and your students and helps in the negotiation of the learning programme.
- It stresses the positive aspects of your students' work; their achievements and competencies as against their weaknesses and limitations.
- It avoids marks and, usually, grades.
- It is formative as against summative: it is arrived at by continuous assessment rather than tests at the end.
- It provides continuous and systematic feedback for tutors of students' activities and progress in other areas.
- It should be a thorough, fair, basis from which prospective employers and course tutors can make decisions regarding the future of your students.

Necessary conditions

- Mutual respect and trust – between students and tutors.
- Sufficient time on a regular basis – to carry out the guidance-and-counselling function while updating the profile with your student.
- A suitable room and privacy.
- A checklist of the syllabus – so that all tutors and supervisors can see the link between the learning activities and competencies to be recorded.
- Regular team meetings – to discuss individual students' progress.
- An organized system of report-back – from tutors and from on-the-job and work-experience supervisors.

Pointers to good practice

- Stick to a negotiated and agreed system, known to tutors and students, so that you will know how often and when the profile will be updated.
- Arrange an initial programme of staff development to ensure that everybody knows the purpose of the profile and feels confident about filling it in.
- Have a follow-up staff-development programme to pick up any signals of unease, to review the profile as a system, and to help any tutor who is unsure about the kind of statements to make and the progress to record.
- If you are designing your own profile, bear in mind that the language used to describe your students' abilities should be accessible for students, tutors, supervisors, and employers.

Notes of caution

- Some profiles require tutors to assess their students' social abilities and personal effectiveness; this is a very sensitive, potentially fraught, area and so you should agree upon a team approach.
- The format that provides a bar to shade across according to the level reached needs to be carefully examined – you will have to decide upon your own criteria for labelling a student's achievement as level 1, 2, 3, etc.
- Sometimes categories overlap and are ambiguous – profile descriptive statements are only guides to help you, and you must work as a team to find the best compromise. Be consistent and communicate your criteria and standards to your students so that they understand how their progress is being recorded.
- There may be disagreement between a student and a tutor or a supervisor on the job or work-experience placement. You may have to be arbitrator and this obviously calls for tact, patience and confidence. Discuss any problem fully with the student and others involved, and be prepared to visit the workplace.

Taking it further

- There are many different formats. Some examination courses allow tutors to decide how many and which competencies or statements to record; others provide tick boxes to shade to record a particular stage or level reached.
- If you are designing your own profile, look at current models.

Appendix 5   Resources list

Tutor's background reading

Induction
Baldwin, J. and H. Wells 1979 *Active Tutorial Work* (Blackwell)
Weston, P.B. 1980 *Negotiating the curriculum* (NFER)
Further Education Unit (planned) *Negotiation* (provisional title) (FEU)

These three publications all deal with the negotiation, contractual and counselling elements of the induction period. For further information, sample timetables, schedules and activities, contact your local Regional Curriculum Base.

Counselling and guidance
The FEU publication *Tutoring* considers in depth all these aspects of counselling and guidance in vocational preparation, with a range of examples from FE which show how and where the activities can be best organized.

Learning to help: basic skills exercises, by Philip Priestley and James McGuire (Tavistock Publications, 1983), provides an informative and practical manual which could provide exercises for self-training or staff-development sessions.

These two publications are basically practical in approach; neither is concerned with putting across a single theoretical viewpoint. Possibly the most influential theoretical book as far as teachers and educational counsellors are concerned is Carl Rogers' *On becoming a person* (Houghton Mifflin, 1961).

Work experience
Work experience and schools, A.G. Watts (ed.; Heinemann Educational Books, 1983) gives an overview of current practice and extended descriptions of the various purposes it can serve.

Learning at work by Linden Hilgendorf and Rosemary Welchman (MSC Research and Development Series No. 9, 1982) gives guidelines for organizing schemes, and reports on current good practice.

Experience, reflection, learning (FEU, April 1978) provides a description of how to ensure that experience-based learning works.

Profiling
The FEU publication *Profiles* (FEU, September 1982) is particularly useful. It discusses the main issues and gives example formats. Another FEU publication, *Computer-aided profiling* (September 1983) will interest you if you have the resources to implement it. See also *Profiles in action* (October 1984).

Index